COUNT NO MAN HAPPY

A BYZANTINE FANTASY

(Revised)

By: Paul Kastenellos

An illustrated introduction to Byzantium and also a narrated version can be viewed on the publisher's website: apuleiusbooks.com

This novel is a work of historical fiction. Any resemblance to modern persons is coincidental.

Published by

Apuleius Books

PO Box 234

Garrison, N.Y. 10524-0234

SAN: 920-0517

ISBN: 978-0-9839108-0-0

Library of Congress Control Number: 2011913936

"Count no man happy until he is dead."

… Herodotus

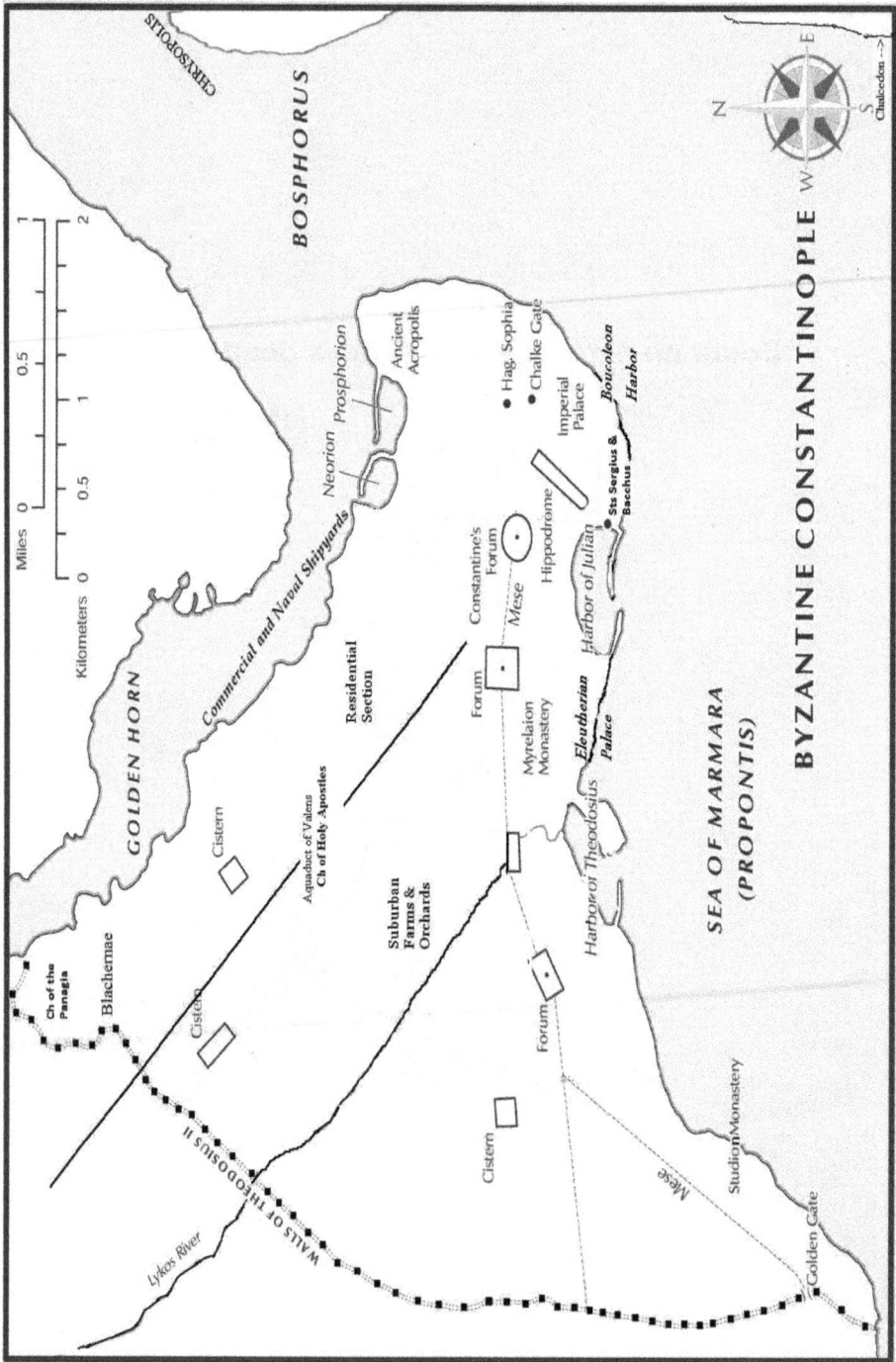

BYZANTINE CONSTANTINOPLE

CHRYSOPOLIS

BOSPHORUS

GOLDEN HORN

Commercial and Naval Shipyards

Neorion Prosphorion

Ancient Acropolis

Hag. Sophia
Chalke Gate
Imperial Palace
Boucoleon Harbor

Sts Sergius & Bacchus

Harbor of Julian

Hippodrome

Constantine's Forum

Mese

Forum
Myrelaion Monastery

Eleutherian Palace

Residential Section

Cistern

Aquaduct of Valens Ch of Holy Apostles

Suburban Farms & Orchards

Cistern

Forum

Mese

Cistern

Harbporoi Theodosius

SEA OF MARMARA (PROPONTIS)

Studion Monastery

Golden Gate

WALLS OF THEODOSIUS II

Lykos River

Ch of the Panagia

Blachernae

Miles
0   0.5   1

Kilometers
0   0.5   1   2

N
W   E
S
Chalcedon —>

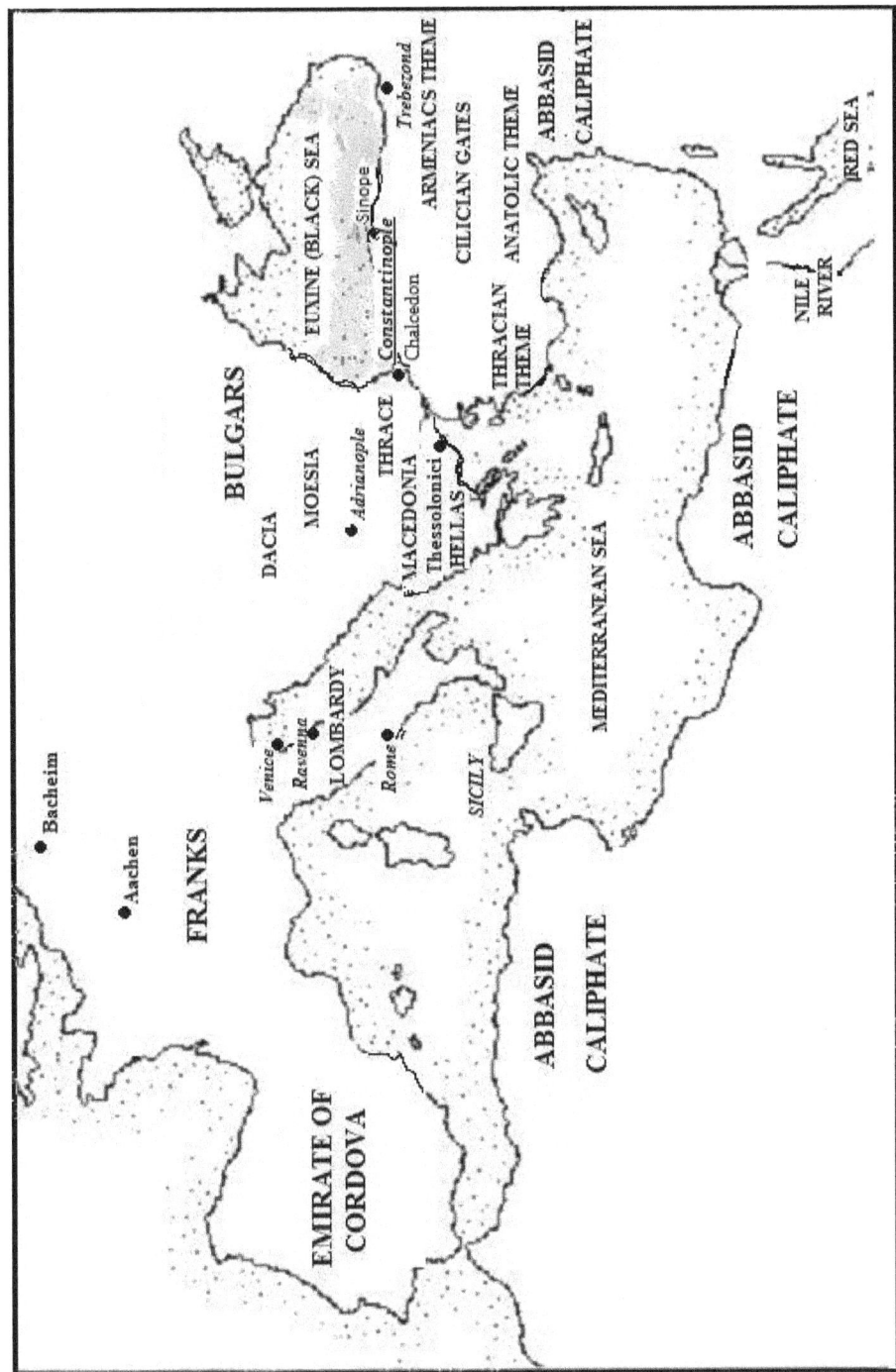

EMIRATE OF CORDOVA

FRANKS

Bacheim

Aachen

Venice

Ravenna

LOMBARDY

Rome

SICILY

MEDITERRANEAN SEA

ABBASID CALIPHATE

BULGARS

DACIA

MOESIA

Adrianople

THRACE

MACEDONIA

Thessolonici

HELLAS

EUXINE (BLACK) SEA

Trebezond

Sinope

Constantinople

Chalcedon

ARMENIACS THEME

CILICIAN GATES

ANATOLIC THEME

THRACIAN THEME

ABBASID CALIPHATE

ABBASID CALIPHATE

NILE RIVER

RED SEA

CHARACTERS

A complete list of characters and persons mentioned, together with a glossary of terms and places appears on the last pages of this book.

An afterword indicating where the novel elaborates on the historical record follows the text of the story.

MAJOR CHARACTERS

Aetius – A eunuch and highly placed advisor and personal favorite of Irene.

Bertmund of Loutern - A younger protégé of Ricolf, six years older than Constantine (fictional).

Beth Pagane - 1950s pinup model (fictional).

Charles, Carolus, Charlemagne, - At this time king of the Franks, later to be crowned by the pope as emperor in the west..

Constantine VI - Son of Byzantine iconoclast Emperor Leo IV and the Empress Irene.

Irene - Succeeds as iconodule empress regent of 10 year old Constantine on the death of the emperor Leo IV.

John Pikridios - Chief tutor and friend of Constantine.

Khardam - Khan of the Bulgars.

Maria of Amnia - First wife of Constantine..

Nicephorus - Uncle 'foros (with four never seen brothers) - Half brother of Leo IV.

Rotrud - Daughter of Charlemagne.

Ricolf of Bacheim - A diplomat and advisor to Charlemagne (fictional).

Stauratius - Eunuch, First minister and general (strategos) of Irene.

Theodote - Handmaiden of Irene and second wife of Constantine.

PRELUDE

It had been fifteen hundred and thirty three years from the founding of the city of Rome, and seven hundred and eighty years from the birth of Jesus of Nazareth. It was now four hundred and fifty years since Constantine the Great had founded a New Rome at Byzantium where Europe meets Asia on the Bosphorus.

With the melting of the last snowfall, infantry from that New Rome, more commonly called Constantinople, were retreating from a small fort on the Dacian frontier, pursued by Bulgar warriors.

It wasn't much of a fort; just a stockaded trading post fifty miles beyond the frontier proper and not very different from a forward post on the U.S. or Canadian frontier in the nineteenth century. It was just a place to trade with the locals or seek refuge if the natives turned enemy.

At first the Byzantines held formation but not for long. The peasants who lived outside the palisade just ran - those able to.

In the past Bulgar raiders would have been content just to kill a few troopers, fire the buildings, grab what loot they could carry, and return east to where a relief army would not follow.

This time they hunted down and butchered both the soldiers and the refugees.

But in the new Rome a beautiful empress reigned in the name of her young son while in Western Europe Charles the Great - Charlemagne - was entangled with warring German tribesmen, A Bulgar incursion hardly stirred the court life of either state. Charles was stretching the boundaries of Christianity and his kingdom, while the courtiers in Constantinople were more concerned with trade, fashion, and forms of worship, than with a minor raid outside the frontier proper.

CHAPTER I

In which are introduced Beth Pagane a nineteen fifties pinup model, and the eighth century feuding that forms the background to our story.

> Who is this arising like the dawn,
> Fair as the moon,
> Resplendent as the sun,
> And terrible as an army with banners?
> .
> *... The Song of Songs*

Beth Pagane climbed the three flights to her one bedroom apartment over a bakery on Broad street in Newark, New Jersey. Balancing a bag of groceries on her hip as a mother might a small child, she unlocked the door and entered. Beth was not a mother, not even married yet, and the clock was ticking. The year was 1956. Women were "girls" until "matronly," or were "ladies," depending upon the circumstances. Men were "boys" until married and "unavailable." Eisenhower was president and *The Great Pretender* by The Platters was the hit song of the month. Beth liked The Platters; everyone did.

Beth put the groceries away and began to undress, slipping out of a pair of well-worn flats, a simple white blouse, and the tan pedal-pushers that accented her rump. Except for that concession to the boys Beth preferred to dress comfortably when not working. But in the mirror wearing only her undies she scrutinized another Beth: the pinup model, the fantasy gal. Beth with the big butt who had to constantly watch her otherwise slim figure or be out of work. She knew she was pretty, but no more so than a lot of other girls. True, God had blessed her with a beautiful body, winning smile, and light blonde braids that fell to her waist when she let them; but still, with her hair up and without makeup she might pass most men unnoticed. That was good. Not that she didn't like men; oh, she surely did, but she didn't like being stared at when she wasn't working.

On her bedside table were some crystal bells, Christmas ornaments she'd bought on a lark some weeks before. She held them, listened, and watched them take the light before placing them in the far back of a drawer behind an Arabian harem pajama and a pair of frilly panties. The panties she's purchased more for their frill than their coverage which was minimal, but she wasn't sure if any of these things really belonged in her trousseau. That would depend on what sort of guy she would marry one day, and at the moment that day seemed to be very far off.

Evening was approaching and she had nothing scheduled for the night. That too was good. Too much partying had become boring. She had to dress for parties and if she did guys drooled all over her, which did little for her popularity with the other girls and wasn't fun for her either. She would have loved a guy who'd ignore her a bit — just a bit — not too much, mind you. Tonight she'd just put on her old jammies and relax. *Perhaps read a bit,* she thought. *Read some history.* Beth had always liked history. If she'd not taken up modeling she'd intended to get a degree in it; probably teach, do some research, maybe specialize in the eighth century when according to historians Charlemagne was inventing Europe.

Tonight there was nothing on her schedule, so after a quick TV Dinner without the TV, Beth grabbed her old blanket and settled herself on the couch to read. If she was hoping for exciting reading Beth was to be disappointed. The first pages were anything but promising.

"In the year 780 of our era the iconoclast emperor Leo IV died in Byzantium, known more commonly as Constantinople, the capital of the Byzantine or Late Roman Empire of the East. Old Rome itself had long since ceased to be the center of the western world and would have been little more than a provincial village were it not for the pontiff's throne being there. The whole West, though technically still a part of a single great Christian state was in practice divided into many principalities with the kingdom of the Franks under Charlemagne by far the most powerful and aggressive. Even the pope relied on Charles for protection from his enemies instead of the emperor in Constantinople, for Charles had crossed the Alps from Germany and subdued much of Lombardy. He was therefore closer and at least as powerful as the pontiff's distant suzerain."

Pretty boring stuff. For a moment Beth considered watching George Gobel on the TV instead of reading, but continued. *Maybe it will get better.*

"Leo passed from this earth unlamented by the clergy, for he and his father's attempts to rid the Eastern Roman-Byzantine empire of icon worship in favor of a more austere Christianity had offended more - and more powerful - people than it had pleased. In particular, they had angered the capital's many fanatical and riot-prone monks. Monks could be a threat to the throne itself when they disputed religious policy with their emperor, known to that Greek-speaking world as their *basilios*; and they wanted their pictures back. St. John of Damascus had written:

10

'Of old, God the incorporeal and uncircumscribed was never depicted. Now, however, when God is seen clothed in flesh, and conversing with men, I make an image of the God whom I see. I do not worship matter, I worship the God of matter, who became matter for my sake, and deigned to inhabit matter, who worked out my salvation through matter. I will not cease from honoring that matter which works my salvation. I venerate it, though not as God. How could God be born out of lifeless things? And if God's body is God by union, it is immutable. The nature of God remains the same as before, the flesh created in time is quickened by a logical and reasoning soul.'"

It's not gonna get better, but I'll do a few pages.

"Leo's widow was the pretty Augusta Irene who would rule in the name of her son, a ten year old boy known to history as Constantine VI. Irene was greatly loved and admired by the monks and women of the city because even while Leo lived it had been an open secret that she still venerated the old pictures, several of which she had secreted in the women's quarters. This despite her solemn oath when she wed Leo never to accept image worship. When her husband discovered images in her chambers she had lied to him and implied that one of her ladies must have hidden them there.

"But though Leo was gone, iconoclasm still had supporters. The armies of Asia Minor, and particularly the Armeniacs, were more sympathetic to iconoclasm than to the cabal of monks, Irene, and her supporters in the western parts of the empire. Upon Irene's acquiring the regency for Constantine they revolted and attempted to place on the throne Leo's half-brother, the caesar Nicephorus, whom they viewed as indifferent to the squabble. Besides the Asiatic troops, Nicephorus was supported by four weaker brothers and much of the intelligentsia.

Forces actually in the capital rallied to Irene however and the revolt was quickly suppressed without bloodshed. The five caesars were ordained priests and sent off to monasteries for awhile, but as *caesars* and *nobilissimi* with strong support in the army, Irene dared not banish them for long. Nicephorus denied having sought the purple, insisting that he and his brothers were loyal to Constantine and the council of regents and had no intention of seeking to rule the empire. When reluctantly returned to favor Nicephorus prostrated most humbly before Irene and Constantine, and that Christmas he and his brothers distributed the Eucharist in the great cathedral of Hagia Sophia. Very soon though, he would be seen once again back in the Great Palace, arrayed in secular garb and offering political advice to whoever would take it. Nicephorus was not to be trusted."

A bitch. Armies. Conspiracy. Maybe it will get better.

"Leo had not been any more mourned in the streets of Constantinople than in its monasteries. Though his religious intolerance had not been so severe as young Constantine's grandfather's, it had still not allowed of any public display of icons. That seemed to take the mystic out of religion – and perhaps the fun too."

Right.

"If Leo had not been quite as doctrinaire as his father, his sins had still been odious in the eyes of the monks. They would accept nothing less than a full return to the old ways and damned the memory of both "false emperors" at every opportunity: in the markets, on street corners, and before the chariot races at the hippodrome."

Did the Byzantines still have chariot races in the eighth century? Like in Ben-Hur?

"These monks and the people of Constantinople identified the iconoclasts with the many heresies of Asia Minor, the demon-inspired Mohammed, and the old law of the Jews. Had not the images of the saints brought security and prosperity to the eastern empire even as the west declined into semi-barbarism? True, in the west the Roman bishops also respected the icons and had bravely spoken out against Leo and the false synod which promulgated iconoclasm; but Charles of the Franks' conviction seemed vacillating, and even Pope Adrian did not seem to recognize that the images were anything more than pictures to delight the eyes of unlettered men and women. *'No;'* Irene would have thought, *'the icons themselves deserve veneration, for there is a bond between the picture and what it represents. In the absence of the actual saint my prayers, directed at the image, may rise to the holy man himself who will place a petition at the foot of Christ's throne.'*"

Give it a rest, lady. Beth pulled her blanket up to her chin and turned her face into the cushions. In no more time than it took to write that line, she was asleep.

CHAPTER 2

The young emperor Constantine and his nasty Uncle Nicephorus are introduced. The threats of advancing Bulgars, and Harun al-Rashid's Arabs are explored, as is Byzantium's relations with Charlemagne of the Franks.

———————————

Beth was late getting home the next day. The trip from Manhattan to Newark was under the river via the Hudson Tubes underground line. She hated having to live so far; the trip could be dangerous late at night when there were few riders and some of them just punks looking for trouble. But the math was simple: Newark housing was cheap, Manhattan expensive. She'd like to have lived in Greenwich Village like some of her friends but she could only afford that if she took a really tiny apartment and shared it with someone. Not an appealing thought.

One might think that, being a model, Beth could have afforded it but such was not the case in the '50s. At that time there were two types of models and no crossover between their jobs. There were fashion models - really thin girls, flat in front and back, who perfectly fitted the size two dresses they modeled - and there were girlie magazine models like Beth - 36 - 22 - 37. Neither were made wealthy by their work. Of course it was easy for a pinup to find a well-to-do guy to help with the rent - some girls did - but that was too much like prostitution. No offense to working girls, but Beth wasn't ready to go that route.

Asleep that night she buckled her leather thong panties to her hips as though to pose and bent to lace her boots. It was getting harder to do this. In a few years she'd be thirty, but she refused to give in and sit to do it. She could still just manage to tie off the laces before the blood rushing to her head would make her feel wobbly. Beth was tall - nearly six feet in her high boots - and yes, her reflection in an antique full-length mirror was as pretty as ever, if in a more mature way. She stood examining her yet tiny waist for longer than was modest. When she had finished, the sleeper slipped into the mirror and lost twelve centuries.

She roamed through corridors of appearances, a jumble of things that are and things that could be, even of dreams and imaginings; of thoughts that were and might be more than thoughts. She was riding through corridors of time. Shades of people past and future were all around her.

There was the Roman emperor Marcus Antonius Aurelius and his wife Faustina, but how she knew them Beth did not know. Nor did it seem strange to her; after all, they were her friends. There was Belisarius who smiled and waved. She knew him though she'd never heard of him. There were saints of long ago and heroes yet to be.

Now she was on horseback riding over brooks and through the forests of Gaul. She stumbled and felt herself falling through the earth until the earth itself was far below ... far, far below. Words cannot describe the world between worlds in which Beth found herself traveling that night. I could write of its peacefulness and try to describe it in terms of a lush hillside in spring, or of gentle breezes on the seashore as evening falls; but any words would fail. The certain characteristic of that world was a complete absence of worry about today or yesterday or tomorrow; about friends, heartache, or death. She was entirely living in the now as though there were no yesterday and there would never need be a tomorrow; in fact it was a world in which the very words of time have no meaning. There might be one way of describing without words that world however, it was like when one is completely lost in some beloved piece of sensuous music which reflects the love of God or the God of love: in Cesar Franck's *Panis Angelicus* or Offenbach's *Barcarolle*, in Wagner's *Liebestod* and Schubert's *Ave Maria*.

Was Beth dreaming? Or was Beth looking upon the earth from outside of time and place? With the dawn even Beth did not know but it had all been beautiful.

Constantinople still claimed suzerainty over the land of the Franks and messengers passed frequently between Constantinople and Aachen where Great Charles - Charlemagne - usually preferred to hold court. Imperial and Frankish couriers would travel from Gaul by horse and by mule and sometimes afoot through the Alps via the Claudia Augusta Pass to north Italy. From there they went on to Ravenna on the Adriatic coast from where a ship could be taken around the Greek Peloponnese to the city named for Constantine the Great who had founded it there on the Bosporus nearly five hundred years before. It would have been quicker to take the old Via Egnasia from Dyrrachium through Macedonia past Thessaloníki and onward from there to where it safely skirted the northern Aegean; but that route was now uncertain. Besides the usual bandits and the Croat warlords who in practice ruled much of the territory, in Macedonia there had been occasional raids by Bulgar tribesmen, who had incorporated in their horde various other west Asiatic tribes.

Over one hundred years before, Bulgars had begun crossing the Danube frontier and the empire had thought it best to accept their presence as a sovereign power. The Byzantines knew their type well enough. They were of the same stock as had attacked venerable and sacred Roma itself under Attila, the scourge of God, three centuries before. Now, however, the Bulgars were not content to harass Roman territory. They threatened Moesia and coveted Thracia and Macedonia where lay the great city of Thessaloníki in which St. Demetrios had died a martyr. The Byzantine court feared an attack on Thracia and even on Constantine's city itself. It had constructed a strong wall across the Thracian Peninsula to protect Constantinople.

The couriers carried news in both directions and besides the official dispatches that were for the eyes of high ministers only, they carried the usual scuttlebutt of travelers. They freely disseminated this to anyone with the price of a goblet of good Chios wine in Roman lands or a pewter flagon of beer in the north. Though there was concern about the Bulgars, the news was not all bad: The Moslem offensive against Christianity had at least been blunted both in the East and in the West. The Justinian plague had not reappeared in recent years as it had regularly for the two previous centuries. The damned Paulitians, who denied the humanity of the Lord, were being driven underground by the empress Irene. Great Charles was bringing learning even to poor villagers, and requiring the clergy to behave in a manner befitting their holy vocation. A marriage alliance between the house of Charles and the Byzantine throne was rumored.

But if the main Arab threat had stalled for now, incursions continued as they had for two centuries. There had been victories and defeats on both sides but on balance it was the Roman side, and with it Christian culture, which were taking the beating. The empire had long since lost the granaries of Egypt which had fed it at its pagan height. It had also lost much of its manpower reserves and just this year Arabs had raided as far as Chalcedon on the Asiatic shore of the Bosphorus. They had taken prisoner Byzantium's logothete of the dromos, Stauratius, who was both Irene's chief of staff and the empire's first minister. Irene had paid a huge ransom for his return but she considered him to be worth every gold solidus. Returned to the palace, Stauratius tried to project an air of confidence. After all, he was far from the only one there who had suffered defeat in battle, though no one man in memory had cost so much gold.

———————————

The caesar Nicephorus walked out of his palace in a black mood. The man was a man of moods. Few of them were particularly noble or honorable and many were dark. At best he might be giddy with delight over some coup he had managed against a rival or enemy, or just some poor dumb clod who got in his way. His idea of showing honor was a bow so humble as to be likened by his detractors to a kowtow from the most eastern parts of Asia. He kowtowed magnificently before those few authorities who stood between his exalted rank and the imperial majesty, all others in the empire did so to his dignity. *Delightful and appropriate*, he felt. Nicephorus had never become so accustomed to the show that he did not enjoy the diffidence that others showed him, nor did he ever cease to detest prostrating himself before the child-emperor, his nephew descended from his father's first wife, a rustic bitch who had born him and died.

Even in the heat and stink of Constantinople's summer Nicephorus rarely dressed comfortably, preferring the stiff robes of state whenever circumstances permitted and only slightly more comfortable dress at other times. It was not only because he was an exceptionally tall and well-built man that both his enemies and the rabble joked that he could easily be spotted from afar, his great frame was exaggerated by the excessive height of the colorful turbans he affected. These monstrosities of fashion from the eastern provinces always complimented the ornate dalmatics that hung, long and stiff with embroidery, nearly to his feet and were decorated with holy images enhanced by pearls and an occasional gemstone. Such holy images were to ward off the evil eye, but also to appear more loyal than he actually was to the iconodules - those supporters of the sacred images who the Augusta Irene had surrounded herself with at court. Those in his retinue dressed equally colorfully though their garments were necessarily less rich. He also insisted his brothers look the part of the great gentlemen they presumed themselves to be, though that presumption was based entirely on birth, with few accomplishments that might have offset the veiled hatred of the augusta-regent or their late half brother. His bodyguards were outfitted in the native dress of their homelands, except that their clothing was of more expensive and more ornate design than the usual Slavic or Scythaean dress. In an unintended parody they looked almost to be wearing the stage armor of a musical comedy. Leather was gilded, belts and scabbards were studded with semiprecious stones, lances bore silken pennants, and their helms were huge plumed things far too heavy to do any real fighting in. But these looked fine carried on the left arm as the warriors flung themselves to their knees before Nicephorus.

It was all too much for the street crowd who would titter behind the exalted dignitary's back. Had Nicephorus ever actually fought a battle? Even had he lost that might not have been a problem if he'd fought bravely. Byzantium could be comfortable with excess when earned. Emperors lived lives of perfume and cosmetics and silk, surrounded by eunuchs in imitation of the angels around the Divine Throne. But they at least were strong, ruling with an iron hand and usually with some justice. Then too, successful

16

generals thought it appropriate to travel about the city in huge parades of armed retainers to impress both citizens and visitors with the power of the empire. The pretty empress regent, though pious, was worldly. Irene enjoyed fine fabrics and jewelry, and was much admired by the court for setting fashion. Like other noble women, she would appear in public wearing an embroidered stola and with the train of a brocaded pallium gracefully draped over her left arm. But her brocades were richer and more beautiful. They were gold and emerald green, or plum, or violet, set with sacred images in cloisonné, and with pearls or amethyst outlining a stiff fold of fabric that fell from waist to foot like a soldier's shield at rest. Her long curling hair would be lightly perfumed, wound tightly as on some Roman bust, and graced with combs of gold. Her eyes were dark with belladonna. Her stiff dalmatics did not quite obscure her graceful walk nor hide a tiny waist.

Not only was it personally delightful to be rich in Constantinople, the court felt that it must impress barbarians with its splendor lest they see its weaknesses. If the emperor's riches were not in fact inexhaustible, that must be kept a state secret more precious than the formula for the fire weapon which burned even on water and could not be extinguished

Now though Nicephorus was a vain man, he was also intelligent. The combination was daunting. To be bullied by a hulking idiot might be frightening, but it is not intimidating in the way Nicephorus, with his size and intellect, intimidated those he wished to impress.

Yet for all that, Nicephorus was neither emperor nor a successful general. He and the other half-brothers were but exalted lackeys and they and the whole city knew it.

"God be with you, Nobilissimus Nicephorus." Some merchant greeted his chief benefactor with a very deep bow, not raising his eyes for some seconds.

"And with you, brother," Nicephorus condescended to reply. "How is it with your family? I trust the Mother of Christ continues to watch over them."

"Indeed, sir, and over my fortunes as well. Thanks to you yourself, the Mother of God, and the holy saints, we prosper." Without waiting to be dismissed the man backed away, hardly rising from his crouch until the patrician had touched a pectoral cross that hung against his dalmatic in benediction and taken his place on a gilded palanquin. Nicephorus moved on through the crowds of smelly people and smellier animals. That was enough of small talk between patron and client when the patron was a proud man. Nicephorus would be glad to get indoors, away from the streets and away from garbage, sweat, and mule shit.

At the baths of Zeuxippos he dismissed the several hundred retainers who accompanied him and with only a few bodyguards and today's suppliants retired for an afternoon's rest where he could listen to the virtues of some saint with one ear while surreptitiously concentrating the mass of his attention on matters of more immediate use to himself and his brothers. *The khan of the Bulgars is perching his ass on Roman territory already and he's long lusted after the Adriatic lands. Stauratius is a fool.* As Irene's first minister Stauratius was the day-by-day administrator of the empire, in his own way more powerful than Irene herself or the council of regents because although Irene might prescribe policy it was Stauratius who would actually carry it out – or not. ... *No he's not a fool,* Nicephorus corrected himself. *To think the man a fool could be a very dangerous mistake. But he fights too many frontier skirmishes with no final result. We might as well accept that a lot of territory is gone to the Arabs and the Bulgars and we'll probably have to give up more ... for our lifetime anyway.*

The lector was reading from Saint Cyril of Jerusalem:

"Even Simon Magus once came to the font. He was baptized, but was not enlightened; and though he dipped his body in water, he enlightened not his heart with the Spirit. His body went down and came up, but his soul was not buried with Christ, nor raised with Him. Now I mention this man's fall that thou mayest not fall, for these things happened to him by way of example, and they are written for the admonition of those who today draw near. Let none of you be found tempting His Grace."

Amen brother. But right now the khan is what must concern me, not Simon Magus. Perhaps someday I may retire to a nice monastery where I can give more time to study, but for now I must consider the Bulgar khan, Arabs, Charles of the Franks ... and our stupid child-emperor as well. Nicephorus ordered a draught of St. Gregory's salt for his occasional gout and spreading baldness and with it he repeated the usual prayer to the saint.

As a young child, Constantine's nurses had been a serious lot, all chosen by his mother as much for their piety as their ability. Even while Leo lived Irene had been determined that from birth the saints would be her son's constant companions even if she could only occasionally and very privately share one of their images with him. Chants were his lullabies and prayers his early education. Flacilla, the nurse with whom he bonded as with a mother, was particularly pious and Irene thought it good that she and the boy spent most days among solemn monks listening to stories of saints and martyrs, many of miracles and demons. Few of the monks thought levity virtuous or any of these stories fanciful. The boy loved Flacilla for in the great palace she was closer to him than either his mother, most of whose time was occupied with the duties of state, or with the other ladies of the court. It was she who would play with him in the grass after religious services on summer afternoons; reward him for his studies, pray to the saints to protect him from the child-devouring demon Lilith; and when need be, spank the future ruler of the world.

At the age of eight the child was given over to male tutors. They taught him the grammar and rhetoric of Greek and Latin, some mathematics, and some science; uncompromisingly exact stuff, but the fate of empires was written in the fixed and moving stars. Irene selected teachers who were inclined to dwell more upon episodes of personal bravery in Greek and Roman wars than the base politics these things disguised. As emperor-of-the-Romans-to-be, Constantine learned the tales of ancient heroes, both real and imagined. It was not always clear which were which; which were true and which were mere stories; which were a mix of the two. It did not matter, he was told; just as it did not matter if all the miracles attributed to the saints had actually occurred - though surely many had - any more than it mattered if there were more relics of these holy men than they had body parts. What mattered were honor and loyalty, faith, piety, and a martyr's courage. Accuracy was necessary in day by day affairs. Reports of his agents and the commanders of his troops would be vital to the survival of the empire but no more so than virtues which were supported by tales of times long ago: legends about Hector on the walls of Troy and Odysseus facing the terrors of the sea, Horatius defending the Tiber Bridge. The humanity of the good son Aeneas and the craftiness of Romulus were obscured by the mists of time as too were the heroes of ancient Israel who by faith alone had brought nationhood out of slavery. Yet their example still encouraged men. His chief tutor, John Pikridios, assured Constantine that the walls of Jericho had fallen to the faith of Joshua. That was certain because it was testified to by scripture; but he asked the boy whether it mattered if the details of Saint Demetrios' death and the miracles wrought by his intercession had been colored a bit by the monks. These were an object of belief to be sure, but not testified to by Holy Writ. That the saint had died a martyr of some sort was sure, however, for it was an ancient tradition; and wasn't that brave act of his all that really mattered?

"You must think for yourself, young emperor. It is not good for the ruler of the world to believe everything he is told, even by me or the priests and monks. No; faith and honor are reliable but the evidence of one's eyes and ears can lead you down false pathways because you do not consider all things. Do you think the world is flat because it seems so? Aristotle said otherwise and proved it, but he had to consider the moon in eclipse to do so. Who among us would think to do that? Those versed in the arts of medicine usually fail to cure. Those in astrology and divination fail in their predictions of the Lord's purpose or predict in so obscure a way that the simplest peasants laugh at them. Lead remains lead, and gold remains gold despite every attempt to persuade the one to become the other. But prayers to the Divine Savior and his saints and angels often bring wondrous cures for those possessed or merely sick. The faith of Christ's people has time and again preserved this city from attack. The heroism of the empire's holy soldiers are its defense against this earth's enemies." Young Constantine listened and began to suspect what had never been suggested to him before: that John had more confidence in the Divine Savior than in His clergy. *But, he thought, Is that not as it should be?*

To John Pikridios' distress, Constantine also developed a liking for the silly stories of Asia. He read or listened to them constantly as a modern boy might prefer comic books to Arthurian legends. To John they were simply rot but they had recently gained popularity among the less-lettered in the capital. Though frowned upon by most of the elite and all of the teachers of rhetoric and literature, Constantine had forced him to admit that they had a certain adventurous and barbaric charm. Mind you, there were too many dragons and magical powers in these for the stories to be believable. Dragons had not been seen for centuries; or at least there had been no verifiable sightings. Even the monks looked with some doubt on such reports; doubts which they never would have had about even the most unlikely miracles of the saints whatever the more worldly tutor might suspect. But God only permitted holy men, alive and dead, to work wonders and always in His name. All other marvels in these stories were either lies or the result not of human but of demonic schemes.

Still, Asiatic tales were fun and without the moral lessons of Constantine's studies.

CHAPTER 3

The only thing happening in Newark on Sunday mornings was mass at St. Stephen's. That was Beth's other side. She rarely revealed that side to her model and photographer friends for Beth was no evangelical. Not that she wouldn't. She didn't hide her faith; it was there for those with eyes to see; but most of her professional friends just wouldn't have been interested. Could a nineteen-fifties girl be both religious and a pinup model? Society was prudish; Beth's spirituality was not. One can only plead that she was "advanced" for the time, if not without doubts, scruples, and some fear for her soul.

After early mass the rest of the day was free. It would be spent in Manhattan. New York is especially nice on a fine Sunday morning. No business was being done in the locked-up office buildings and all the people from Queens and Brooklyn and the Bronx were in their homes attending to their own weekend pursuits. The hectic atmosphere is lifted on Sunday mornings except in the tourist spots; worse there than during the week.

It was too early for discussions over coffee of Ferlinghetti and Dostoevsky and Sartre. The beat crowd was still recovering from Saturday night. She'd just walk along the riverside and try to recall something of the strange dreams she'd been having lately. Not details. It is usually impossible to remember the details of dreams and when one does they're a nonsensical mess. No, not details but feelings. She did remember a pleasant emptiness. She did remember that she had felt entirely comfortable and very special.

Beth had reservations about some of the pictures she posed for. Not the bikini shots, the leather stuff that guys no doubt masturbated to. Still, she felt sorry for guys who needed pictures, thinking: *It must be really tough being a guy with all those hormones building up, want it or not.* Yet any reservations she might be entertaining this morning melted away with the sun and Beth's mind was drawn to the peaceful world she'd dreamt of where none of that mattered so long as she remained good in herself. "*As you judge, so shall you be judged. As you are kind, so shall kindness be shown to you.*" (Luke 6:37) There was a liveliness in her steps. She skipped down the street as though she were very much younger than she was. Of course she was young; young of heart and young in spirit. The day was fine. She'd nothing that had to be done. A shopkeeper watching her smiled. She would have a cookie. Like a kid she wanted a cookie.

———————

But in Constantinople Irene was prostrate alone in the Pharos chapel. Most of the palace buildings were in large part open to the fresh breezes of the Bosphorus. Not so this holy place. It was beautiful but dark, hung round with heavy draperies, and with the odor of candles mixed with lingering incense from that morning's service. The beautiful and holy Irene was with her saints, the images of whom were all around her; painted icons encrusted with jewels on silver and brought forth from many hiding places now that Leo was dead and it was safe to venerate them. The thoughts of the empress were a mix of passionate devotion to these holy men of the church and of how best to reconcile the future of the church with the needs of the state.

For Irene the two were one; but the regrettable fact remained that beneath their protestations most men - even good orthodox men – were far more concerned with success in life than with the success of their lives before Christ. Irene felt it her sacred mission to recall them constantly to their true duty not only so that the saints might be honored as they ought to be, but also that the orthodox state might face its enemies secure in its faithfulness to the Divine Will; that Christ's Holy Order might prevail among all men.

But there were so many enemies and potential enemies; some, like Nicephorus, even in the palace. There were the horrid Paulicians who hated God. There were also many people in the eastern provinces who, infected with the heresies of Mohammed or the Monophysites, wanted to again strip the church of its saints, burn the holy icons, and destroy even the beautiful and precious mosaics of the palace churches and the other churches that Irene was restoring throughout the land. They would ban even those simple pictures poor people still kept by their beds and on their persons to ward off disease and demonic attacks, and to remind them of the necessity of devotion. The iconoclasts had for a time succeeded. The empire had been nearly denuded of sacred images. Many monasteries had been closed and many good monks and nuns had been martyred in their defense. Had not the holy Theodosa and her companions been killed right here in Constantinople for defending Christ's image at the Chalke gate? Now the whole of the eastern provinces were infected with the monophysite heresy which denied the very humanity of Christ; but Christ was a man and so could rightly be depicted and his image venerated. So too, then, could the holy saints and martyrs, through whose intercession sinners might implore forgiveness. The restored images would be an ever-present sermon to all the people. As John of Damascus had written: " A scripture, concise and easy to interpret."

These priorities and the ambition necessary to carry out God's work so dominated the empress' thoughts and actions that her soul was at ease, knowing that what must be done for the true faith must be done regardless of consequences. It was the Divine Will that she – though a mere woman and weak of flesh – fully restore the images that the iconoclasts had destroyed.

Or so the woman told herself. She would do whatever she must to insure God's holy rule through her person. The holy Augustine himself had blessed coercion to orthodoxy for the sinners' own good and that of the church; but it would take commitment and strength. Her son might reign with her but she would be the man in all their public actions. There were many who would not accept this though, and so she must be constantly on guard against plotters; not only ferreting them out but forestalling them by her own intrigues ... for the sake of Christ's church.

Not far away, John Pikridios had left a quote from the pagan emperor Marcus Aurelius for his pupil.

"If you are doing what is right, never mind whether you are freezing with cold or beside a good fire; heavy-eyed, or fresh from a sound sleep; reviled or applauded; in the act of dying, or about some other piece of business, for even dying is part of the business of life; and there too no more is required of us than to see the moment's work well done. "

It was a shame that a ten-year old should have to deal with such heavy things as death and duty but the lad would one day be the ruler of the world. It was necessary that he learn honor and duty now. A true sense of honor and duty were not things one could easily acquire later in life. *As a twig is bent by the wind so will the tree grow.*

He must also be charitable as Christ had taught. John feared that he would not learn true charity from the unruly monks or palace priests - or from the empress-regent either. Yet as emperor he must be kind, and it was they - not his tutor - who were obligated to teach him this. They weren't doing it so he must, but John was saddened as he left the palace schoolroom thinking over the words of the Savior: *"As you judge, so shall you be judged; as you are kind, so shall kindness be shown to you."*

Irene was most beloved by the very religious and very superstitious of Constantinople, for she had taken no time after her husband's death to begin undoing his work. On the very same Christmas day that Nicephorus and his brothers were made to distribute the Eucharist in the cathedral church of Hagia Sophia, she traveled in pious procession there to return to its rightful place a votive crown of gold and jewels which her late husband had appropriated. Those who most hated the emperor were sure that his fever and death were God's righteous penalty for this impiety, an opinion which Irene shared. She would have endorsed it even had she not, for it focused the attention of the people on her intent to restore all the old ways. Constantine rode beside her on her chariot that fine December day through the joyous crowds of the monks and women of the city. Soon they would be able to touch and kiss the holy pictures again. All the relics of the saints would be recovered from where the martyrs of the Iconoclastic period had hidden them. Once again there would be sacred song and incense enough to satisfy the most reactionary, if not kindness and understanding. Though he was too young to fully understand the theology, Constantine accepted his mother's explanation of how his father had been misled by heretics and the impious. After all, had not God already blessed the return of images to the palace by defeating a huge force of the Abbasid Caliph in the mountain passes between their realms? The Lord had sent the enemy fleeing back to Baghdad pursued by Constantine's noble cataphracts, the empire's heavy cavalry.

While he lived Leo had associated Constantine with himself on the throne so it was important that he, and not the empress-regent alone, be present at all major state ceremonies and functions. It was assumed by everyone except Irene herself that as the boy matured he would begin to take precedence in affairs of state. But it did not really matter that fine day in December. The boy would be what he would be. The people of the city saw he had a saintly mother to guide him along the path of orthodoxy. Meanwhile, until he was old enough to rule as well as reign, the good augusta could be trusted to right the wrongs against the holy icons, the saints to whom they were bonded, and the many monks, nuns, and priests who had suffered grievously under the iconoclastic emperors.

At about this same time, Irene - or rather Stauratius in whom she placed all faith - appointed the patrician Elpidios to be governor of Sicily; but within months his enemies reported to the throne that Elpidios was a friend and supporter of Nicephorus. Stauratius sent a small force to bring him back to Constantinople to answer charges of having been involved in the recent coup attempt but instead Elpidios' troops stood between him and the Constantinoplian guard and would not give up their commander.

"What do you suggest, Stauratius?" The empress-regent had not bothered to request that the other ministers and bishops on the council of regents attend the conference.

"It is vital that we hold Sicily. It is desired both by the Saracens in Africa and Charles of the Franks. Charles is extending his hold ever further south of the Alps. If Elipidios' troops love him then we must be discreet in how we deal with him. We do not want to throw Sicily into the hands of either the Arabs or the Franks."

"You are too subtle and too worried, Stauratius. Crush him. Send additional troops to Sicily and see how long his soldiers' love lasts when they are bleeding."

"But Highness ..."

"No, my friend; we must show strength against all our enemies and particularly those within the empire. Some of our troops opposed the restoration of the icons. Let us give them an opportunity to amend themselves in my sight. ... And Elpidios has a wife and children in the city. Arrest them. For the sake of the holy saints and Christ's empire we must be firm before we show them our love. Whip them, then let them join the holy monks. That is better for their souls than living with a husband and father who is a traitor. As for Charles, I will bind him to the empire in other ways. He will not support the traitor."

Stauratius appointed a reliable leader, the patrician Theophilos, and sent him with a large force against the rebel garrison. Negotiations and intimidation failed as did bribery and appeals to patriotism from both leaders. There remained no other way to settle the rebellion but civil war. The forces of the rebels and the empire were evenly matched. Both were primarily heavy cataphracts carrying bows, axes, and maces as well as the spathion, a long double edged sword well suited to cavalry use.

Both were mounted on good horses and both were well led. The Byzantine military at this time was divided into two parts: a central army based in Constantinople ready to go where needed, and armies in each military province, called themes (or themata in Greek), who were not only the first to defend against foreign invaders but could join together and form as formidable a force as the Constantinoplian guard. The patrician Theophilios' Constantinopolitan cavalry outnumbered Elpidios' thematic horsemen four to three but their numerical advantage was reduced by Elpidios' employment of local levies of infantry with knowledge of the land; and no doubt too by his certainty that a loss would mean his execution, or possibly the loss of his eyes if he were more fortunate. Before joining battle Elpidios prayed for victory in a simple village church. The commander of the imperial army prayed too, but for him it was a formality. He was distracted, his mind going over his battle plan again and again.

The armies joined battle in mid morning sweating beneath the hot Sicilian sun. With his greater numbers Theophilos expected to easily turn his opponent's flank and roll back a battle line strung out for nearly a mile through a hillside olive grove. His lancers did take Elpidios' right flank but were then confronted by an unexpected maneuver.

For a while Elpidios' flank had held. With the imperial troopers bunched up on his right, Elpidios emplaced his locals on the line and was able to swing his disengaged cavalry through ninety degrees, pivoting on that flank. Now the imperial army was facing an enemy above it on the hillside and with the dazzling sun at their backs. Elpidios' battered right had now become the head of a column instead of the end of a battle line — hazardous in the extreme if Theophilios could regroup. Elpidios ordered that the part of the column not actually engaged with the enemy should form line abreast and charge the crowded mass of horsemen further down the slope.

The Constantinopolitan troopers reformed their line as best they could and prepared to receive the shock. The armies clashed with lances. The imperial troops were stunned but recovered. Now it was spathion against spathion and war-ax against mace. The government troopers were forced back against a bramble wood behind which Elpidios moved his infantry archers. Their heavy bows were far more effective against cataphract armor than the light ones carried by cavalry. They also far outranged them. The imperial cavalry found itself between two enemies and their horses stumbling through the briers. For a time the fighting between cataphracts was hand to hand, ax to ax, lance against shield, and fist against face. Despite their lamellar armor, both sides suffered severe losses as the sound of clashing weapons mixed with the screeching of wild birds in the trees, the screams of mutilated soldiers, and the neighing of terrified or wounded horses as they ran back and forth across the battlefield. Each time the imperial force recovered and formed a mounted battle line Elpidios would sound retreat and his rebel army would disengage. Then the slaughter would be one-sided as his archers took over. Christian soldier slew Christian soldier amid prayer and cursing. Theophilos had no choice but to disengage and Elpidios had no choice but to allow it, for he dared not pursue the larger imperial army outside the range of his archers.

By mid afternoon the battle was over and each side retired to bivouac in nearby villages where they had set up field hospitals for the wounded. By agreement local priests and army chaplains took their turn on the field of gore and did their best to shrive and comfort the dying. Local farmers were forced to become grave diggers; local women made to tend both Elpidios' friends and enemies. Some took revenge on the wounded for the rape and robbery that accompanies passing armies, and they died; but most just fed and washed the troopers. Imperial politics did not concern them.

What Theophilos did not expect was that night Elpidios would slip away.

In the following months he was pursued about the island by the army of the empire; but he did not tremble. Finally he and his army again met Theophilos in open battle and for a time his men held their own, not deserting their leader because they were outnumbered. Eventually numbers began to tell however. Still they did not desert him nor betray him but fell back in disciplined order, the heavy cavalry protecting the retreat of his infantry and auxiliaries till they were able to disengage and retreat into the hills. There - like so many other armies in Sicilian history - they waged guerrilla warfare and harassed Theophilos. They gave Elpidios time to collect what wealth he could from the island; then with his army he fled across the sea to Africa.

As Stauratius had feared, the defeated were warmly greeted by the Arab enemy of Byzantium. On orders from the caliph in Baghdad Elpidios was given gifts and treated as honorable and a friend. A Christian church was chosen and the proper imperial symbols fashioned. Then he was crowned as Roman emperor - a puppet shadow emperor whom the caliph hoped he might one day install in a Constantinople which was wracked by internal feuding between the supporters and enemies of images, and by nobles and generals with little more fondness for each other than for the empress-regent. Meanwhile he would be a useful thorn in the side of the Romans.

With Byzantium's attention directed towards Sicily, the caliph sent his son, Aaron - later to be known as Harun al-Rashid of *Arabian Nights* fame - to attack the empire's eastern frontier. Harun's army was large, composed of cavalry from Syria, Mesopotamia, and the Arabian desert. They came unexpectedly out of the mountains, overwhelming Roman garrisons and, because of the treachery of another Roman commander who hated Stauratius, drove as far as Chrysopolis within sight of Constantinople on the opposite shore of the Bosphorus which separates Europe from Asia. Of course, Harun could not long hold a position deep within Roman territory with only his light cavalry and with heavy imperial warships between himself and the walls of the city. These were armed with Byzantium's secret fire-weapon; he soon had to retreat. Then, the strategos of the Thrakesion theme was able to trap an Arab army of thirty thousand Saracens at Darenos and kill half the enemy.

In Constantinople Irene was angry.

"Fools! How did a bunch of camel herders get so near the city? Are my generals idiots? I'm surrounded by traitors. Where is Lachanodrakon? He's an evil man but at least he's not a fool or a traitor."

"He has destroyed Harun's army at Darenos and is even now returning to cut the infidel Harun's safe route back to his lair in Baghdad, Augusta." Stauratius spoke with some fear for his life. Irene trusted in him but the enemy was close. "You have only been betrayed by Tatzantes."

"Only! Only by Tatzantes!" Irene sneered. "Tatzantes defected because you treated him like a slave. And what about Elpidios in Africa? Doesn't he matter? Thank God for Lachanodrakon. I have to rely on an iconoclast. Holy Mother, have the Saracens better generals than I? Thank Christ in heaven for the navy, fool. The enemy will not be able to cross the Bosphorus, and if they try our ships will burn them and send them to hell; but why must I rely on sailors to do the army's work? Damn, this will cost us but pay the Arabs what we must to get them out of here permanently. I have more important work than fighting Arabs."

Upon payment of a humiliating bribe, peace was signed. Harun withdrew and boasted that he had forced the Romans to pay the caliphate tribute. But the city was safe and Irene's first minister was secure. Irene forgot her anger. She seemed no longer to care the heavy cost.

The child-emperor was not quite so pleased. *We are humiliated and still Stauratius thinks himself brilliant. Why?* Yet Constantine was ten and his mother was his mother, so he put such questions away and concentrated on petting the cat in his imperial lap who was itself insecurely eying a much larger cat, one of the hunting cheetahs kept in the imperial complex. His mother's purchased peace would more or less hold during his minority, but warfare would break out again when he came of age. The boy would not be so inclined as his mother to appease enemies.

The usually leaden skies over Aachen in the land of the Franks were clear a few days later and Great Charles felt the pains of middle age less. He relaxed enough to ask his friend Ricolf of Bacheim to stroll with him in the menagerie adjoining the rambling, stockaded palace that Charles called home when in Aachen. Though larger overall, the palace did not differ much in appearance from the many monasteries which he had ordered built throughout the Frankish kingdom, consisting of a long two-story main structure and a chapel. These buildings were connected by shelters to the many outbuildings needed to serve the king. There were kitchens and storerooms, granaries, stables, a bakery, a scriptorium for the clerks of course, and housing for his immediate bodyguards - the larger part of his personal troops living with their families in wooden barracks outside the palisade. This fair day workmen were, as usual, busy on the great cathedral that Charles had ordered to be built nearby, not only to impress visitors but out of honest piety also.

In the menagerie the king petted and played with the strange animals that other sovereigns had sent as gifts, and not always as tribute. His liking for exotic beasts was one of the things about Charles that was well known even in foreign lands. He was also known for the strength of his will and the armies of unusually well-disciplined warriors that he commanded. He was grudgingly recognized for his intellect, this even in the few kingdoms that were still greater than his. That was something rarely granted by the intelligentsia of Constantinople and Baghdad to these barbarians who had usurped imperial rule in the western empire.

As usual the king gave at least an outward appearance of being happy and self-assured if not quite carefree. Also as usual he wore simple Frankish garb: a linen shirt and breeches and a simple tunic fringed with a little silk to indicate his kingship; but with hose wrapped with bands just like any peasant. At his side hung the sword *Joyosa,* for he trusted his own strong arm more than guards in any last defense should an assassin get into the palace. In his purse rested a bit of bone from St. James the Greater, brought to him from Hispania for the pains of many years in the saddle.

Here in Charles' court his nobles might learn much, as Charles himself did, from visiting and resident scholars and from the books which Charles had read to them during meals. Ricolf was one of the most attentive students.

Even without armor Ricolf of Bacheim was an impressive man; tall even for a Frank and - unusual for Charlemagne's court - with a well-trimmed beard which was long and cut square much as one sometimes sees in paintings of Eastern saints. His hair, which had begun to recede, was of a dark hue that took on some redness in the beard. His arms were obviously strong but without the excess of those vain courtiers whose strength came not from soldiering but from time-wasting exercises intended to flatter themselves. He was a widower; his deeply beloved wife had died of a fever five years before. He bathed often.

Ricolf had learned much as a youth when his farsighted parents had sent him for schooling in Italy; but he had learned more here, especially of the ancient world including the career of the noble Belisarius whom he much admired. That general had lived three hundred years before and for a time had reunited all Italy to Constantinople under the great emperor Justinian. But that had been centuries before when the empire was still something of its ancient self. Now it was very different. Leo was dead and a woman and a child sat on the thrones in Constantine's city.

"Tell me, Ricolf, this Irene in Constantinople; what do you think of her? You were in Constantine's city some years ago; that's the only reason I permit you that hairy face. They don't trust men with only a mustache in the city. But tell me, you must have an opinion about Leo's widow?"

"In truth, mi-lord, I don't like her. They say she is a fanatic."

"She is restoring the holy images at great risk. She is pious." Charles' voice rose momentarily and his face darkened. "…Though I admit I have some concern that plain people may overvalue images. I will not have idolatry in the land."

"Yes, mi-lord, she is pious ... and ambitious, and narrow-minded; devious even for a Greek."

"Indeed? You really don't like her." Charles feigned a look of horror but then grinned. "But do you think she'd make me a good wife?"

"She's pushing thirty, I think. Pretty, but not quite your type. Besides you're on your third wife now and Irene is very pious."

Charles looked at the knight and a queer look of shared understanding briefly lit his face: "Perhaps an older woman would be good for me. She's not as old as I am, not quite; and they say she can be a raunchy devil when she's not praying."

"You're up to something, mi-lord"

"You'll recall, my friend, that the pope told my father that he who ruled had the right to be called king in Frankland. Well, I've restored much of the empire in the west and Irene can never rule in her own right because she's a woman…"

"You would marry her and be proclaimed co-emperor with her son here and in the east?"

"I expect I'd not have much say about what happens in the east. But I've heard that Irene worries what will happen to the empire when her son comes of age to reign alone. If we were to wed, she and I could greatly assist him - she in the east and me here and in Rome. When we get old he will not be so young any more and will be better able to rule. It is just a thought though."

CHAPTER 4

Usually Beth worked in midtown Manhattan, in what's known as the garment district. The lofts of old factory buildings often served as inexpensive artists' and photographers' studios. They had a lot of space; and a lot of light entered through the tall windows that before electric lighting had supplied the only illumination. Today, however, she was uptown for a shoot outside St. Patrick's Cathedral. She was clothed; for once she wasn't posing for girlie rags like *Titter* and *Wow* but for a real magazine, one that wouldn't be quickly slipped into the buyer's pocket. It happened; not often enough, but it did happen. When the work ended and the sun was going down, the photographer offered a few cheery words and invited the girls for a drink in one of the better local bars. Beth chose not to join the others. She didn't like socializing in bars and she saw the girls often enough anyway. Instead she opted to spend a few minutes in the great church.

Putting on a scarf, she walked down the side aisle to the altar of Mary and knelt. She took a rosary from her purse - all Catholic girls carried a rosary at all times in the fifties, along with a safety pin for broken bra straps and "mad money" for escaping over-stimulated dates. She asked herself if she was good. The priests would say she was living a life of sin so she dared not receive communion; but couldn't she still be good? She went to church; and after all, Jesus himself had prostitutes for friends. She hoped she was good but wasn't sure. Certainly her family didn't think so. Oh, they loved her; but they worried for her safety, her future, their reputation, and certainly her soul. She worried about the last too, for she hadn't quite reconciled her own feeling that there was nothing bad about helping lonely guys "get off", with what she'd learned about chastity, abstinence, and cold showers from the nuns when she'd been a child.

She hadn't realized either, just how troubled she'd been about other things until now: wondering where her life was going ... a modeling career on its way down, a bunch of artsy beatnik friends who talked a lot but weren't actually accomplishing much, and no real boyfriend. Soon she'd be too old for modeling and she hated the thought of working a regular job in some office, or waiting tables in a diner. She'd been able to put away a few dollars but not that much. There might be enough to pay for a simple vacation abroad but afterward there'd be nothing left.

She'd need to work at something. She'd long since given up the fantasy that she'd meet someone rich and nice like girls met Cary Grant in the movies. That wasn't going to happen. Oh, there were nice guys and there were rich guys, but the "nice" guys weren't bringing a pinup model home to momma and the rich ones only wanted a mistress. Besides she was a fantasy to them all. They didn't want her; they wanted an animated pinup.

She gave it up; she couldn't keep her mind focused. She put the beads away and went and sat in a pew to think. The Gothic decoration around her was nice but not, she found herself thinking, as nice as the elegant mosaic decorations of eastern churches. Gothic was pretty but too realistic. *It is impossible to represent the unrepresentable, so why try? Eastern churches*, Beth thought. *I've never actually been inside one, just seen them in books: all gold and icons that only hint at representation.* Gold was the primary impression that Eastern Christendom had made on her artistic mind in school: gold and incense, and ritual. But there was something else about the mystic air which surrounds Eastern Christendom that now seemed to call her to itself in a way that St. Patrick's couldn't. She didn't know what, but she did know that recently she'd been reading and dreaming about the middle ages; maybe that had something to do with it.

Beth thought about a real friend of many years. Eddy Miller was her friend, just a friend. Neither wanted anything more. He was a photographer whom Beth had sometimes worked for when they'd both come to the city eight years before. Edward worked as a freelance photographer for whatever publication would hire him that day. At first he'd also waited tables at a forty-sixth street restaurant but now his photography was enough to earn a living, if only barely enough. In those early days he'd had dreams of being a great portrait photographer as Beth had of becoming an actress. Just earning a living had frustrated both ambitions; or to be more accurate, those ambitions had been put off too often to have much life in them anymore. In Edward's studio was a sad reminder of his ambition: an expensive view camera with which he'd taken an occasional portrait of Beth's pretty face, just for her.

Beth found herself wondering what they could do in the future. Eddy would be OK. There was always need for good photographers, if not artsy ones. He could open a photo shop or work for a newspaper, maybe do advertising. For herself though? study? Was she thinking about medieval Europe because she was regretting that she'd given up her history studies? No, that wasn't it. There seemed to be more. She sensed that something inside her wanted to do its part for others and that didn't involve study. It didn't mean giving more to charity either, or working in the missions, though the thought of her posing for mission magazines brought a not-too-innocent smile to her lips. No, that stuff was good, but not for her. She wouldn't worry anymore about her future though, at least not today. It would be what it would be. These things always worked out all right if one took Christ's teaching seriously about the birds of the air, and the lilies of the field: *"Your Father knoweth that you have need of these things. ... Therefore be not solicitous for tomorrow, for the morrow will be solicitous for itself."* No, right now she would concentrate on right now; model some more while she still could, and - a really weird thought - dream dreams. *How could dreaming be important?* Yet, she felt it somehow was. *Whatever*, Beth told herself, *I've not much to say about tomorrow anyway ... 'cept okay. If I feel right dreaming then let the dreams come.* She nearly laughed as an image struck her hard with an immediacy that daydream images ought not to have: herself in her knee-high, high-heel boots and leather thong panty wandering the courts of medieval Europe. She caught herself because she wouldn't laugh aloud in this holy place; but she did smile. It wasn't the famous smile she smiled for the camera. It was more innocent, more beautiful still.

"Marry that Frank? Of course not. Send him some princess if you like, but the empress herself... ?" The master of horse stuttered at the thought. "Honored Aetius, can you imagine Her Sacred Majesty out in the forest with a barbarous warrior? Why he can't even read."

"But he can, a little anyway, Illustrious Sir." A well educated man, the empress-regent's advisor and personal favorite, the protospatharius Aetius spoke the finest Greek; not the *koine* of the streets but something very like the classical language of literature, laced with a cadence inherited from the empire of the caesars. "Besides, reading and writing are not the Franks' way. The barons see no purpose in a warrior wasting his time with them. They may have a point too. They have little written literature of their own to read, you know, and their warriors see no reason to learn to keep records in the forest. They have clerics for such mundane things. Anyway, Charles is quite unusual for a Frank. Not only has he taught himself to read a little but he speaks good Latin and even some Greek as well as the old Teuton tongue. They say that he understands things well when they are read to him."

"Christ help us."

"Besides, I doubt he means to have the augusta riding around Gaul with him. Most of the time he is at war somewhere. I expect he'd just keep a vacant throne here in the city next to hers."

"Christ help us all."

"Anyway, don't worry overly. Our Sacred Majesty likes a little roughness in men."

"And how would you know? You've no beard. Are you privy to Irene's taste in men?"

Suddenly the conversation had degenerated and the two officials were talking about a Roman empress as though she were just another woman. This could be a very dangerous thing to do. Irene was not only known for her piety and comeliness but for her vindictiveness as well. Aetius could get away with much however. For many years he had been the empress' closest friend and if she could match him in subtleties and intrigue as well as in pettiness and brutality when cornered, he and his rival, the logothete of the dromos, Stauratius, were by far her masters in bravery and diplomacy.

"Even a eunuch can appreciate beauty," was all that Aetius would say in answer. But both men knew that on more than a few occasions Irene had sent her servants away so that her favorite minister could relax from his duties of state to comb and put gold highlights in her hair.

After their conversation, Aetius thought long about his future. The master of horse might be right. Where would he be if the augusta married the barbarian king? Aetius was a person of rank and authority, clever and able. He would have liked to see one of his own nieces marry into the imperial family someday. If this Charles were wed to the empress he could forget about that. In fact he would be fortunate to escape with his life. Charles was vigorous. He would not tolerate a competitor, least of all one who had combed his wife's hair. *No, a marriage between them will not do, but perhaps one between their heirs. It will be years before the children will be old enough to rule. Many things can be done in that time. The Franks' suggestion should be politely turned..... Yes, perhaps a marriage between His Serenity and a Frankish princess. It would be best for the empire. It would not hurt my future either if I were to find the little emperor a nice little blonde bride. I doubt my family will wear the purple any time soon anyway and at least that will put an end to Stauratius' plans for his family also.* Aetius seated himself by one of the many palace fountains. The sun was bright and the air was fresh. The palace was situated high above the waters of the fast-flowing Bosphorus that brought with them a cooling breeze from the Black Sea. That breeze was pushing the fetid air of the city away from the palace quarter and back upon itself.

This is no day for worries. Leave those for winter. There will be time later to consider such affairs of state as little girls with blonde braids. ... Yet, "a councilor ought not to sleep the whole night through." Aetius quoted Homer to himself for he knew full well that he'd never wait more than a day to deal with his duties and opportunities. Still, this fine day his thoughts amused the minister in a most innocent way. *Perhaps seeing to Constantine's happiness can be a pleasant duty.* For now, however, a rubdown would be in order. The fresh air would feel even better afterward. Though Aetius was a eunuch like almost all the palace staff near to the throne, he did not fit the stereotype of one. He was neither fleshy-fat nor lazy, but an active man with a successful record. True, his diplomatic career had not the glory and flash of his rival Stauratius' military successes nor did he have quite the power; but he had done as much for the empire and the empress, and he had no military embarrassments to answer for. - *"Envy is the ulcer of the soul,"* - a quote from Socrates. He was still strong and handsome for his age which was approaching the middle years. He had no hesitation about appearing naked in the baths.

Such was politics in eighth century Byzantium. The Caesar Nicephorus would have brought Irene down were he able to. He was not; and for their own safety neither Aetius nor Stauratius would ever betray the woman to whom they owed everything. Irene was their protectress against their own potential enemies, the many other ambitious eunuchs about the palace. These would not be loyal to the two out of a feeling of empathy or companionship; but to challenge the authority of either of them was to challenge the augusta herself. Their very lives and certainly the fortunes of their families would be at risk were they to oppose them. So the chief eunuchs were safe in Irene's protection, while their strength was her protection against usurpers.

None of this precluded constant infighting between supporters of the two chief ministers. Though Aetius and Stauratius feigned being above the fray themselves, they allowed the fight for power to swirl below them. While Leo had lived and exercised all power he had kept the fighting between these minions of his wife controlled; yet even on his death neither camp attempted to totally unseat the other. Stauratius had military and executive ability and it was he who wielded day-to-day authority under Irene, but Aetius was the more loved by the augusta. He also coddled the boy who would one day rule the Roman world. There was continual jockeying for position but neither camp would go for the kill. They combined in a cool alliance to forestall the efforts of Nicephorus to take the throne, and of the traitor Elpidios to entice other commanders to ally with his exile throne in North Africa.

Young Constantine was in the church of Saints Sergius and Bacchus, located above the sunny Sea of Marmara. It had been only a short walk from his quarters in the Great Palace to the south coast of a peninsula that also contained the city and a few small farms and vineyards, all protected by the most formidable fortifications in the world. Centuries in the past the city's population had been larger, but now fruit trees and vegetable gardens grew amid the ruins of some of the ancient houses. Everything about the empire was smaller now, including its reach. The blood of the city and state had always been trade. There was still a lot of that and Byzantium was still wealthy, but not so rich as before Mohammedan pirates began roaming the Mediterranean.

Constantine had walked, only accompanied by a minimum of guards; nor at ten years old was he inclined to affect a perfumed handkerchief against the city's stench. Once he would have run but mother had ordered him to act more grown-up after the death of his father. Soon he would be compelled to ride or be carried everywhere; then he would need to do boring exercises to keep fit for war. *It makes no sense,* the boy-emperor was already quick thinking enough to observe. He was also astute enough to appreciate what successful emperors had always known: It was politically necessary to be seen personally leading their armies from time to time, whether they were militarily capable or not, whether they were afraid or not.

The church was not as dark or brooding as some. The golden walls were decorated with bright colorful mosaics of nature which shone in the rays of the sun. They had been put there under the iconoclastic emperors to replace older images of the saints and martyrs and archangels. The sun lit everything; even the air itself, it seemed. It burst from large windows high in the barrel dome. It illuminated the whole of the church in a way that, beautiful as it was, so huge a structure as Hagia Sofia never could be, either by the sun or when lit by thousands of lamps and candles. Twenty-six years before, all the mosaic portraits, together with what his mother still called the "holy icons," had been removed from all the churches in towns and countryside firmly under imperial control in accordance with the theology of his father and grandfather. Soon they would be restored here as had already been done for his mother in the Pharos chapel. *They might look nice,* the boy thought, for he had grown bored with the pretty pictures of trees and fruits and birds. He knew that in the city there were other people who, though they had not dared to support the sacred images while his father lived, yet referred to the iconoclast decorations as resembling market scenes. The humor was not lost on the boy and had elicited a regal smile from his mother.

Constantine was ten years old but he prayed like someone ten years older. He prayed in fear for himself for he knew he had enemies. Even friends and relatives like Uncle Nicephorus might envy his throne despite their protestations and overt friendliness. Uncle 'Foros brought him toys whenever he visited …. real toys that had nothing to do with learning to rule the empire. He would also sneak him sweets to "rot his teeth," the man would joke. But Constantine always put them aside as mother had instructed. An emperor must learn early to be on guard against treachery even by - especially by - friends and relatives, his mother had told him. "Trust your mother and no one else save the holy saints." He would trust in Saints Sergius and Bacchus, soldiers who had died for the faith, for as emperor he would need to be a soldier too. This church named for them would be his personal favorite even if he were required to attend the cathedral more often. *What matter?*, he thought, recalling the advise of his chief tutor. *I must learn to live like an emperor, as Marcus Aurelius did ... and I must learn to die like one too as he prepared himself to. There are so many enemies. Marcus was not brave like a soldier and he knew it. But he was brave like an emperor. Duty. But it is not enough that I die well. I must live well, for emperor or farmer we must all make an accounting to Christ, and it is likely that I shall do so while still young.* The thought aged him some more.

Constantine also prayed for his father as he knew he should. Particularly, his mother had directed him to pray ceaselessly – even night and day in his heart – that the Divine Master would forgive the late emperor for all the evil he had been led to do. Not only had he destroyed thousands of sacred images, allowing only a simple if huge cross to differentiate the interiors of churches from secular buildings, he had flogged monks and even bishops who had dared try to protect God's saints. He had closed many convents and monasteries. His enforcer, Lachanodrakon, had forced monks and nuns to marry one another.

Constantine heard footfalls coming near. They were not the pace of his guards but those of his mother. The boy-emperor turned his head as Irene knelt beside him, prostrating herself before Christ's cross for a few moments before speaking to her son. It was one of those too-rare occasions when affairs of state were not pressing and mother and son could be alone together. Irene had always been too busy to be with him as much as they would have wished. Now Constantine was growing and there was a widening distance between them. Today, however, Constantine - still depressed at the loss of his father - was buoyed by the strength of the woman beside him.

"It is a good day for a walk, Constantine, though I took a litter here. It is good that you have sought out a holy place for yourself and I know you like to get away sometimes and just be a boy. But always let me or Aetius know when you do.

"Pray for your father, my son. I fear for his soul. But in only seven years you will reach your maturity. Perhaps Christ will listen to the prayers of a child destined to be the Isapostle - the very equal of His apostles - and the temporal head of His Church on this earth.

"I came to tell you, my son, that I have today heard from a most pious monk that a farmer working near the Thracian wall drew from the ground a wondrous omen: a sarcophagus with an inscription that the holy man within would be unearthed in our reign. I know that Christ has appointed us to rebuild His Holy Church here in accordance with the ancient ways. I feel it within me. There is much to be done, but since I have managed to secure leadership of the council of regents do not fear the burden. I will lead and you need only agree. It is most important that the extremism of the icon-breakers be eased or they will pave a path for the Paulitians who venerate the sun and moon and hate the Eucharist. Just watch; you will see what good your mother can do for Christ's empire."

Irene left but Constantine remained. *Does it really matter? So what, so long as each man seeks God.* Constantine had heard many of the arguments for icons both pro and con. He just didn't know why it mattered so much that men killed and imprisoned each other in Christ's name.

CHAPTER 5

From the heavens a lovely lady looked upon the sleeping daughter of Charlemagne. Her smile was bright as the sun for she knew that she loved God and He loved her. Nothing else mattered. She felt that she was clothed in a gown of nebulae. She was wearing sandals and her sandals shone in the light that she shed wherever she walked, bringing erotic love with an innocence which would have shocked Charles and Irene and the desert saints and church fathers, but not the Lord they worshiped. Even her thoughts were noble and near poetic now. The princess Rotrud could not know it but her identity would be borrowed by Beth this night and others. It was in the best of causes. *You are a fine young girl, Rotrud. You will find joy with the saints and be the very best of friends with a boy who will dream of you. You will learn in eternal life to love him as what he is, and he you for what you are. But eldest daughter of Charles the Great, I must borrow your name for awhile. The dreamer has need of me, Princess.* She hummed a German song for the sleeping German child:

"Heiaha! Der freude!	"Aha! What joy!
Hell am tage	Now through the daylight
Zu mir Isolde."	Comes my Isolde."

To her day and night were one. The night was as lively as the day and day as lovely as the night. Soon dawn would be on the world and everywhere life would be awakening.

That was all that Rotrud would recall when she slept and woke: grassy fields wet with dew, and the sky, without cloud or mist, as sharp a blue as the fields were green; perhaps the lingering notes of a song which would not be written for another thousand years. But it was enough; she lay happy in her bed of warm furs.

There was a flurry of diplomacy between emissaries who'd meet, usually in Italy, to discuss informally the needs of the two most powerful states in Europe: Byzantium, like an old woman, dignified and proud of her heritage both from Rome and from Greece - and from further east too; and the upstart Carolinian kingdom with a pugnacious ruler who, however, sought not to further diminish the Roman Empire but to revitalize it, reign over it with Irene, and rule in the west as its emperor.

This was not to be. Charles was too much involved with conquest of the Lombards to his south and the Saxons to his north to be courting the empress of the east. For their part, the Byzantines: monks, courtiers and tradesmen alike, were unwilling to let an unlettered barbarian sit on their throne beside their saintly Irene. The diplomats tried heroically and with some success to further improve relations but there had been feuding over who would control Sicily and North Italy. This might have been reason to bring the two monarchs together but instead it irritated both. There were skirmishes between their troops. Charles reluctantly accepted that his fate lay in the west, not in the east. If he were to overreach, the conquests he had already made for the Christian faith might slip away. But as he held the bargaining chips of former Byzantine territory in Lombardy and the exarchate of Ravenna (which he had taken but not yet determined to hold), it had been suggested by the empire's emissaries that he might still consider the honor and profitability of one day having a grandson rule from Constantinople.

To Irene, Charles seemed not to have the belly to thoroughly wipe out iconoclasm. *There must be "one fold and one Shepherd," one empire worldwide under Christ, the ruler of all; at peace with itself because cleansed of all heresy. Then there will be true Christian love and peace through understanding of the one truth, not a false and temporal peace bought by cowardly compromises with false doctrines. Let us make it so. Charles is too kindly toward iconoclasm but if a grandson of his should rule a reunited empire ... one educated here?*

The two states shared real interests – neutralizing the heretics within and the barbarians outside their frontiers. They must not wage serious war upon each other. Oh, a province here or there might change hands, peacefully or otherwise; but the Byzantines had learned a hard lesson when after a thousand years of warfare between Rome and Persia, Byzantine armies had finally defeated the Persians. They had won but the effort had exhausted both. A few years later the armies of Islam quickly devoured all of the Persian lands and much of the Roman when they rode out of the deserts of Arabia where they had never before been more than a nuisance to either state. That holy fight wore on and on. Now there was another and equally dangerous enemy: pagan Bulgars in the north who might devour more imperial territory if the empire were further weakened by a conflict with Charles. So, although Charles and Irene were never to regally frolic in the imperial bedchamber, the diplomats still had much to do. The mutual problem which constantly came under discussion was the Bulgars and their aggression-minded Khan Khardam. If these warriors from Asia were a growing but poorly understood threat to the Franks, they were better known to the Byzantines who had watched with concern the victories of their khans as the tribes moved steadily south and west into Roman territory. Already they had marched along the Black Sea into semi autonomous parts of Dacia. The empire had accepted this reality decades before but now they were threatening Moesia and Macedonia.

Charles held court throughout Frankland, not only at Aachen, staying for a time at the fief of one or another of the great lords. Only occasionally would he gather all, or most, of them together in one place. Unlike the chief ministers of Irene who were always together in Constantinople, Frankish barons did not hold their titles and lands from the crown. Powerful as he was, Charles effectively held his kingship at the will of the nobles of the land. From time-to-time one or another of these would declare his independence and then it was the work of war or diplomacy - usually both - to bring his loyalty back to the king. Not so in the east. The dukes there held their appointments from the empire and it was both treason and sacrilege to go against the child-emperor and the empress-regent. Few would dare do that unless he felt strong enough to make himself emperor, and no such *doux* dared confront the power of Aetius and Stauratius in the capital even with an army at his back. The threat to the rulers of the world was not so much armed insurrection as court intrigue.

This winter Charles was staying at Ricolf's fortress at Bacheim. He regularly visited many of the towns and castles of the realm to insure his authority and to spread the cost of lodging the king's entourage among as many nobles as possible. He was not in the great hall which he merely tolerated, but more at home in a small room sitting on a plain wooden chair improved somewhat with a cushion. His wife, Hildegarde, and several of his many children were nearby. The day's work was ended and he watched absent mindedly as a servant tended the fire over which a pot of good cabbage soup still simmered. It would do for his breakfast too, he had said; rather upsetting Ricolf's cook's menu for the next morning. The fireplace smoked badly and everyone in the room coughed. But they were used to it. Two of Charles' younger daughters had helped him remove his heavy cloak and sword belt for there were many days now, particularly here under the leaden skies of cold and wet Bacheim, when he felt the aches of creeping middle age more than he liked to admit. As he sat, half sleeping and half musing on some business, his eldest daughter, Rotrud, entered crying.

"Oh Daddy, it's cold; there's nothing to do; and Alcuin* is going to Italy where it is sunny and warm and there is lots to do."

* See note: pg. 206

"Ha!" Charles snorted. He tried not to laugh, for despite the snort Charles loved Rotrud above all things on earth. "There is plenty for you here. You have your studies, don't you? You should learn proper Latin so that you can read the Church fathers and some of the better Romans too. You have your spinning to attend."

"Daddy, I am a princess. We can buy cloth or have it woven."

"Of course, child. But what kind of example is that to set. Listen to your father. If the king's household do not do the same chores as the people, at least so far as time allows, then every noble in the land will think that he doesn't have to either. Soon they will feel it is below their dignity. Then where will our people be? To the chieftains they will be nothing but servants to do their bidding as in some other lands. And daughter, know this secret: No matter how strong a king may be, he is no stronger than his barons together. His natural allies are not the lords he is surrounded by, but his people. He must serve them while letting the nobles think of him as one of them."

"I know, Daddy." Rotrud had heard it before and knew it to be true. She started to drag herself toward the fire looking as grumpy and disappointed as she dare.

"But, daughter, I do have a surprise for you." The king produced a pretty ring and with it the picture of a boy perhaps two years younger than she. "This ring is a gift from that Constantine who reigns and who will be the next to rule in Constantinople.... There it is sunny and warm."

"He is the son of the augusta, Daddy. Is that his picture?"

"Do you think he is handsome, Rotrud?"

"He's a kid."

"He is only a little younger than you; but he probably knows more, living in the great city as he does. You must understand that I do what I can for you children. I've brought us teachers from Britain and Italy. But Aachen and Bacheim are not the capital of the world, dearest. In Constantinople there are great schools with famous scholars, and even the clergy know far more than what is in the church's books." Charles thought to add how sitting on an unsteady throne would also mature the lad quickly. *No. I need not frighten her. I'm sure Constantine has friends as well as enemies. May God grant him the wisdom to know the difference.*

"What has this to do with us? Are you sending me to Constantinople? That would be fun."

"No, daughter; not yet at least. But I spoke with two of the empire's highest officials who had come all the way to Italy to visit me when I was in Rome. They are sending a famous tutor to teach you Greek. His name is Elissaeus and he is a great scholar."

"Daddy, I've enough to study now."

"Rotrud, you are to marry Constantine when he is a little older. This ring is his troth. I will write to him and his mother to tell them that we look forward to visiting them some day. Would you like that? Would you like to be empress of the Romans sitting on an ivory throne in the great city with this handsome young man beside you?"

The young princess, not yet quite twelve years old herself, thought for a moment. Confusion and worry showed on her pretty face. She realized now more than ever what it meant to be the child of Charles, called the Great. Should she argue that she should have some say in the choice of a husband? That was not necessary. Daddy would never force her into a marriage and there was time enough ahead to confirm or back away from the agreement. How could she know? She had never met the boy. What would he be like? Some spoiled royal brat? Perhaps not. She had heard of him from Ricolf who spoke Greek, and knew a lot, and who rather liked him after hearing the reports of her father's agents. Then she remembered a verse from the bible and her face brightened. She had no intention to be sacrilegious so she did not say it aloud, but the verse was so fitting: "*Be it done unto me according to Thy word.*"

In time spring came even to North Germany

"Ricolf, I have a job for you."

"Certainly, mi-lord What is it?" Great Charles was more relaxed than he had been in days. Word had arrived from the northern front that operations against the Saxons were going well. As important, the local people were accepting the priests sent among them, or at least not assassinating them in the night. That was good. It pained Charles to have to chastise peasants but he would order whatever was necessary to stamp out idolatry in his growing realm. There would be one Christian world at least so far as he could achieve that in the life which the Father had given him. Forced migrations and a trail of blood through the north had demonstrated that early in the war. This determination, if no other, he shared with the Augusta Irene.

"A marriage alliance has been discussed between my house and the empress regent's. No, not us: our children. There is no need for a formal betrothal or to exchange provinces, or anything like that at this point; but I want you to bring my assurance to the empress and her son. My Rotrud is a sweet little thing and I think she and the basilios will get on very well together. Then, when I am gone, my liege will be the more inclined to give Constantine their allegiance knowing that one day a grandson of mine will sit on the imperial throne. That will be good for all the world, Ricolf. Do you not agree?"

"Certainly, mi-lord."

"Ricolf, I want you to take young Bertmund of Loutern with you to Constantinople. He can serve you for a squire until you get there. Then, I'm afraid, you'll have to respect the importance his family ties give him. He is a good lad and will not mind serving under you en route. He is also smart enough to do what you say before the lords of the east when he may technically outrank you. I'm sure they will understand the arrangement."

"I understand. He is indeed a fine boy. But why me, Seigneur?"

"You, because I want Bertmund to learn about the world; I doubt he will ever be particularly able in battle. He is the studious type, which is good; but he has not had the benefit of your wide education. Perhaps you can pass some of that learning to him on a long trip. Take your time, visit the holy shrines of the saints; but also let him see something of what the empire was in ages past."

"Indeed it would be educational, sire. Indeed it would. But has this mission anything to do with Bertmund other than to educate him?"

"In a way. We must raise the caliber of our liege here, Ricolf. I can't have my grandson thinking of Frankland as just some barbaric province. You know I've started what I can and I hope the next generation of lords will get off their war-horses long enough to travel and study some. Then, perhaps, they will be fit to take places among the emperor's closer friends and advisors. That will only happen if we work at it. Bertmund's father rules a lot of territory and will rule more if the Saxon war continues well. Bertmund will be a very important man. It would serve us and the whole empire if when he takes over for his father he were a good friend to the emperor and perhaps spent his time in Constantine's city instead of on the frontier. We can leave that for the more warlike."

"But why Bertmund, mi-lord? There are others even in your own household."

"Yes, but my sons will be busy here. We need a man who is free to roam but also one who is good. Constantine will have many very intelligent advisors but he also needs that one of them be a good and loyal friend. I would have that friend be a Frank and we agree young Bertmund qualifies. He shows intelligence, but as important, he is six years older than Constantine; both young enough and old enough for the young emperor to confide in. ...And as you say, he is a fine good youth."

It was not long before knight and squire were on the road. Clearly the future of both East and West for many decades to come were at stake. Besides, summer would soon be upon the land. That was the best time to cross the Alps, after the mud and before the snow which would come all too soon. They took the best-traveled path to Italy, descending from the mountains into the marshes that had once given refuge to Romans fleeing their city before Attila. This was the site of what would one day be beautiful Venetia, the pride of maritime Italy, but in the eighth century it was little more than a notable market town and a run-down lair for bandits.

"We have work to do, Bertmund. We must get to Ravenna and find a good ship and a trustworthy captain. I should not like explaining to Great Charles that I lost you because the captain thought you comely enough to sell to some Arab slaver."

Bertmund was still young enough to blush. He'd heard of such things happening and he was, in fact, pretty in a boyish way. He knew it and wished it were otherwise which was why the youth was growing his first mustache and hoping it would show some fullness by the time they reached Constantinople.

"I had a dream, mi-lord."

"You dreamed of some pretty lass. I hope."

"No Seigneur. I fear I do that too though." The blush upon the teen's face was shadowed by a look of fear. "It was a terrible dream. There were demons in it and they were chasing me."

"But they did not catch you, Bertmund?"

"No mi-lord. But I fear for my soul. I try to do what the priests say; but it is hard. I carry a little holy water to chase away the evil one; but it is hard. I fear the demons will catch me weak some night and that will be the end of it. I will go to hell."

Ricolf put on a serious face. It was well that the youth worried for his soul, but it were better that he do what was good for the ideals which churchmen had taught him. *Live well, do good; not merely for your own salvation but for the sake of others. That is how one loves and serves the Lord. Charles is right; there are enough mere warriors among his liege. The king ... and the emperor too ... need men who will always advise them what is right - for the sake of their souls to be sure; but better, to do so because Christ has given them that duty; has put them mounted and armor-clad above the multitude of men, not for their own sake but that of his empire on earth.*

"Listen Bertmund. I have lived many years and fought in many battles. The worst of these were not against warriors but against demons. Let me assure you that they were not dreams. The demons had no horns and were hard to recognize as such. They looked like you and me because they were men like us, but men who had forgotten to love the Lord in His people. I suppose I sound like a priest but believe me, the demons we must defeat are those who give our lord Charles advice that will advance themselves, not the good of the Frankish host; those who fawn upon great Charles but care only for their own advancement. There are enough of these without worrying when awake about creatures of our dreams. Perhaps it is the Lord himself or your angel who sends you these visions to warn you not to be like such men. One day you will die and then, indeed, devils will be awaiting the souls of the evil and the weak. Be good. Do good and you need not fear the judgment. That is what Christ asks of Charles' liege. Now give me that blessed water." Bertmund took a little stone bottle which hung under his tunic and opened it. Ricolf touched a drop of the water to his finger and drew the sign of the cross on his squire's forehead. "I stand in your father's stead, Bertmund, and in his name I ask our Lord Jesus to give you strength, in the name of the Father and the Son and the Holy Spirit."

In a few days they reached Ravenna.

"Now lad, we have work to do. There's not much left of the port here but there are galleys and men who know the waters to Constantine's city .... Ah! But first some sightseeing." The two Franks left the local palace where a vassal of Charles held court; a Longobard of no great virtue save the wisdom to remain loyal to his faraway lord. They began to walk the streets, most of which were far less grand than those near the palace. The houses were mere wooden shacks and much of the town stank of shit and marsh water. Some old boards thrown in the mire were generally all that kept the Franks' feet out of the muck and Ricolf thought of how much more civilized the cities of the empire had once been, where stone blocks had provided a way to stay out of the mud and excrement in the street. Very few of these remained in place. "This was once a great city, Bertmund, the second or third city of the western empire for centuries. Before that, when it was but a village, great Caesar marched from here to end the Republic. The emperors ruled from here when Rome itself was threatened by the Goths. The churches are marvels of mosaic decoration. In San Vitale there's one showing the emperor Justinian with the Illustrious Belisarius who returned this city to him. Ah! Have I ever told you of Belisarius, lad?"

No, he had not. In fact the only things in that history lesson that Bertmund recognized were Caesar and Goths.

"Belisarius was the finest man ever to lead an army; absolutely loyal to the emperor. If some men are demons in disguise, Belisarius was a saint in armor. He could have taken the imperial throne himself, or at least ruled over the Goths here. That's what they themselves wanted. Instead he remained loyal to the emperor Justinian .... a fine man, a great commander, pious, fair to his men and to the peoples he conquered; generous, not a meanness in him. But that was long ago."

"I've heard of Caesar and Justinian but not this Belisarius."

"Caesar! A brilliant general it is true, but pagan, and vainglorious like Alexander. Fighting is a lamentable business. It must be done sometimes to bring Christ's holy Gospel to devil-worshipers, but not .... Jesu forbid .... for your own glory."

Ricolf was unusual for a Frank in that he at all honored Belisarius, a foreigner; and for regarding him as much for his character as his success in

46

battle. Most of the Frankish liege would hardly have heard of the great general and certainly would not have agreed with Ricolf's assessment of warfare. Though Christian they looked forward to combat as relief from the boredom of administering their lands and villages and wives. If successful they would get booty and ass. If killed … well, to die in battle was a proper way to end a life. At the annual *Campus Martius* the great lords would confirm who would be their enemy that year and Charles would issue the *heriban* requiring that his local officials choose men at arms and arm them well for that year's campaign against some pagan enemy. War was their life.

Some days passed before the ambassadors could take ship but finally they rented a galley. A war galley was far safer than going with the wind since Moslem pirates had begun to infest the Mediterranean and even the Adriatic sea; though in Greek waters the imperial Navy still ruled. Ricolf did not forget the boy's dream though he made no more mention of it. Dreams did not always signify anything, he knew, even if some people didn't. Of course when younger, like Bertmund, he'd been frightened often enough by the holy stories of Christian priests and by the demon-summoning of those pagans who still remained in the realm. But after nearly forty years of life nothing really bad had yet happened to him, save for the loss of his wife through the impersonal plague. Ricolf was inclined to relax. *The devils are not nearly so active as our imaginations,* he'd concluded, *or the plots of simply bad people … men and women both. Perhaps women more than men as the holy fathers of the Church have often written.* Anyway, tomorrow they would go aboard the *Clement* and sail for Constantinople. The priest they'd met at San Apollinare near the port was an educated man like so many of the Italian priests, at least those from the higher classes. He would bless their ship and their mission as a priest ought, with sensible prayers that the Lord might actually attend His ear to; prayers sincerely asking for Christ's help to achieve a good purpose, not drivel about demons and serpents, with an excess of blessed water and smoke.

In the event, the good father merely repeated the words spoken by Pope Clement I, patron of boatmen, for whom their ship was named: "Charity unites us to God. There is nothing mean in charity, nothing arrogant. Charity knows no schism, does not rebel, does all things in concord. In charity all the elect of God have been made perfect." It seemed an appropriate message for a Christianity in peril of being pulled apart by the rulers and churchmen whom Christ had set over it.

CHAPTER 6

On the other side of the seas Nicephorus waited in the Anadendradion, an ancient garden in the imperial palace. It should not be supposed that the Sacred Palace was some single immense building after the style of western royal castles in later centuries. Rather it was styled much in the manner of the Turkish Topkapi complex now standing near the same spot, a collection of buildings built at various times and in varying styles, of pavilions of stone and silk; of formal gardens, walkways, carefully tended herbs, fountains, delicately screened bathing pools, storehouses, and chapels. This garden, dating from the time of Justinian if not the blessed Constantine I, was the delight of the court, with tall cypress trees and several ancient oaks flanking the porticoes through which the child-emperor would often enter preceded and flanked by angelic eunuchs – their hair cut short or in ringlets, pretty maidens, and courtiers from the extremities of his empire. A field of green grasses and vinca minor interspersed with marble fountains and beds of lilies, hyacinth, and narcissus fell away towards the Bosphorus. The air was not only fresh, it was perfumed by the flowers which could actually be smelled here where no donkeys or sweating porters mingled with those who ruled. Had Nicephorus not been preoccupied he might have compared the songs of nature's own birds with their clockwork counterparts that decorated several of the fountains and sat on ivy-covered walls that separated anyone in the garden from the city's stink on the opposite side.

But today he was preoccupied and it was not his imperial nephew that Nicephorus waited for but Eustathius of Dalmatia, an acquaintance of many years - *stupid but useful*. For a few moments only, before he must turn his mind to matters of state, the caesar allowed himself to dwell on a cherished fantasy that he dare not indulge. Were he a common soldier he might from time-to-time enjoy some pillage and rape, particularly the rape – some buxom peasant girl trying to outrun him; while he, mounted on a war horse, could easily run her to earth. Easily yes, but it would be more satisfying to take his time and play with her like a cat plays with a mouse. *A cat does not play with a rat,* he thought, *far too dangerous; but a young frightened mouse-girl. ... Some nice rope work while she watches with terrified eyes, and the lunge.* However Nicephorus wasn't a common soldier. He was a caesar and nobilissimus and far too well known to indulge such tastes, particularly now that he had been forced to take Holy Orders. That had not always been so. When young he had dared chance the fantasy a few times. A large payment to a discreet pimp. No questions. He'd taken a few girls that way. *Very few, too few.* And their struggling had not been entirely faked. He'd made sure of that.

Eustathius was approaching. As soon as Nicephorus was certain that Eustathius had also sighted him, he crossed himself and slipped into a chapel where they would be alone.

"Caesar Nicephorus," Eustathius made the accustomed kowtow. "Last week I was visited by a stranger. The man said that he is a house carpenter but I doubt it. He is quite fair skinned. I doubt he has spent much time under the sun. More likely he is a spy."

"But for whom, Eustathius?" Eustathius had information so Nicephorus spoke kindly..

"He is neither from the east nor the west; nor is he a foreigner. I think he may be of Moesian blood. Many there are disloyal to their Sacred Majesties. Some prefer western rites, others are Paulitian heretics. Some have contact with the Bulgars."

"Yes." Though Eustathius had stated what was well known Nicephorus determined to be charming. "What was he visiting about, my friend?"

"He ... the man gave the name of Pamphilus and that is a Greek name but he was certainly not a Greek. ... He wanted me to introduce him to somebody who could help him get a job at the palace. I believe he might have sought me out because I, myself, have a poor reputation. There are those who think I am disloyal."

"You have crafted a fine mask, Eustathius, and we appreciate what you have done to your own reputation for the sake of Christ's holy empire. Pursue these possibilities, good friend, particularly any Bulgar connection. I am forever in your debt for your concern for us. If you are right he is probably up to no good ... a spy as you think perhaps, or worse. Their Sacred Majesties will be enormously grateful if you have helped secure the Christian empire against our enemies."

Nicephorus just barely emphasized the word "enormously."

"Ah, but now it is time to relax. Will you join me in the therma?" He was being polite. He knew what answer to expect: "It is not good for you to be seen being too friendly to me." Eustathius excused himself with a grovel.

Constantine's city came into view from the Bosphorus just as dawn broke over the hills of Anatolia. This was the world-famous view spoken of by pilgrims and other travelers: the merchants of Italia, the wandering tradesmen of Thracia, and an occasional slave trader from barbaric Bohemia. From the boat it appeared that everything in the city had just been painted. In fact, the city looked like a painting in the early rays of the sun. The seaward walls were bright white, like marble although surely built of some humbler stone, and the houses were white as the walls and roofed with tiles of blue or red clay. Most spectacular of all to Franks from the forests of northern Gaul, dozens of churches reflected the dawn on their golden domes.

Oarsmen had driven the galley through the night to reach the city before word of the ambassadors arrival could reach possible enemies of their king at the Byzantine court; for certainly they had been sighted as the ship passed through the Hellespont to cross the Marmara sea. Now they approached a quay in the palace harbor of Boucoleon, an honor indeed not to have to land at some naval dock far from the palace. The appearance of the city had not been entirely a figment of the sun's rays, for at least this harbor was indeed of white marble. Below the bright walls was a large sculptured lion seizing a bull by the horn, pulling its head back and setting his teeth in its throat. "Probably the work of some ancient artist," Ricolf said to his squire. "The city is full of such stuff." The knight knew this for a certainty for he had been there when he himself had been a youth in the service of Pepin, Charles' father, the man who had taken the Frankish throne from the Merovingian line.

"Such stuff," the knight rethought what he had just said. *I should not deprecate these arts before the boy. They have their place, even if these Greeks make too much of them.*

"I am a simple old battle-ax, Bertmund. I serve our king and try to serve Christ. But these Greeks have much to teach us. Be careful not to let stupid ignorant knights tell you otherwise. Charles is quite right about the need to learn from the ancients, and these people can tell us how they made the great artificial water courses, built amphitheaters which stand till this day, and constructed the marvels of Rome and Ravenna."

"We have seen the churches of Ravenna, mi-lord"

"Yes. What did you think of them? The original mosaics are still there… and well cared for. For that we must thank the clergy and the Holy Father in Rome, but mostly artisans sent from Constantinople to care for them when an exarch had that Lombard's palace."

"Very beautiful, mi-lord, but Charles' new church in Aachen shall match them and give as great glory to God."

"Perhaps, Bertmund, but they are nothing to what you are about to see in Constantinople. The cathedral ... The locals just call it the "Great Church" but it's Hagia Sophia in Greek … The cathedral could hold Charles' church, great as it is, under its dome; and craftsmen from here will oversee the artwork in the Aachen cathedral. This week I will take you to see the city walls; not these sea walls, fine as they are, but those which protect the city from the land side. I don't think we could make such fortifications in Gaul now."

The knight might call himself a mere battle-ax before his squire but he was far less rude than the lords who generally served Charles. These, indeed, were mostly crude fellows from estates cut out of the northern forests ... or not even that ... tribesmen from east of the Rhine who had been newly brought into the Frankish empire by the reach of the king's ambition and the success of his armies. Ricolf had been educated in the schools of Italy; better educated than the Frankish clerics who were entrusted with routine matters. That was why Charles had chosen him to go to the Empress Irene; not because of a reputation for valor, for his was modest; nor for the prestige of his land holdings, which were fairly modest also; but because he could talk like an educated man to the Greeks. At least he'd know enough to be silent when conversation went beyond his understanding; instead of insulting his hosts with some crude comment intended to show the warlike character of the Franks, but that instead would show their ignorance. In a few hours Bertmund would take up the role of co-ambassador and everyone would recognize that he had been chosen for the prestige of his family, and to learn; whilst Ricolf represented the will of the barbarian king. The court would remember that Ricolf, himself, had first visited when not much older than Bertmund was now. In his turn, Bertmund would become a diplomat too. That would be borne in mind and the lad be given a good impression of the empire, of its rulers, of its power, of its good intentions, and of its status as the center of the four quarters of the earth.

"I just called these people 'Greeks', Bertmund. That was a bad mistake and doubly so for a messenger of the king. We must not forget that this city is still the Roman capital even if the augusta has no real power in Rome itself. Charles still honors the young basilios as temporal head of the whole Christian world, at least in spirit. He would do that only for a Roman autocrator whatever his lineage and home, so long as he rules in Constantine's city in an unbroken succession of emperors ... never for a mere Greek."

"Very complex, mi-lord; but I will try not to insult the vanities of the ... Romans here."

"See to that." Ricolf made his face stern to impress the importance of what they were discussing on the boy. Bertmund nodded. Truly, he was not quite a boy or thought himself not to be. He had seen his sixteenth birthday at Ravenna which he and his master had celebrated with much good Italian wine and fish dishes unknown in Gaul.

The ambassadors were kept waiting for several weeks in the comfort of a large villa that was quite near to the Great Palace. Bertmund was delighted with the delicacy with which they were treated and the dress and manners of the populace. Dignitaries of the empire wore rather oriental clothing, often turbans. Women drew a kind of veil across their faces when in the company of strange men. They were spied upon constantly but that was to be expected in any court. Nor were Ricolf and Bertmund particularly secretive. There are those things that one cannot officially speak of before the thing is done yet does want revealed, so the young Bertmund made no great secret of his happy mission to affirm a proposition of marriage between the boy-emperor of Byzantium and the eldest daughter of Charles. Nor did he make it any secret that Charles felt such a union would benefit both. Charles did rule the western empire in fact if not in name and this was a soreness to the imperial throne. In Roman law he was king only of the Frankish people there. He was the emperor's designated authority over all others in Gaul. An alliance of blood would give real authority to his position. He could expect to be appointed a caesar. His power might even require he be made augustus in the west and co-emperor with his son-in-law. For the empire: the young emperor's mother would gain a secure frontier in the west and firm peace with the Franks in Italy, a son happily occupied with western ways, and free reign to confront the Arab menace in the east and the Bulgar threat to the north ... as well as the freedom to destroy the Iconoclasts, the Paulicians, and the Monophysites; to her the worst enemies of the Christian state. True the emperor was only ten years old and the princess only twelve. It would be seven years before their marriage but it was not too early for the couple to begin to know each other. Ricolf hoped that better understanding between the two peoples would lead to better relations. *Although we cannot begin to match these Greeks in knowledge of the arts and sciences, our barons would be fine allies for them ... They may even learn to like us; at least our women go about unveiled.*

There were titters in the streets and more raucous humor in the wine shops as rumors spread about the probable future of the child-emperor with a barbarian bride tutored in barbarian bridal customs; but there was also far less pleasant news. Another small fort south of the Danube had fallen to a Bulgar advance detachment and the garrison had been massacred. They had fought but had not felt it necessary to fight to their deaths in a hopeless defense of a minor strong point. After a three day defense the garrison surrendered. That was a mistake. The captive soldiers did not simply have their hands tied to be sold as farm labor somewhere to the east, their arms had been painfully crossed behind them and each hand forced to its opposite elbow. Feeling as though they no longer had hands or arms at all but simply torsos they were drawn to their captors' campfires to watch as the holy icons of their regiment were added as firewood. Then one by one the Roman troopers were thrust in. Without hands they could only squirm like worms. If one managed to roll his burning face out of the coals the Bulgars pushed him back into the flames with sticks, poking at him as one might a rather large piece of firewood. Their screams meant nothing. The Bulgars did not even laugh or joke, they simply drank their beers, and watched, and poked absent mindedly as with a piece of wood. The stench was awful but the Bulgars seemed hardly to notice. Only a group of children, awake past their proper bedtime, held their noses and made faces, making a game of it as they ran between the fires.

The Bulgars did not only murder captive soldiers. They swept through a village that lay in the shadow of the fort, mutilating the men with axes and raping the women and children - especially the children that they might attach more terror to their khan Khardam's name. Even those Christians who tried to refuse the crown of martyrdom died. When Irene was informed of the atrocities the empress retired to the Pharos chapel to beg forgiveness for the souls of these apostates.

Still, the raid had been only a minor incursion, a probe. The frontier of Christ's empire was threatened but certainly it would hold. Irene was certain of this; Stauratius and her generals were only hopeful.

CHAPTER 7

Asleep, Beth dreamed a dream like none she had dreamt before. She was standing on the battlements of a fine stone castle that overlooked a white city beside a warm sea. She did not know why but she sensed that she was needed here. She knew that there would be some joy and much sadness, a long deep sadness that she thought should make her feel as bad as the boy in the city below. Somehow it didn't though. What would happen would happen and be of no importance. *"Weeping may endure for a night, but joy cometh in the morning.* "(Psalm 30:5). Beth looked out from the castle battlements and launched herself. She stretched up and out until it seemed to her that she covered the earth and that she herself had become so thin, so vapor-like, so like a net that the stars in her gown were the only reality about her. She saw below her the earth in night: villages, cities and lonely farm houses, the occasional shepherd on a hill and fishermen earning their pay at sea. Beth knew their personal agonies: The loss of parents ... or so it seemed to them; they would learn. The depression of losing, if not one's loved ones, than all else a man or woman or child might value in their world. She knew their thoughts all at once and had she dwelt on the pain Beth, now so frail, would have dissolved in her own tears. She felt each fully yet all together, none more important or less than another, for whatever the details, each was suffering to his capacity. There was need of her this night and Beth was all softness. In kindness she blew the clouds away that a child might look upon the tiara in her hair, a soldier her jeweled sandals, a lonely woman waiting for her husband who would not come home, the belt that clasped her waist. Each would see such bright and sharp stars as ever he had seen before and in them know the peace that comes with the perspective of endless ages and infinite distance. Beth awoke. She was at home again in her own bed. *What a strange dream, but beautiful.*

"We can confirm the agreement reached in Aachen then?" Ricolf and Bertmund were listening to a perfumed and rouged eunuch; obviously a learned man since no monkish translator was needed as would be the case in their other meetings.

"Yes. If you will, please convey it to the augusta. If it is acceptable to Her Serenity, I expect king Charles will be most pleased. He admires the augusta, you know, not only for her holiness and protection of her people from the heresy of the iconoclasts, but for the skill with which she has devoted herself to the council of regents in the emperor's minority."

"Thank you, Seigneur Ricolf." The eunuch used the respectful term that was gaining popularity among the Franks. "If I may dictate the terms to Brother Iosephius here."

"That there may be one fold and one shepherd as Christ Jesus prophesied, and for their great love and admiration, and that the Roman empire may again be a single Christian and orthodox body under one administration in the city of Constantine, with one body of law throughout both east and west; the Augusta Irene, as mother and regent, has agreed to the proposal of a marriage between the basilios Constantine, and Rotrud the daughter of Carolus, the empire's patricius in Gaul and king of the Frankish people there.

"The wedding of the emperor and the princess shall be in the New Rome, which is Constantinople, when the emperor shall have attained his majority.

"King Charles shall take his throne as caesar and father-in-law of the basilios. Those provinces which the king now administers for the empire and those which he may recover north of the Danube and east of the Rhine River he will continue to directly administer for His Serenity.

"Since the empire shall once again be one unbroken state subject to Roman law and custom, with the consent of the Roman senate the blessed Constantine and his successors shall exercise sole rule of the entire of the Roman empire in the east and in the west and Charles' sons shall forfeit any rights to rule under the law and customs of the Franks, yet shall be deemed caesars of the empire and as such administer as his *comes* such provinces of the empire as the basilios shall think fit and also such lands as they may recover from idolaters and usurpers."

At their good-byes Ricolf spoke warmly and tried to hide his dislike for most eunuchs. There were eunuchs in Charles' court too, but fewer and with less power for mischief. "We will see you again soon, I hope. My king has asked that I show Bertmund some of the Roman constructions and he thinks it would be good for Bertmund to speak with some of the clergy too. For Bertmund's sake we took our time coming through northern Italy. Regrettably, too many Frankish lords know little of the... of the emperor's domains south of the Alps. I promised to show Bertmund your defenses - not the details, of course - but the land walls as an enemy would face them."

The ambassadors' acceptance into Roman society was signaled by an invitation passed on by the eunuch to dine with the emperor's uncle Nicephorus. After the Frankish ambassadors escaped the eunuch - who looked as happy to escape the barbarians - they began a long but leisurely stroll through the city. They had already seen the hippodrome, the great brick and stone race course which was near to both the Great Palace and the cathedral. They had been warned not to take sides in the fierce rivalry between the two factions there: the Blues and the Greens. For centuries these rivals had disputed everything from horses to theology to politics, very often with riotous and deadly result. They were a good deal weaker and more ornamental now, but in the time of the emperor Justinian, Belisarius had put down a revolt in the hippodrome which had nearly toppled Justinian from the throne. True to form, the emperor had not long appreciated the general's personal devotion for he always feared that Belisarius would himself seize the throne since he was perhaps the more capable and certainly the more popular. "How little he understood Belisarius," Ricolf lectured Bertmund. "True, his best friends can become a monarch's deadly enemies, so he must choose his friends well. Justinian chose well but then failed to respect his own choice."

The ambassadors left their residence and wandered awhile the side streets near the Golden Horn, that inlet from the Bosphorus where much of the city's trade as well as the Roman navy made port. Here there were no palaces but only wharves, workshops, and slums. The naval shipyard and arms depots were appropriately clean and orderly and the warehouses businesslike. The slums were slums however, so accompanied by a troop of Vigla guards which the empress had insisted on providing, they turned south toward the main thoroughfare of the city. It was a wide street that ran from the Great Palace, under the arches of a fine aqueduct such as Bertmund had only seen the remains of in Italy and southern Gaul, straight to the city walls. They passed monuments and statuary, and homes built after the Roman style for the aristocracy and merchant classes with windowless exterior walls but sunlit interior courtyards. There were also numerous tenements of several stories to house the poorer citizens. There were parks, forums, and uncounted monasteries. Several of the monasteries were located outside the urban area itself, among vineyards but still inside the circumference of the city's defenses. These were large edifices comprised of chapels and housing for the monks; but also of refectories for the poor, hospitals for the city's sick, and hostels for merchant visitors to the city. The *Mese*, for such the street was called, ran past the famous monastery of Studion straight to a polished brass gate which shone like gold in the walls of the city. The Golden Gate, which was normally opened for the emperor alone, was near to a substantial fort that anchored the southern limit of the land walls where they met the sea wall at the Sea of Marmara. From there a coasting ferry brought the tourists back to the palace precinct before dark.

Had they lingered at the fort until after sunset they might have noted how bright the stars were on the sea that night.

The following day Nicephorus sent litter bearers, a translator, and a large force of guards to accompany them to his palace. The ambassadors would have preferred to walk again but they could hardly dismiss this formidable entourage without giving insult. The caesar Nicephorus had been delegated as tour guide not because of the rank or worthiness of the Franks - he would not have bothered to stand to greet them - but because the basilios was to wed the child of their master. After lunching at the palace Nicephorus ordered a carriage that would hold the three of them and they continued their tour of the capital of the world. Perhaps because they were to be friends and allies now, or perhaps because it seemed wise to have the ambassadors broadcast the strength of the empire's defenses, Nicephorus allowed Ricolf and Bertmund wide freedom of movement. They climbed to the battlements of the fort they had seen the day before. From there they could see for several miles an unbroken stretch of stone defenses: white walls three deep, a wet moat, and towers every few hundred feet. Behind the walls was a wide roadway on which troops could move quickly to any threatened section. On the towers heavy ballistae waited. There were wheeled vehicles on the middlemost of the walls. These they were told carried the fire weapon. Ricolf thought better than to ask to examine one close up for such a request would surely be politely refused amid embarrassed explanations.

It was nearly nightfall when the party arrived back at the caesar's palace. Nicephorus did his best to be pleasant at dinner that evening, explaining that the delay in obtaining an audience with the basilios and his mother was regrettably unavoidable et cetera. In truth the empire neither wished nor dared to seem hurried before barbarians, even somewhat cultured allies.

In the following days Ricolf, Bertmund, and the caesar Nicephorus together with a host of that prince's followers had little to do but continue touring the city. Ricolf had seen some of its wonders before but Nicephorus was a good guide to the younger Frank and enjoyed or pretended to enjoy the role. The Franks had already been inside the great cathedral but Nicephorus was able to give them a more detailed understanding, pointing out some of the engineering feats of the architect Anthemius of Tralles which had gone into its construction some two hundred and-fifty years earlier. "Even now," he noted, "no one has constructed a larger dome anywhere, nor - with the protection of the Blessed Mother of God - one so immune to the earthquakes which from time-to-time trouble this city." Nicephorus beckoned to a retainer. "Comantes can quote the historians from memory."

"Procopius was the first to write of the Great Church for he lived in the time of Justinian who built it: 'Who could recount the beauty of the columns and the marbles with which the church is adorned? One might imagine that one has chanced upon a meadow in full bloom, for one would marvel at the purple hue of some, the green of others, at those on which the crimson blooms, at those that flash with white, at those, too, which Nature, like a painter, has varied with the most contrasting colors. Whenever one goes to the church to pray, one realizes at once that it is not by human power or skill, but by Divine influence that this church has been so wonderfully built. The visitor's mind is lifted up on high to God, feeling that He cannot be far away, but must love to dwell in this place He himself has chosen. All this does not happen only when one sees the church for the first time, but the same thing occurs to the visitor on each successive occasion, as if the sight were ever a new one. No one has ever had a surfeit of this spectacle.'

"The writer of the *kontakion* composed for the inauguration of the church describes the light: 'This sacred church of Christ evidently outstrips in glory even the firmament above, for it does not offer a lamp of merely sensible light, but the shine of it bears aloft the divine illumination of the Sun of Truth and it is splendidly illumined throughout by day and by night by the rays of the Word of the Spirit, through which the eyes of the mind are enlightened by Him who said 'Let there be light!'.

"Paul the Silentiary sang a hymn of praise: 'Above all rises into the immeasurable air the great helmet of the dome, which, bending over, like the radiant heavens, embraces the church. A thousand other lamps within the temple show their gleaming light, hanging aloft by chains of many windings. The night seems to flaunt the light of day, and be itself as rosy as the dawn ... Thus through the spaces of the great church come rays of light, expelling clouds of care, and filling the mind with joy.'"

"Enough now, Comantes," Nicephorus interrupted. "Thank you. I'm sure our guests can observe the truth of these verses themselves."

Outside, Nicephorus dismissed most of his entourage except for a few score Slavic bodyguards, and the group began strolling past the great hippodrome and nearby palaces. Nicephorus tried to keep them distant from the huge odoriferous stables of the household cataphracts, for the air was still and the day was hot. They observed the aqueducts which supplied water to the city itself as well as to the fountains and baths and toilets of the imperial residences. Ricolf noted the great number of granaries and huge subterranean reservoirs. *This city cannot be starved out,* he thought. They strolled again along the Golden Horn where a fleet lay tied up at the naval shipyard. The air on the piers stank here too, but this was the clean aroma of pitch. Many busy hands were at work loading some warships which were preparing for action against pirates in the Aegean sea. Nicephorus pointed out the massive armories and factories where the fleet's weapons were made and stored, including the fire weapon which burned on water of which, however, he would say no more. "A state secret, you know. I'm a caesar of the empire and even I am refused the formula." *Nor can the city be taken by sea, much less by land behind the triple wall,* Ricolf was thinking when the noise of a nearby marketplace attracted Bertmund's attention and he requested to see how a typical city dweller lived in this part of the world.

What they saw was an amazement to the young man. The trade goods for sale were even richer than what he had seen in Italy, brought from the farthest quarters of the empire and from its barbarous neighbors, even from the Arab-controlled provinces with which Byzantium was usually feuding. There were textiles, weapons, and furs. There were spices and perfumes such as Bertmund had never known; but what most attracted his attention were the many craftsmen gathered here in one place, not scattered across many fiefs as in his homeland. It was while observing some copper smiths that the characters of Ricolf and Nicephorus were clearly distinguishable to him. Though the Greek would point out the artistry of a design, Ricolf was as interested in the technique which created it and would engage the craftsmen in friendly, even respectful conversation; admiring not only the beauty of the finished pieces but the skill and imagination which had created them. By the time the group moved on, almost an hour later, Ricolf and Bertmund knew more about copper smithing than Nicephorus would ever have cared to learn and also a good deal about the smiths' families and homes, their small triumphs and failures. Nor did young Bertmund fail in his first small attempt at diplomacy. The smiths were surprised when Bertmund promised to send to them a relic of Saint Maurus, the patron of copper smiths, from the abbey at Glanfeuil in Gaul … a promise he kept. Unlike most Byzantines who broadly characterized Franks as uncouth and barbarous, these men now had a broader vision opened to them and each would ever afterward speak of the day when he had entertained noble visitors from the far-off kingdom of Carolus - Charles called the Great.

Finally the day of audience arrived. The ambassadors were not the only visitors to the Chrysotriklinos palace on a September morning. The empress-regent and her son had been busy. Besides the usual courtiers, bishops, and dignitaries of various types, certain Asian traders had presented themselves after a hazardous and arduous trip from the Celestial Throne of Cathay. They had brought with them besides the usual rich gifts, a letter sealed with the Tang emperor's own seal offering peace and trade, and advice about the ways of war of the Turkish tribesmen who lived between the two greatest empires of the world. Interesting observations to be sure but not unlike the ways of other barbarous nations that had threatened Rome before. Of more concern to the strategoi near the imperial throne was to find a way to reverse the nation's losses to the nearby Arabs. These Moslems had seized half the empire, and more, and had even dared to attack the capital itself. Worse to Irene, their strict prohibition on images had infected the eastern provinces of her empire and furthered if not instigated the iconoclasts.

When Ricolf and Bertmund arrived, young eunuchs, chosen for their angelic beauty, led them a winding way past many of the palace attractions, stopping to let them admire - or gawk in Bertmund's case - at the mechanical birds that competed with nature's own in song. There was statuary by Phidias and Praxitiles. There was a menagerie which Bertmund would have liked to compare with Charles', but time was not sufficient for visiting a zoo. Though they certainly were not rushed, protocol and promptness were paramount and strictly enforced. Yet once inside the building, the ambassadors were kept waiting five hours, enough time to indicate their subservient position as barbarians, but remarkably short by imperial standards where even great notables often had to wait days for an audience. They waited in a pretty antechamber, fussed over by other *angels* who brought teas and sweets to help them pass the time. A senator - a man of some substance and position if little authority - was detached to engage the foreigners with pleasantries. Of true Roman ancestry, he prided himself on his mastery of classical Latin and spoke to them in that language. He entertained Bertmund especially with stories of his ancestors who had been among the original immigrants to Constantinople, brought there by the emperor Constantine the Great when he had founded the city five hundred years before.

The ambassadors had brought gifts for the imperial family. There were ornaments of fine workmanship and a great broadsword such as the Frankish cavalry had begun to employ, but this one richer and more ornate even than Charles' own. There were also the first fruits of the Aachen palace's new scriptorium, a Psalter of fine workmanship modeled after Celtic originals - It certainly would have been unimpressive to bring one fashioned after the Byzantine style though these were the more plentiful products of the scribes. Yet all in all there was not much that was Frankish that would impress the court at Constantinople so these gifts were supplemented with a fine reliquary holding a bone of St. Hospicius of Thier, the authenticity of which had been vouched for by Pope Adrian himself.

These things were effusively accepted by eunuchs who prepared them to be displayed artistically for presentation. Then Ricolf and Bertmund were called to the throne room where they were immediately plunged into a world of particularly rich incense, gold and silver fixtures, marble columns, and sparkling jeweled mosaic walls newly depicting Christ and the saints. The room was a domed octagon and similar in construction to Constantine's favorite church, that of Saints Sergius and Bacchus. It was bright because of the many windows in the octagon compared to the relatively small size of the overall room. Bright, but certainly not in a lighthearted way. The impression was severe and yet assuring. As with Victorian furnishings, in the hands of lesser craftsmen the overall effect might have been poor, but the artists who had made and improved the effect over five hundred years were the best in the empire. Bertmund now knew how primitive his homeland was. At his majority the young emperor would be the anointed of Christ, His chosen representative on earth. Though enemies without and heretics within might continually attack, they could never prevail.

Not an audible word would be spoken by the rulers of the world and few by others. At a sign from one of the white-robed *angels* Ricolf and Bertmund prostrated themselves in accordance with the tradition of the court. From somewhere the strains of an organ roiled and a choir intoned something in Greek. Ricolf might have understood some of it but Bertmund could only recognize the *Kyrie Eliason* repeated after every stanza. Kneeling face down on the floor the ambassadors could see nothing but did hear the cries of mechanical beasts and birds such as they had earlier observed in the imperial gardens. A touch on the shoulder advised them to rise and look upon the serene rulers, mother and son, who sat silent and glorious on high marble thrones like the Madonna and Child, wearing stiff vestments of gold cloth ornamented with holy images and adorned with precious stones. Beside the emperor was an empty throne reserved for Christ, the true Ruler Of All; whilst the whole scene was illuminated by shafts of sunlight as though from paradise itself.

The audience did not last long. *Angels* whispered to the emissaries but there was really nothing to discuss. All details had been prearranged and the audience was but to put the Augusta's authority and the future Basilios' acceptance to the agreement in the presence of the patricians and senators of the empire. Afterward in a palace garden there was more informality, much hugging and even some joking. Constantine was the star and for once his mother allowed him to shine. Ricolf spoke to him of Rotrud and Charles, but it was Bertmund, a teenager, only six years older than Constantine, who spoke longest and most earnestly to the emperor. His congratulations were heartfelt. Ricolf had spoken of Rotrud's intellect, her modesty, and her piety. He had also allowed that she had a well-favored face; but Bertmund, without any artifice, used words like "fun" and "laughs" and "cutie" to describe Rotrud. In fact Bertmund stopped just short of saying something about a nice ass. That would be far too undiplomatic. After all, he was describing a twelve year old future empress and wife to the ruler of the world, and he only ten years old himself. It was what might be expected of a barbarian and that was why he held his tongue.

Constantine believed what he heard about his fiancé: that she was pretty and vivacious, and with a high humor more befitting a mistress than a wife. That last was good but probably not something to be shared with mother.

CHAPTER 8

Beth was without fear or worry. She had a mission to be sure, but no care. She was entirely young and pretty in both the eyes of God and his children. Her image began to float earthward. On his bed Constantine sensed her. As the priests taught, he forced his mind to matters not of the flesh

"In the morning when thou art sluggish at rousing, let this thought be present: I am rising to a man's work." Constantine tried but it was not easy to emulate Marcus Aurelius. *Come to think of it, Marcus must have had the same problem getting up, otherwise he'd not have had to encourage himself.* "Flinch not, neither give up nor despair if the achievement of every act in accordance with right principle is not always continuous with thee." Constantine rolled out of bed with a small smile on his lips. *Maybe the old emperor wasn't such a perfect model after all. Stodgy though.*

He was growing up and he knew it. Last year he had been betrothed to the daughter of Charles of the Franks and this year his military training had begun in earnest. For two hours each day he trained with sword and ax and bow. For another hour he studied strategy and tactics at the palace command school. This was the first time in his life that he had shared a classroom with other boys rather than studying alone with a tutor; but these things were not arts to be studied alone. He had to match and hone his own skill and insights against other boys in argument and tabletop war games. Then too, when he would come to command armies he would need subordinate commanders whose judgment and abilities he understood as well as he did his own. Commanders in the Byzantine army came from many places, including the ranks, but it was those he knew now who he would most trust in battle because he knew what they would do. As a later commander would say: "The battle of Waterloo was won on the playing fields of Eton."

Yet Constantine was not so old that he did not enjoy lying abed with a pet cat and that was what he would do this fine morning. Old Furface was not just any palace cat. A social climber, she had somehow become the emperor's own pet many years before when they had both been very young. Not that Constantine wouldn't stoop his serene self to chuck a rival under the chin; but there was a special place in his heart for this animal which shared the imperial bed and could be counted on to wake beside him each morning with an annoyed look, wondering no doubt why her friend had to always rise so early.

They both had breakfast and, although it was not the usual thing, Constantine then returned to his chambers with Furface, or rather he followed the cat back to the bed. The sun was bright and warm through the marble lattice and while they'd been eating breakfast the pale green and white marble room had been cleaned and decorated with small sculptures and brightly colored flowers. *Just as it should be,* the cat was probably thinking if it was thinking anything at all. Her eyes were slowly closing and the emperor lay quietly so as not to disturb her. Though Constantine was still young, Furface was not as the lives of felines go. At best she was middle aged going on elderly and the emperor dreaded the day which must come when she would die. Of course being emperor, he already had enemies. It was possible that she would outlive him. He was unsure which thought depressed him more.

Am I brave or a coward?, the young emperor questioned himself. He did not know and Furface, if she knew, was not answering either. *When will death come? When I am young or old, or sometime in between?* The question was pointless as Marcus would have noted. It would come at God's chosen moment and that was that. But how he would meet it worried the boy. A shepherd or farmer, even a soldier, might die crying and soon no one would remember either him or his death; not so one born to the purple. He must die well as he must live well. It must have troubled old Marcus Aurelius despite all his protestations. After all, their memory among men was all the pagan emperors had to trust in. For a certainty, he too had known fear and been uncertain of his own bravery. *"Do not worry about it,"* the patriarch had assured Constantine: *"You will die well if you have lived well."*

Is that so? Constantine hoped so, for he was trying his best to live well. The priests had given him the martyrs to emulate and John Pikridios had given him old Marcus. *What was it Homer sang? "It is not unseemly for a man to die fighting in defense of his country."* He could try to die well if he died in some battle against some enemy of his people – he owed them that. But how would he face some assassin in the night without his friends and comrades about him to steady his resolve? What if he were wounded and his dying took days or weeks? *How can a man die well like that? I am not an ancient hero. I will try, but I am not a hero. What if I am tortured?*

It did not take long for trusted agents of Nicephorus to determine the tribe and purpose of the spy who had approached Eustathius of Dalmatia and less time to turn him into a double agent, or more precisely a conduit. The man was of Macedonian, not Moesian, stock but had lived many years north of the Danube in an area for some time now under Bulgar control. That the Bulgar khan would have spies in Constantinople was to be expected. That he would use someone who, though obviously not Greek, still might pass as one of the empire's subjects was likewise to be expected. But that a mysterious person acting on behalf of a high but unknown official of the empire would recruit the spy as a two-way conduit of information was more than Khan Khardam had hoped for, though it was certainly not without many precedents. What was troubling to Khardam was the high official's purpose. Was he a potential ally within the enemy's palace or a loyal Roman probing a growing threat to the empire?

Nicephorus was both, of course. As a Roman he hoped for the defeat of the Bulgar threat and would cooperate with the empire's military and foreign service. But a day might come when the khan could be helpful. To his mind Irene had stolen the throne from him. As Leo's half-brother he was the late emperor's nearest blood relative save for a boy under his mother's thumb, who prayed for peace between iconoclasts and iconodules and would never be fit to rule. *The future is not to be known*, Nicephorus concluded. He crossed himself out of old habit. It cost him nothing and signified little. *But not to be prepared for whatever opportunities the fates may provide would be foolish and stupid.*

Nor was it necessary to hide his interests from officialdom. Nicephorus, even as a young man, had recognized the growing danger north of the Black Sea and had made the language and customs of the Bulgars a study. Now he was considered expert on them and was welcome in those conferences which discussed them. That he had spies and contacts in the Khan's camp, while never mentioned, was assumed.

One source of power for Irene - one which a man like Nicephorus would never understand, care to understand, or even think important - was the delight she took in showing herself before the people of Constantinople; and the pleasure that the ordinary man and woman took in seeing their beautiful and adored benefactor step from the heights of power to be with them; much as Evita Peron would do twelve hundred years later in Argentina. Had she not been so lovely, to look upon her stola alone would have delighted the crowd; but the great lady took care that her every hair was where it belonged and that every graceful fold of her garments hung just as it should. Irene had everything. She was blessed in form and face. She was pious, educated, and powerful. She seemed caring of the people. On occasion she would distribute coins to the poor as she rode ceremoniously through her city on a brightly gilded chariot drawn by four fine white horses. Even more frequently she would travel in holy procession to some monastery to seduce the monks with her undoubted piety, and perhaps her smile.

It is not that vanity was one of her faults; these were ambition, and even brutality, when a more subtle and disarming manner failed to advance her aims. But she had been told since she was twelve that men found her beautiful, and not only by those who sought to flatter. She accepted this beauty as another gift from God, one to be used for higher purposes.

What was not obvious to the crowds she waved to with almost a teenager's *joie de vivre* was that in the Great Palace their saintly augusta was mean-spirited and petty. She was sly. She held tightly to those things which made her powerful, like riding through the streets while waving to the populace and tossing coins among them.

Irene ordered and happily planned the decoration of a new retreat for herself, the Eleutherian Palace overlooking the sea on the southern limits of the city. It was between the two places that were her other sources of strength: the villa of Stauratius and the monastery of Studion -- the sanctuary of which still stands, a group of verde pillars amid the squalor of modern Istanbul. Those palace buildings which had been completed were magnificent. The people of the city could see that and they roundly approved the extravagance. When completed the gardens would rival those of the Great Palace itself. The chapel was a glory of gold and silver and fine marble. Portraits of the saints and archangels rose to its ceiling and covered the spaces between finely worked columns. Christ Pantocrator watched with stern approval from above.

Arabs had always been a formidable enemy but now the Bulgars were becoming increasingly troublesome. Reports from spies were becoming fewer. Their presence had become known and they had been killed. Yet everyone had spies. Why were so many being killed now instead of earlier or later? The Bulgar khan was making a statement for they were not simply axed to death. They died martyrs for the Christian empire, torn apart by horses. It was as though Khardam wanted the screams in Dacia to be heard in Constantinople.

The three who ruled the empire met in one of the consistoria, a small meeting room that looked out upon a large courtyard, or would have had the lattice shutters not been drawn. Their guards were Slavic ax-men from far north of the imperial frontier with no loyalties to be compromised and a poor knowledge of court Greek. But they would hear any commotion from there far better than in a fully enclosed room if an assassin were to sneak in. The emperor was not present and the usual formalities of the court had been relaxed at the wish of the empress-regent. Irene stood with Aetius and

Stauratius at a table covered with maps instead of sitting alone on a high throne. Aside from the usual terms of respect and diffidence to her, the three behaved almost as equals which in fact they nearly were.

The maps were of several types. There were ornate scrolls dating from the centuries when Rome actually ruled the northern provinces in fact as well as name. Other, simpler ones, had been prepared over the past several decades by *curiosi* and *agentes in rebus* -- secret agents in the provinces -- to show not physical sites but rather problems and opportunities: places where stronger fortifications might hamper an invader or where Byzantium's own armies might meet stiff resistance. Still others were quite recent and had been compiled by the foreign office. These were mere sketches with rough approximations gleaned from merchant-travelers, barbarian captives, slaves, and returning missionary priests.

Stauratius, as the foremost strategos of the empire, as well as the day-to-day *de facto* ruler, was obviously in charge despite his bows to the empress-regent to whom he would occasionally look for a sign of approval. These signs were always forthcoming, for Irene knew and cared far more for the theological disputes within her realm than she did for annoying foreign enemies: "You take care of the Arabs and Bulgars," she had often said to Stauratius, "I will deal with our enemies within."

Aetius listened to what the logothete of the dromos had to say. Aetius was certainly not Stauratius' friend but neither did he want him for a full-blown enemy. Then too, Aetius for all his own ambition was a politician, not a soldier. He knew that and secretly cursed his rival for being good at both - well, fairly good. Stauratius had his victories. He had also had defeats and that perhaps more than anything else kept him from having total influence over the empress-regent. He ruled in Irene's name but Irene was no fool. She listened to the advice of others too. He was Irene's most powerful minister, but not so good a friend as Aetius. If she took a disliking to him he could lose his eyes as many other ministers had in Byzantine history. Though Stauratius loathed Aetius as much as Aetius did him, the Logothete would listen carefully to his rival and even pretend he was a friend. Both Aetius and Stauratius knew there would be failures. *"Zeus does not bring all men's plans to fulfillment,"* Homer had written. Failures were inevitable and it were best for Stauratius to share some of the glory of plans made in conference that led to victories. That was the price of sharing responsibility for those that ended in defeat.

"Here is the problem," Stauratius continued. "Your Serenity, the northern frontier is wilder than in centuries past when there were infantry legions to defend it. The forts are nearly denuded and what troops we have there are no longer locals but from other parts of the empire. The Bulgars are not welcome there but neither are our own soldiers. I must admit some sympathy for the farmers. Anatolian cavalry can be a rough lot to live next to.. "

"Then the Bulgars can take Thrace? Is it that serious?"

"Perhaps not Thrace, Majesty. They will raid there but with the help of the saints we can hold. However, Macedonia is another matter and we've no reinforcements to send. Harun is making too much trouble in the east."

"Yes." It would be disastrous to let more of Asia fall to the Arabs, even temporally." Irene spoke and her ministers listened politely. "The simple folk can be seduced to become Moslem. Then, even if we win the provinces back, the poison remains and strengthens the iconoclast argument."

"The Bulgars, Augusta?"

"Stall them. Send gifts. Let Khardam think it tribute if he likes. Promise him one of Leo's nieces and a title if he will give up idolatry and conquest. Talk to Nicephorus."

CHAPTER 9

Rotrud lay on her bed in a room directly above her father's rather larger quarters at Aachen. Grander; but not by all that much, for while great Charles' taste was simple he could deny his daughters little, and Rotrud, his favorite, almost nothing. Fortunately for peace in the family, gentle Rotrud requested little beyond the treats her father showered on her. It was a warm night and her maid had opened the draperies to let in some air. The healthy aroma of hay and horses drifted up from the courtyard of the manor. *Perhaps it will make Daddy's aches better.*

She lay on her bed and thought of Constantine. Ricolf and Bertmund had spoken well of him on their return from the city. Ricolf had spoken fondly as a proud father might of a fine son, describing Constantine in such manly terms that Rotrud near forgot that he was still but a boy. "He will be older soon," Bertmund had said, and "he is grown beyond his years in many ways. I guess having such responsibilities ahead of him does that." Both had also spoken diplomatically but with considerably less fondness of the empress-regent

Rotrud on her bed knew that she must grow in strength to be a fit wife to the emperor. Would that mother of his be a help or a problem? A problem, she feared. Even though young, Rotrud could read between Ricolf's phrases a concern. Irene was "pious and strong." Pious was used too often to describe her. Was she as fanatical as her reputation had her to be? "Strong?" That meant domineering. That might be good for the empire. It would be bad for her and Constantine. Ricolf had spoken guardedly of the boy emperor's wish, and her own father's too, to find a position on the image problem that would keep peace without angering Greek monks and the pope on the one hand; or on the other, the fanatic iconoclasts of the Anatolian desert, supported as they were by a large part of the provincial armies. Such conciliation would not please Constantine's mother.

Rotrud had other thoughts about Constantine. He was growing older; old enough, she reckoned, to be thinking of her and wondering if she were pretty. *How would he like me to be? Sweet? Vivacious? Smart? Big or little in front and behind?* There was nothing Rotrud could do about the last, but for the rest.... And how would he act toward her? Rotrud looked at the very formal portrait that the empress had sent of her son and which Bertmund had assured her was very stiff and unnatural ... a particularly poor likeness. He and Ricolf had described him in fonder terms which put Rotrud in mind of the Solomon Song:

"I see my love leaping upon the mountains,
Like a young stag, skipping over the hills."

She fell off to sleep. Her hand moved of itself to touch herself, and Rotrud dreamed a dream of him.

"Let him kiss me with the kiss of his mouth...
A bundle of myrrh is my beloved to me;
He shall abide between my breasts..."

At twelve Constantine was now experiencing the first uncontrollable throbbing of puberty. He was expecting it but of course the child had not expected it as it is. He was not certain that what he felt was even good. That especially when the protospatharius Aetius suggested that as a man he should now move from his child's rooms into his late father's imperial suite. The bed was huge. Aetius showed the youth the hidden door: "To escape an assassin," he had diplomatically – but also frighteningly - put it. But the door opened both ways into the women's quarters and not all the unmarried palace girls were aged frumps.

The patriarch had warned him of the sins of the flesh without a great deal of passion. Several monks, on the other hand, had painted word pictures of hell with its demons, and with sinners falling into pits of fire. They had not failed to include that emperors too, though they ruled Christ's church on earth, were still subject to the judgment. Iconoclastic bishops were suffering there now; as were those emperors who had forced marriage upon monks and nuns; except in the unlikely event that Christ Jesus had accepted a deathbed repentance by his father or grandfather. They told of holy virgins who had died under colorful tortures rather than share a pagan governor's bed. Indeed they made the bed in Constantine's new sleeping chamber seem more a trap door to hell than a place of rest.

None of this jibed with Constantine's dreams. More than a few were of pretty girls, innocent but exciting. Why should it be that he was excited merely by the sight of some lass in a dream? After all, they weren't doing anything wrong. They weren't unclothed. Sometimes they were just running around, playing games. But his dream-girls were always more happy, carefree, and smiling than the real girls he knew. "Demons, none the less," the holy monk Platon of Saccudion on the Asiatic shore of the Bosphorus assured him. He must awaken and do penance to learn control of his earthly flesh.

He tried. But in truth Constantine did not want to control his dreams; nor did he wish to control his urge to wrestle with several girls of the court of about his own age. But he must. "Be patient, Your Serenity," Aetius had advised. It seemed curious that a eunuch should be so understanding. "They are gentle and weak, I know," he had said, "and they smell so nice when they come from the baths, all cheerful and full of life. They move differently." That was so. The boys that Constantine knew were full of life too, but it was an aggressive life with a hard edge. In their games his friends were like young bulls competing to head the herd. There was something of play missing in teen boys but very present in girls. Aetius understood. Still, unlike the monks he had urged patience, not abstinence, and Aetius was a wise (if cunning and often amoral) counselor.

The words of John Pikridios echoed those of Aetius: "Be patient, Your Serenity. That door will always be there. But the monks are right about sin if only because to sin is foolishness. Do not rush merely because as emperor you can have whatever you wish. Would you be a Nero or a Caligula, or some other monster who because he was born to rule the world never thought to rule himself?" As usual he had a quotation from Marcus Aurelius at hand: "'How many pleasures have been enjoyed by robbers, patricides, tyrants! Take care that thou art not dyed with this dye; for such things happen. Keep thyself then simple, good, pure, serious, free from affectation; a friend of justice, a worshiper of the gods; kind, affectionate, strenuous in all proper acts. Strive to continue to be such as philosophy would make thee.'"

Like the monks and Aetius, John was right, and Marcus was right ... but boring. Constantine lay himself on his father's bed and retreated into dream. The dream he dreamt now was not quite so innocent as well-clothed young girls running in his courtyard ... giggling and their legs flailing left and right beneath their skirts. Or to be more exact, it was erotic but innocent still. There was one girl only; a girl – older than he was – who curiously appeared only in flashes. She did not move but was like a painting, yet far more lifelike. A figure caught in motion except that, curiously again, there was no color to the image. Still, that did not matter. The figure which was all black and shades of gray was unlike anything the young emperor had ever seen or could ever imagine; a smiling lady in very little clothes and holding a whip as though it were a flower. *She should be wearing more clothes,* Constantine knew. *Still, this dream is not evil. It is as though the sun walks beside her.* Waking, Constantine knew that the apparition was not evil no matter what the monks might say. After all, they hadn't dreamt his dream. *They think only of self-mortification in some dark cell. What would they think if she were to use that whip on their bare asses?* That image amused Constantine more than he thought it should. *Would they die of shame or chase her away yelling "demon"?* Constantine refused to think of the lady as anything but good - not an angel to be sure, but good. He could not think otherwise of her, and each night he fell asleep hoping to dream the dream again. He did. When Constantine confided his dream and his thoughts to the patriarch, his All Holiness restrained a smile in loyalty to the monks but wondered himself what they'd do in the face of such eroticism. *Oh, they can resist a painted whore well enough, but a smiling young thing whom the sun itself walks beside ...?*

CHAPTER 10

Two more years passed and life at the two courts continued with each primarily interested in affairs on its own borders. While Rotrud flowered into a pretty and intelligent princess - a fitting wife for the ruler of the world if a little unlettered by the high standards of Greek nobility - Constantine was also growing. It is impossible now to be certain why, but he developed a passionate fondness for his fiancé, though they had not yet met. One may assume it was what was told him about her, and the few carefully prepared letters that she wrote. Then too, it may have resulted from his imaginings of a strange and barbarous land; but it is tempting to think it was also influenced by dreams. Of course when awake the teenager knew that his dreams were only dreams, and that his fair Rotrud - while pretty, and bright, and cheerful - no doubt wore bulky dresses, not the little things he dreamt of her in; and that if she carried a whip like the lady of his dreams, she thought of it as having no other purpose than to hurry a horse. Still, he could hope.

Meanwhile there were occasional frontier skirmishes with the Arab enemy. The court - and particularly Nicephorus - also kept a close eye on the approaching Bulgar threat. In Aachen, the expansion of Charles' empire into the German forests occupied him and his armies for most of each year.

On a sunny afternoon Constantine sat under a tree in an imperial garden, his own tree in his own garden. Six years before, he and his late father had planted this tree with their own hands while imperial gardeners and an army of courtiers looked on smiling, chatting politely and encouraging the emperor and the emperor-to-be; the courtiers all the while being careful not to dirty their silk garments. It had been a pleasant retreat for the entire court from the strain of diplomacy, strategy, and the ever underlying intrigues of the officials; these usually being petty spats, but more than occasionally compromising the crown. Military and civil leaders with no liking for each other had, that day, happily, even merrily, joined together in drinking toasts of fruit punch, dancing peasant dances on the grass, and chiding the emperor Leo in ways that protocol would not normally permit. There were limits, of course, to the informality, but none were so stupid as to breach these. Young Constantine and his father, dressed in gardener's clothes and gloved with leather mitts, had succeeded in digging out the softened soil of the garden and entrenching the willow with only slight help from the professionals whose ancestors had been imperial gardeners for many more generations than the Isaurian dynasty had ruled.

But that had been six long years before when in Constantine's own mind he had been a child. Now he was fourteen; his papa was dead, and his mother ruled in his name. His days were not so carefree.... *Or had they ever been carefree?*, he thought. His own safety had always depended upon him knowing that there were men who would prefer him dead. He had been warned over and over not to trust anyone, no matter how close; not even close relatives, especially not his uncle 'Foros.

Nicephorus was away now and Constantine's mother was busy inside the Sacred Palace. Except for a few guards slightly relaxing at the gate as much for the teen's sake as for their own comfort, Constantine was alone on the grass under his willow. *How big it has grown so fast*, he suddenly realized. *It has been six years it is true, but other trees have not grown so tall in six years as has mine. I am growing too. If I were not to be emperor I would be working in the fields all day by now ... or fishing. I suppose that isn't much fun if you have to do it every day. Other boys have their work to do and I have mine. Attic, Latin, a bit of Persian and the vile Bulgar tongue to look like I know more than I do ...and mathematics, rhetoric, geography, navigation, astronomy. Theology especially. Why must I know all about old heresies that no one cares about anymore? I'd rather do football or race with Phillippus and Meletius... or Rotrud.* Constantine did not need to look at the portrait he always carried now of Charles the Frank's daughter to see her features in his mind's eye, but he chose to. At fourteen he could see the girl was pretty. *She has a nice smile and those barbaric braids would be oh so nice to steer her by... Get along Rotrud; we have to be home by dark. I wonder if she would want to be with me or just sit on a cushion being a princess all day long? We could play victorious emperor and his barbarian girlfriend, or maybe I could be a cataphract with a war-horse and Rotrud could be my captive. No, I am growing too old to play.*

The boy put away the picture but did not cease to think of his fiancé. *We will rule the west again. Her papa can visit here and I can go to Italy on a big dromon. We'll be able to catch fish along the way and she can cook them herself in the Frankish style. Bertmund said that her papa made her learn to cook and sew just like a peasant woman. He said that she is sweet and that she doesn't smell of perfume at all but only of the pine forests when she comes home after riding all day; or of herself, I suppose, when she has bathed in a mountain stream.* The boy felt good, very good; better than he had ever felt before. He did not know why but was sure it had something to do with the fair Rotrud.

76

"My most excellent and exalted pupil." The voice was that of John Pikridios. He had approached unnoticed by the youth who had begun throwing clumps of dry dirt into the grass, imagining the explosions of dust to be the navy's fire-weapon which had saved the empire before and probably would again. "Your Serenity, wake up. It is time for us to be trying to make sense out of the Gnostic heresy."

"Sir, I can understand why the Nestorians were important. They held half the empire. I think I understand why the eastern provinces disagree with us about icons. But the Gnostics were silly devil-worshipers."

"Perhaps." The tutor did not condescend. The boy's question was serious and deserved a serious answer. He must understand the dualist heresy without becoming frightened by its excesses; or worse, falling under its seductive philosophy. As the emperor's tutor since he was eight, John was allowed a more relaxed demeanor in his presence than anyone else in the palace, save his mother and his old nursemaid. With barely a hint of bowing away John began walking toward where the guards stood, the boy's eyes following him. One hurried to meet John part way across the field. He borrowed a cape and returning to Constantine's tree, lay it on the sward. "Perhaps here in the sun is the best place to discuss such dark matters. Do you think the Persians silly?"

"No. They hate us and they fought us for thirteen hundred years, as you've said; but they are not devil worshipers."

"No. No one but an idiot would worship devils. But they do believe there are two great powers, God and Ahriman. God is good, but he is only the God of the spiritual world. Ahriman is the creator of everything material. The Gnostics believe much the same. There is the Father who is the God of the spiritual and there is Ahriman, the Demiurge, who created the material world. But they go much further than the Persians. The Gnostics believe that the God of the Old Testament is the Demiurge and that he is evil. They believe that everything Moses taught should be opposed and fought against."

"Moses gave us the Commandments."

"Exactly." John paused a long time. "To them law is from the evil one; marriage is from the evil one; property is from the evil one; your authority and the state itself is from him. Churches are homes for devils; lust is bad but better than marriage; lying and stealing are justified. It is better to have sex out of wedlock like the animals than to marry, and best to kill the children of that union."

"You say 'believe', not believed. Are there still Gnostics? These Gnostics sound like Paulicians."

"Yes, and there always will be Gnostics who make too much of mystery, and other dualists under one name or another. But a greater threat are good Christians who unknowingly are tainted by their teaching, men who would give the devil more credit than he is due. This world is not a battlefield between forces of the spiritual and the material, of good and evil. The Devil is not that strong. He is not lord of things but only of confusion. Life is an opportunity for us all to reach a higher spiritual state using the material world, and that is especially important for you."

"Everyone must strive for salvation."

"Yes, but not everyone can affect how the whole world approaches God. An emperor can. Your mother, the holy augusta, understands that. An emperor must keep the whole society focused on Divine perfection, not upon small things. You, as emperor, will control many things, the material things that the Gnostics and Paulicians... and many we think of as good Christians also decry. You must use them as God's instrument of good and put the lie to these heretics. That means you must make it possible for men to devote as much of themselves as possible to building and learning; for progress is good. You must wage peace when possible instead of war. You must be a teacher as much as a general."

John thought but did not add: *Progress is good whatever the monks might think.*

"And I suppose a monk too."

"No. Your place is as a leader of men. It is not for you to concentrate on self as monks do." *Or should do*, the tutor thought but did not say. "You are Christ's anointed in His earthly empire, the very equal of the apostles in power and influence. You must keep the empire directed towards God. The monks too often drag Christendom into bickering. Even the holy fathers did that. The emperor must keep the clergy's discussions and arguments directed toward unity and away from conflict and confrontation. Do that and God will show the right; but only if men - monks and bishops especially - so behave among themselves as to deserve that grace."

"That is a heavy burden."

"In our day, your most difficult challenge will be to keep those who do not think it appropriate to venerate the holy icons, and those who do, from killing each other in Christ's name." John did not say more. He was on dangerous ground. Should the augusta hear him she would not be pleased and the augusta had spies everywhere.

"I am only fourteen."

A child shall lead them. Let us pray, Divine Savior, that this child will be better for the world than his predecessors. John picked up the soldier's cloak and brought it back to its owner. *Enough of lessons. That was heavy enough for one day.* Despite the future ruler's opinion of him, John was not actually old though he affected a full beard to give that impression. He called across the field to Constantine: "Have a guard call your friends, Your Sovereignty. Five laps around the track. Perhaps one of you will finally outrun me today."

78

None did. Constantine would be a man before he could do that, for John took seriously the Hellenic tradition of both athletics and the arts being appropriate activities for a citizen. Like a very few of his day in Constantinople, he saw no conflict between Christian faith and humanism and regretted the closing of the schools of pagan philosophy two centuries before. Mortification of the flesh was not for him. It smacked of the dualism that he had just decried. *Genesis* said it all: "In the beginning God created the heavens and the earth." Christ was lord of all, and all included sports and drinking, and dance; as much as the study of philosophy and theology. But he worried about the boy whose education had been put in his care. Fortunately, his mother, despite her great piety, had wisely not restricted his tutors to monks and priests. "They have their place," Aetius too had said, "but they are too prejudiced. Even though we agree - most of the time - the other side must be given a fair hearing, else one will be forever battling straw men. That may be all right for the citizens, but not for an emperor. Too much is at stake."

As the afternoon wound down Constantine continued his studies under his tree but his thoughts were often interrupted. More than once he touched his tunic as though to assure himself that the image of Rotrud was still against his breast. *I should have a holy relic here against my heart. Instead I have the picture of a girl I've never even met. I can't even talk to her and I can't possibly learn Teutonic. Elissaios and the Lombard deacon report that she is doing well in Greek but I think it will always be a strange language for her. Rotrud speaks good Latin though, so I must try to do well in Latin too. Until she really masters our language it will be best if I can speak Latin as well as she does. ...Perhaps we could bring back Latin in some state affairs here when the empire is reunited. That would be good for the peace and unity that John spoke of being my duty. I wonder what he would think of that? Hey! I've had an idea worthy of a statesman ... I think.*

Ah, another idea!

When next they met, Constantine carefully posed a question to his tutor. "Master John, Do you know any Latin poems? Not ones about Troy; something gentle."

"Yes, but most of the good ones are too crude for a youth and an emperor.... downright filthy actually. But there is one from Horace that occurs to me:

Neu desint epulis rosae	Give us roses all to twine,
Neu uiuax apium neu breue lilium.	and parsley green, and lilies white.
Omnes in Damalin putres	Every melting eye will rest,
Deponent oculos nec Damalis nouo	on Damalis' lovely face; But none may part

79

Diuelletur adultero	Damalis from our
	newfound guest;
Lasciuis hederis ambitiosior	She clings, and clings,
	like ivy round his heart.

John Pikridios grinned and Constantine understood that his teacher knew more of what was on his mind than he had realized. *That is good. I need someone to talk with about real stuff.*

Life and love and war and piety went on as usual. Rotrud, however, seemed different than she had been and not merely with the differences that might be expected in the years between twelve and sixteen in any girl. She remained as sweet and as pious as ever, a constant joy to her father. But Rotrud sometimes seemed very different even from the other girls of the court, more independent than one might expect from her disposition. Then too she was given to study far more than most, and with something more than the diffidence to the arts that Alcuin of York's other students showed. After all, they all agreed, the knowledge of the classics which this learned monk of Albion poured out was quite interesting and good for a lady to know, yet hardly important in the grand scheme of Frankish affairs. Rotrud seemed to see it differently. Not only did she stay awake late at night reading the holy fathers and the poets of antiquity but she also read books of no use, like a *Strategecon* and a *Tactica* in Greek, and the *Wars of Belisarius* by Procopius. It was understandable that she might be interested in the Greek empire since she was to marry its emperor, but why the *Wars of Belisarius* rather than the *History* of the architectural achievements of the emperor Justinian whom Belisarius had served, or books of the court ceremonies, or church music, or of Greek drama. These things would be more interesting and would serve her needs better as empress. War was man's work, and that was that. Even her doting father could not understand, though he humored the girl in this, as in all things possible.

CHAPTER 11

The fall from his horse had not seemed bad. Constantine had been stunned for only a moment, or so he thought. His companions had quickly gathered around him. Even Stauratius and Aetius had laid aside their hot rivalry and cold courtesy to tend the boy together. Nicephorus himself brought cool water from the stream the party had been about to cross. He wiped off a trickle of blood and made a compress to cool the emperor's head. At everyone's urging Constantine agreed to rest awhile under a large elm while the others gathered in concerned groups talking together.

Alone under the elm Constantine allowed his mind to wander, or rather urged it to wander away from the groups of old people talking together and into another view. The scenery was the same: the stream, the trees, the undergrowth; but he chose to imagine that he was in Rotrud's homeland with all their courtiers and guards gone.

"Hi!"

Had he been standing Constantine would have spun on his heel. But he was lying under the elm and could only look up into the sky as a grin bore down on him.

"Rotrud?" the boy stammered.

It was Rotrud, but not at all as Constantine had expected her. True she was blonde and pretty and had long braids and her face was that of the image he carried against his heart, but this girl who flashed a smile like the sun, seemed no retiring daughter of the Frankish court, happiest surrounded by books and pets. This Rotrud was out of the northern legends themselves, or from his dreams. She bent over him and let her braids touch his face. Her skirt, which did not come even near to her knees, was all of black leather. It snugly hugged a large round rump. Her bodice was mostly black leather straps, and it too was filled to overflow. Rotrud had been but twelve when first they had been engaged, but obviously in the several years since, the child had changed. In her hand she held a whip. Vaguely Constantine recalled some images, all black and shades of gray.

"Do you like your wife, *my lord Emperor of the Romans*?" Rotrud spoke in a bright, cheerful laugh of a voice. Her bright wide eyes lit the smile she smiled on her husband-to-be. Nor did Constantine take any offense at her playfully mocking tone. How could he beneath that sunshine grin?

Constantine said nothing; he had never seen anything like the girl who stood before him gently swinging a whip. Even in the theater women dressed more modestly even if actresses did not often behave so.

"Hey, it is the fault of the great autocrator himself, *Your Sovereignty*, if I'm not like the picture you've carried for so long. It was you who wanted to see me here in my woods. I'd have been more than happy to go to your city, *Illustrious Sir*. In fact I was looking forward to it. Then I'd have dressed like a proper princess for your stuffy friends. Would you rather that? I can leave you...."

"No. Absolutely no." Constantine jumped to his feet. He was so stimulated to actually see the fiancé whom he'd only dreamed of until now that his superheated mind and glands raced with each other, neither winning his undivided attention. He was so overwhelmed by that smile that his bowels became queasy in his belly. He actually liked the disrespectful tone this Frankish bride took with his august self.

"Dare you to catch me!" Rotrud took off like a deer and Constantine chased after her bouncing leather-clad bottom. She spun round in a clearing and grabbed her future mate as he almost plowed into her. Briefly she looked into his eyes. Then she slipped to the ground under him and pulled him down onto herself. She felt so nice that they play-wrestled for many minutes till finally Rotrud ceased squirming and Constantine lay quiet on his stomach next to her, not thinking of anything but what fun married life would be. Then, unexpectedly. she jumped onto his back and bounced again and again while he feigned pain and fear. But it was all play-acting like his cheetahs' cubs playing at fighting. After a few long seconds she stopped bouncing and lay her golden head next to his. The fifteen year old emperor heard Rotrud whisper in his ear. "You are sweet, mi-lord; not at all like an emperor should be." Then she was gone.

When Constantine awoke he was being carried on an improvised litter by four of his guardsmen back to the city where court physicians would worry over him hourly for a week before they agreed that the mild concussion had done the emperor no lasting harm. Strangely, the empress-regent continued her usual routine at court showing little more than formal concern for her son. He hardly cared.

A few months later the main Bulgar army began moving along the Black Sea coast far south of the Danube to where sovereignty was still disputed with the empire. Its cavalry units were split ahead of the infantry and behind the baggage train. Khan Khardam rode with the forward units as though daring the Romans to ambush him. Soon villages which were slow to send him lavish greetings would be set burning; and the word of his movements would reach the empire's garrisons at their forts in Moesia. Khardam could then expect harassing attacks from thematic cataphracts while Stauratius gathered his main forces and moved north along the coastal road.

In the capital, the young emperor and his mother listened to the reports and to the advise of the various strategoi who had hurried to the palace. After the Holy Liturgy they had gathered not in one of the rooms kept to impress foreign visitors but in a still ornate but smaller chamber. There the empress and Constantine could listen to the debate from less ornamental but more comfortable thrones. Stauratius outlined the defensive situation and contrary to Khardam's expectations advised caution. "The Bulgar khan can be bought off after a minor face-saving confrontation and his thrust turned against the Franks in the west. Then we can retake the exarchate in Italy while Charles is occupied."

"No, that will not do," Nicephorus interrupted. The prince did not often give military advice which was perhaps why the assemblage fell silent to hear him out this time. If Nicephorus was no military leader, he was credited with being a crafty politician known to have studied the Bulgar threat. That was the only reason why this semi-outcast of the imperial family had been invited. "True, this land of the Romans has always been better served by exploiting the dislikes and jealousies of its enemies than by confronting them militarily when that was unnecessary; but eventually we must deal with Khardam and we should do that when he reaches Thrace. Besides, Would you have His Serenity disavow his future father-in-law?

"Stauratius, you well know the danger of Khardam and you are right not to wish to confront him so far from here, where our back is as vulnerable to discontents and Sklavanians as our front is to the enemy. But he will not be turned west except by defeat in Thrace. The khan is a proud man who has not come so far to be bought off at a barbarous province. He knows he cannot take this city, protected by Christ and Our Lady, but the nearer he comes the better price we will pay and he knows it. Yet closer we have the advantage.

"That is indeed as it is." Aetius added in support of the prince. He hoped to recover not only the exarchate of Ravenna but the whole of Italy and the lost western provinces by the marriage alliance with the Franks. "Properly played we may even be able to enlist the Franks on our side in a very few years. Nothing could be more natural once they realize that Khardam is a danger to both themselves and to us. It is not to our long term advantage to try to turn the Bulgars against them now."

Constantine, who until this day had never spoken at these conferences, looked down from his throne on a dais besides Irene and dared it that all might know he was no longer a child, if not yet a man. He summoned up his best imperial manner: "We are in communication with our patricius Carolus who is lord of the Frankish host. It is our desire for peace with those provinces under his authority." Then Constantine looked at his mother for approval.

Prostrate before the thrones, the stratagoi could not see her reaction. It was Aetius, who alone with Stauratius, Nicephorus, and a few ministering eunuchs, was allowed to stand who finally spoke for her. "It is as our Blessed Basilios says. Our interests in Italy require friendship with the Franks, for if there is not peace between us Charles might assimilate the whole of Lombardy as well as keep the exarchate, and even join with the rebel Elpidios in Africa - Bulgars or no Bulgars. We agree with you, Stauratius. It would be difficult to fight a war in Moesia, especially as troops from our Asian themes are at the present unreliable; but I assure you, Illustrious Sir, we will not allow Khardam too near. Someday the army will have to meet him midway. He will not be permitted to approach so far as the Thracian wall. In the meantime, we'll send gifts to delay his progress."

One of the generals overstepped: "It could be many months or even years before Khardam feels strong enough to attack in Thrace. If he is not to be turned away we should give him a beating now…"

"Indeed we shall beat the evil man well," Aetius resumed, directing his words at the teenager on the throne. "But I urge some caution, Your Serenity. We will send gifts - that may stall him for awhile - but we will not try to turn him west. In time the Asian troops shall learn to love and respect thy holy self and the augusta. then we shall destroy him in Thrace. He may grow stronger but so will we. Your Serenity has an alliance with the Franks. We will not now turn the Bulgars against a strong and Christian ally."

Constantine said nothing more. For now all was well but he was both young and powerless. These men who supposedly served him could destroy all his hopes of joy with Rotrud.

So, for a time Khardam had his way. Gifts from the capital were accepted while the khan consolidated his hold on northern Moesia. But he was not the empire's only enemy. The war with the Arabs would surely break out again.

CHAPTER 12

For months before Constantine turned fifteen it had worried the court that he seemed - well, distracted at times. Oh he did well at lessons and was a goodhearted youth. Perhaps that was the problem. Whatever the priests might say about rule by saintly monarchs, and the philosophers about philosopher kings, the unfortunate fact was that the world was not fit for such. It might be if men were basically good, but they weren't. One might blame Adam for that fall from grace, but it was the main fact circumscribing a ruler's world. A later courtier in the west, Niccolo Machiavelli, would be forever damned for facing the problem head on. One could be a saint or one could rule. The duty of one born to the purple was to rule. That meant being as deceitful and brutal as others who ruled or would rule if they had the opportunity; men like Nicephorus. If a prince could not do that he should resign and retire to a monastery in favor of one who would put the good of the country before his own holiness. But that was unlikely to happen if for no other reason than the good man would hope to use his position to show others the way to God. In fact, according to the theories both priests and tutors had taught to Constantine, this was the first responsibility of the basilios.

Then too, there was a dreaminess about Constantine which though attractive in the very young. could be a distraction in one who must one day devote his whole being to ruling. It was one thing for the monarch to admire painting or sculpture or music or poetry, but quite another to be overly concerned with their mechanics. Constantine loved the finer things. He did not simply accept them as the trappings of his position. He loved the arts for themselves. That still might have been acceptable if he had limited this interest to the ancients. It was good in a ruler to be cultivated. However the teenager invited to the palace the disreputable scum who sang their sentimental songs for pennies in the marketplace, and Asiatic bards who did not recite the ancient poems but made up their own silly tales of monsters and heroes for the multitude.

He even painted. He played the lavouto like a peasant on Sunday. And he wrote silly love poems about a girl whom he'd not yet met.

The court wondered which would come first, maturity or assassination.

Constantine's valets were all eunuchs or high dignitaries from the oldest aristocracy, and most of them unsuitable for anything else. On a bright early spring morning they prepared Constantine for a most unusual event in the hippodrome, where chariot races usually held the attention of the populace.

Constantine was still too young to lead troops in battle and his mother could not, so in his stead Stauratius, as logothete of the dromos, had just recently led their army against Sklavian marauders in Macedonia and ancient Hellas itself. He had returned victorious, laden with plunder and captives. The embarrassment of his capture by Arabs under the young Harun al-Rashid, and the huge ransom which Irene had paid for the release of her highly valued advisor were entirely forgotten now. He was to be rewarded with a triumph after today's races; not as lavish as an emperor would have received, but unusual for an officer and therefore quite special.

"We'll leave leading armies to men and to the Amazons of legend," Irene had joked to her ministers a few days before, "…and to the barbarians. You do remember that woman in Britain who defeated a legion?"

"Boudicca, Your Highness."

"Yes, Boudicca. A real bitch."

Constantine had been horrified to hear such language from his mother. But he forgave her it later when John Pikridios described the evil woman's bloody slaughter and tortures. Female collaborators with Rome had their nipples sewn to their own lips on her orders. "Yuuch," was all the youth could say.

Constantine did not like Stauratius who, it seemed, not only had his mother's ear but with it all the power of the throne. He had reservations about Aetius too. Aetius was too close to the augusta even for a eunuch; but at least Aetius did not affect an insultingly haughty air in his presence. Indeed, the eunuch would sometimes play at football with him and the other palace lads, something that would never have occurred to Stauratius. Beyond formal obeisance, Stauratius never seemed to give any serious consideration to Constantine except occasionally on Irene's order. This was maddening to the emperor. In two years he would be seventeen; old enough to rule in his own right, yet Stauratius did not seem troubled by the ill will he was courting in his sovereign. Why? Constantine began to wonder if he would ever be allowed to rule. More than one boy-emperor had died before coming of age in Roman history. Would that happen to him? *No, I don't like Stauratius but mother would not let me be harmed and Stauratius is nothing without her.*

Stauratius and his troops of armored cataphracts paraded through the race course. They were smiled upon by the stately Irene who looked as beautiful as the day. They received garlands of victory from the hands of Constantine and were lauded by the jealous Aetius. Behind Stauratius' troops came wagon-loads of booty and a disorderly mass of disarmed enemy. Many of these would now be enrolled in the empire's own armies. In accordance with Christian custom the leaders of the captives, who in an earlier time would have been beheaded by the Romans, were instead offered baptism and rewarded with estates upon their pledge of good behavior. In the great church Stauratius received the thanks and blessing of the patriarch.

The next day Aetius suggested that the empress-regent and her son visit the effected provinces. It would be good to show the rulers' concern for the populace there and the hardships which they had recently endured. They would also confirm victory over the paganism of the enemy by impressing the people with the wealth and authority of Christ's Church. Surely, even simple folk would realize that a God who could grant victory to a widow and her child must indeed be the true Lord of the universe.

In May they rode forth with an impressive host of troops, with musicians, and even portable organs, with banners and crosses and icons. It was the first time since he had been an infant that Constantine and his mother would spend a great deal of time in each other's company. Irene had always been too busy as the augusta to spend much time with her son. No doubt she had been tired. It would be pleasing to write that they spent the days together with fondness, but such was not to be. The two had long since grown distant and Constantine, while not yet grown, was yet no longer a child. He was an active and energetic youth, with ideas and conclusions and intentions of his own. These might someday compromise Irene's own plans.

"The boy is simple," his mother lamented to Aetius, "He does not see the dangers; only dreams of bringing all our subjects together without intimidation. How I wish that could be so. But right belief must sometimes be imposed for the sake of the state and the deluded themselves. I fear he would be a poor ruler, a dreamer led by opportunists. He will reign, but it is necessary that I continue to rule so long as the Father gives me breath. Perhaps by then he shall have learned … or have a smarter son than himself to rule. …But not, I think, by that Frankish girl unless her father has a serious change of heart. Pray for him; the deacon, Lombard Paul, has sent me troubling messages about Charles. He continues to have iconoclast sympathies and discourages true veneration of the holy images."

Aetius did not let despair show on his face. Despite his intrigues, until this day he had still hoped for eternal life with the saints. *How am I to do what must be done for Christ's empire without sinning against His emperor on earth? You are wrong, Dear Lady. You care too much for your pictures. Constantine would be a worthy leader, and Rotrud would be best for him. But you are my empress.*

"Be patient, Your Serenity. An alliance with Charles is most desirable." This was as much as he dared to say.

Tutors who accompanied the procession as it passed through Macedonia tried to point out to the teenager what marvels still remained from ancient days and fortify his understanding of history. Philip, and his son Alexander who conquered the world, had been Macedonian. At Adrianople the empire's infantry legions for the first time met defeat before mounted Goths. In Thessaloníki Saint Demitrios had been martyred for the Christian faith, and in Stagira the philosopher Aristotle had been born. It was all very much like Constantine's studies. His mother, for her part, seemed bent on making an imprint on the province, demonstrating that her own person was the senior of the two monarchs, even though in two years Constantine should rule alone. Irene gave the impression not of a mother and regent for the boy-emperor, but of an empress; this despite the fact that in law she was powerless in her own right since the death of her husband. Local dignitaries were quietly advised that it was to their advantage to give their obeisance to the regent before the emperor, and no sin to refer to her not only by the title of augusta, due to her as Leo's widow, but even as "basilia" – ruler. In Broia, Irene took it upon herself to rename the town Irenopolis, insisting that it was to be understood as meaning 'City of Peace' in remembrance of those who had died in the war, and not "City of Irene." Yet many wondered about the double meaning, the future of the empire, and Constantine's fate. Officials who should have taken advantage of the long trip to give advice to him on foreign policy, strategy, and politics, began showing Constantine only the pleasures and personal prerogatives of reigning.

When they returned from the Peloponnese, Constantine was effusively greeted by those dignitaries and major household staff who had not joined the mission; and by his cat. For a moment she ran across the courtyard to see her friend - perhaps she thought he'd been eaten - but then, recalling her dignity, she stopped, washed, and pretended to ignore him. She also ignored the laughing fellowship of the palace. Furface had earned a fond place in the court by her affection for the emperor; for Furface called Constantine to bed each evening and would sit waiting - her tail swishing in displeasure - if studies or ceremonies kept him at his desk or in conference beyond the usual hour. But when her friend was sound asleep, she would leave his bed, walk past the sentries who had become humorously accustomed to her nightly prowl, and disappear out a palace window. Then as the pre-dawn light brightened enough for others to see by, the cat would return by the same route. She had long years past decided that it was her duty to be on Constantine's bed when he awoke. She may also have been, along with John Pikridios, his truest friend in that huge imperial complex.

CHAPTER 13

It was a Friday. Beth had finished work for the week. She'd made enough money to pass up posing for the camera club guys this Saturday. Some of them were okay; at least they didn't have the all-business attitude of the professionals who posed her during the week for spreads in *Rogue* and *Titter* and *Wink*. But most of the nicer guys were too shy to ask a fantasy gal out.

It was early evening and Beth was in Greenwich Village. She was too tired for the jazz clubs; some caffeine at a coffee shop was more her style tonight. She headed for Bleecker Street letting the usual crowd of tourists pass her by, along with would-be beatniks and guys looking for some free love and not finding it. Beth liked the Village on an autumn night. It was a nice mixture of quiet side streets with street lamps casting yellow circles of light through which the people passed in and out, with livelier main streets filled with simple cafes, tourist shops, and downscale nightclubs. It was pleasant; very pleasant. She was about to pass one of the many second hand bookstores that lined the Village streets in those days (before the hippies with their simplistic philosophy of love beads and drugs made them passé) when, for no particular reason except curiosity, Beth went in - *just for a moment*. The shop was a basement; the counter a simple table. The books were arranged on wooden racks. There was not enough light and too much dust. But there was a good history section and a big art book collection including even a few of the new Abrams publications with their bright colorful illustrations, far better than the books of even a few years before - a few years before generally meaning prepared before the war but not printed until afterward. Color photography had improved a lot in recent years. Beth knew about things like that for her photographer friend Eddy Miller talked too much about it. In the medieval history shelves Beth found something special, O. M. Dalton's 1911 *Byzantine Art and Archeology*. The illustrations were all black and white, of course, and many of them of particularly poor quality. That couldn't be helped though; there would be no new-technology color photographs of all too many of these places. Two world wars had destroyed much of what the Greek-Turkish wars had missed. She'd studied the Byzantines and their art - not an easy thing to do in the nineteen-fifties when most people had never heard of the Later Roman Empire of the East; or if they had, they'd dismissed it as a minor and decadent state. That was a prejudice inherited from Gibbon and one hundred percent wrong. Beth knew better. Still, it seemed to her that what she knew, or more accurately, what she felt about the Byzantines was something more than book learning. It was something like a forgotten dream.

Constantine received a letter from Rotrud:

Most honored Constantine:

I am sending this note by a good friend, so I know that it will reach you. I can trust him so he will make a copy in good Greek for you if you have difficulty with my poor Frankish Latin. Things have not been very good for us lately. My father has fears that your mother is excessive in her attachment to the holy pictures. He and the pope agree that they are a fine way to encourage devotion, but fear that such language as "holy icons" and the stories of miracles wrought, not by Our Savior, but by the images themselves are idolatrous. I do not want troubles between my dear father and the augusta; I care too much for you. Ricolf has told me more about you. He would not tell you himself ... I suppose it wouldn't be diplomatic ... but he told me what a fine, handsome man you are growing to be. He says that he'd learned that you have killed a boar by yourself, that you study the great Marcus Aurelius - great even though a pagan and a persecutor. He says you have tried to learn all you can about the great generals of the empire, especially your Belisarius. Ricolf reveres Belisarius but tries not to bore me too much with stories about him. He assumes it is a manly interest. Ricolf doesn't think that I need be content with sewing and singing, which is good, but he doesn't think I need to know about strategy and tactics either. Would your mother disagree? Someday when we are married I must ask her. He says that you are both strong and smart. That is good in an emperor because you will have enemies. But he says you are very busy, with many things to learn. Do not fret too much if your Latin is a little poor too. I am studying your language and Elissaeus tells me that I am a quick study. I am anxious to read the Greek Fathers in their original language, and I want to be able to speak to you with as little foreignness as I can.

I am writing this letter in my own hand. The chief scribe at the convent of Chelles is visiting us at Aachen to try to get Papa to buy some books that he doesn't approve of. She says that we must preserve all knowledge, not just what we agree with, because we might be wrong. Daddy doesn't like that argument, but they do agree that there is more to be preserved than just the holy writings. Strange though, when they start discussing what works should be copied I am shooed away. Anyway, this learned sister says that I have very nice writing and should come and study for a time at Chelles someday. I might like to do that. Would you mind if sometimes I visited my homeland once we are married? You could come too, Papa says, so long as you leave your army at home. I think he is joking.

Constantine read the letter at his desk, books around him and with a football, looking as lonely as its owner, waiting for him on a chair. For awhile he thought upon his bride-to-be. They were happy thoughts. Her letter had been serious, not mere female twittering. Her letters confirmed what he had been told about Rotrud's mind; he could only fantasize a bit about the rest. She wouldn't be like his dreams, he knew; but just maybe, she'd be a little like them.

At last Constantine turned his mind to studies. He hated studying strategy and tactics but they would be his life's work soon. He tried to pick up *Caesar's Gallic Wars*. After all, ancient Gaul was now ruled by Charles but one day soon it would be his when he married the fair Rotrud. ... "Fair", John Pikridios had called her, and his chief tutor was far too good a friend to have lied. Besides, Constantine had Rotrud's picture which he had removed from under his tunic and which now looked back at him from a corner of the desk. *If it is a true likeness, she is fair. The monks would say that is superficial. I should look to her virtues. OK. She is kind, I'm told, and well educated for a Frank, and artistic too, and she is the daughter of the man who rules half our lands ... And she is beautiful. I think she is far prettier than the hags they still call beautiful around here; some of them must be thirty at least.*

Omnia Gallia in tres partes divisa est. – *The whole of Gaul is divided into three parts; one of which the Belgae inhabit, the Aquitani another, those who in their language are called Celts, the third.*

The ancient tribes and divisions were mostly just names now, but geography doesn't change. Some of Charles' forts were in places with old Roman names; rivers often determined those things. On the far wall of Constantine's study was a large mosaic map of the world indicating the military thema or provinces of the empire. On a table were more accurate if less ornate scrolls with the rivers and roadways of his empire laid out in detail. These Constantine found more interesting than Caesar's history. *I will want to know all about the west of Rotrud. We can manage to speak in Latin together. I will go to Aachen and go to services in her father's church. If her father is tainted by iconoclasm I hope we can reach an agreement of some sort. Perhaps more attention can be given icons here, less in the west. Why not less in the Armeniac theme too? In time the beneficence of venerating the holy images will speak for itself, Momma says, and she is probably right.*

But though she speaks of patience, she is impatient.

Rotrud! You are pretty and you will be mine someday, but I need you here now. Or do I just need a girl? Yes, that too, but if you are as much fun to be with as Elissaeus writes, we will laugh and play together and do great things for the people. And you will be warm and soft and smile and laugh when we're alone together. I will hold you and braid your golden hair. We will not be wearing anything.

This much only can be described in words, and this was the least of what the young emperor felt as he tried to make himself study. The patriarch, himself, had explained the queasiness that Constantine felt when thinking of his fiancé. He had also warned the youth not to take too seriously what the monks said about it and about the attractions of women generally. *I am growing up. I see the changes. I feel funny. I should go out and play football with the guys. …. I'd rather feel like this. I wish Rotrud were here.*

Even as Rotrud and Constantine exchanged many letters and came to know each other a bit, the Bulgars were again on the move. This was no raiding party but thousands of fighting men, with their women, their children, old people, and animals. They were marching down the coast toward Thrace long before the empire expected. The bulk of the army was Slav infantry from conquered territories. These were headed and protected by a large Druzhina cavalry force amounting to one-third of the total according to Byzantine spies: more, if one put any faith in the reports of the peasantry fleeing before them.

They were not civilized. The ethics of Christ would not reach these people for another hundred years. Villages and towns were burned and their inhabitants put to torture if too brave or slow to flee. Some militia were simply murdered outright with the great axes that the Bulgars favored; but others who were slow or too strong to die quickly in battle might be burnt or be disemboweled alive to delight the Bulgar women with their screams. Children were encouraged to throw excrement at them as these wounded were pulled on ropes into the burning ground. Some died by pieces: fingers, tongues, and eyes, removed one by one.

A special death was prepared for true soldiers. Mailed warriors were laid out in their armor upon a platform of tree trunks. Another platform was laid across them, with yet another layer of armored men upon it - and so forth until the men at the bottom began to die from the weight of trees and men upon them. Khan Khardam and his chief Boyars would feast, sitting upon this moaning platform. When finished the whole was set afire and the victims roasted in their armor.

92

After one of these feasts, Khardam retired early to his tent. It may be that the khan was past enjoying such events. He continued them only to encourage the blood-lust of his army and to attach yet more terror to his name. Love too was good. He hoped his own people loved him but fear was a quicker way to gain obedience among the newly conquered.

A young girl named Lucia had been chosen from Khardam's tribute to spend this night with the great chief. She had been waiting many days, staying awake all night and sleeping by day so that she would not fall asleep with him when her turn came. Lucia was small breasted even for a Kotrag but she hoped that might interest her lord. So many gifts to him had the biggest breasts that could be found in his subject peoples, at least among the prettier girls. *Besides*, she thought, *I have long nipples*. Indeed she did. They stuck out nearly an inch which may have been why this small-breasted girl had been chosen to be Khardam's concubine by the chiefs of the Kotrag. *I've a big bottom too.*

Lucia was not the girl's birth name. She had assumed it because in fine Latin speech it meant "light." She wanted to be the light of the Bulgars. She knew that someday even Rome would be their subject though for now it was free. She would become a lady there if Khardam favored her; a great lady with beautiful silks and fine enamel jewelry, and servants of her own.

When Khardam was spent and asleep, the lord of a hundred thousand lay on his side. As quietly as she could Lucia moved herself until she could take his now-flaccid penis in her mouth. She planned to spend the night this way, awake and occasionally flicking her tongue, careful not to wake him, but to give him good dreams..

Near dawn Khardam was restless and Lucia swirled her tongue, but he only told her to bring a long-necked jug that was near their bed of furs. She did not obey for an idea had lit her mind, one by which she might set herself above the khan's other women. She held him more tightly with her lips and began to swallow quickly and often. *This girl might be good for many nights*, the sleepy barbarian thought as he emptied his bladder.*

Though the areas under control of the empire were nearly entirely Christian yet its frontiers were Moslem, or as pagan as those of King Charles in the west. Pagan lore infiltrated the capital itself. In Constantinople priests riled against foreign superstition but were blind to it when it had a Christian face. Science was unreliable; the unseen powers, both good and bad, were not. The future might be known to Christians who correctly interpreted the stars which reflected the Divine will, or from dreams. Less respectably it might be made known to those versed in Bulgar

---

* See note on Urophagia. Pg: 230.

lore who could interpret thunder or the flight of birds. Pagan superstition and custom was seen as demonic and evil; yet not fraudulent. For a price, a Bulgar shaman would prophesise anything to a Christian.

When the horde approached within several hundred miles of Constantinople Khardam stopped his advance and waited. There was skirmishing but the Romans made no serious attempt to dislodge him from the conquests he had made. They only placed large forces at the Thracian wall and refortified some outlying fortifications. It was not a time of peace but not really a time of war. In 1939 another generation would term such a pause in combat a "phony war." Winter came and went but still the Bulgars did not resume their advance. There were taunts but only minor clashes. There were, however, a series of visits to the khan's camp by tradesmen of the empire. Guardedly worded messages were discreetly exchanged.

CHAPTER 14

As time passes, dreams fade.

One would expect that Constantine would have forgotten the hallucination when he'd fallen while hunting. He had not. Maybe that was because he did not want to; maybe it was because he was not convinced that he had been hallucinating. Now he'd gone to bed with nothing more on his mind than that day's soccer game with Phillipus and Meletius and some other youths of the palace. True, he'd read a bit about Frankland before falling asleep, but the book had been a dry and boring recitation of the kings and archbishops of the Franks - not a valkyrie or a good bloody battle in it. It was, however, an excellent soporific, and soon the emperor was asleep.

"Wake up, husband."

"I am awake, Rotrud. I just don't want to get up this morning. I'm ruler of the world; shouldn't I be able to sleep a little late?"

"No, mi-lord *I* want *you* awake."

Constantine loved it when his wife spoke to him so disrespectfully. It excited him and he lost all desire to turn over, put his head in the pillows, and let his mind go blank.

Rotrud was next to him on the bed, tickling him with the ends of her golden braids and with one thigh over his. She wasn't naked, but then, she hadn't much clothing on either and that was more exciting. Her dress, if such it should be called, was after the fashion of ancient Roman armor and the iron plates on her skirt rattled delightfully with her every movement. The breastplate fit her curves and her feet were shod with iron-studded boots. Just as she turned to give Constantine a better view, he awoke.

"Damn!" The teen-emperor spoke his first profanity.

Charles had a special mission for Ricolf of Bacheim and Lord Bertmund. Bertmund had grown into a bright young man and a baron of great estates, but he was only six years older than the emperor. Wise Charles reasoned that he might be better able to talk to Constantine than some long of tooth elder knight whose motives not only might be questioned by the emperor, but might quite correctly be questioned. After all, Charles' high barons were not simple minions. They had ambitions and schemes of their

95

own.

This would be Bertmund's second trip to the great city and Ricolf's third. Ricolf might be considered by the Greeks to be more worthy than the typical barbarian. His estates were modest so in himself he posed no threat; and on his previous visits Roman officials had praised his diffidence to them and to their culture, never demeaning it but always querying great and small with a curiosity which did not appear to hide any ill will or designs upon the empire. In fact, they cheerfully reported, he had seemed as interested in their ancient history as in present politics, rivalries, or matters of defense. It was not that these things escaped him, for understandably they were most relevant to a diplomat; however, they did not so preoccupy him as to seem to have any threat behind them.

Now it was early spring in Aachen and the weather was good by the standards of the Rhine country. The two nobles looked forward to being across the Alps and on their way. Both knights could almost taste the fresh fruits and vegetables of Italia and Grecia after a winter of hoarded potatoes and apples, and the root vegetables which could stand the winter months of Frankland; but these were hardly enjoyable. Ricolf, who had gained quite a bit of unattractive weight on a diet of venison and venison and venison, yearned for something more healthy and fresh out of God's good ground.

Such a trip by high officials and friends of the Frankish king was more than a goodwill visit. The king was worried. He was well informed of the Bulgar advance. He knew that they would enter Byzantine controlled territory in Thrace well before becoming a threat to his own realm. But he also knew the Greek penchant for a purchased peace over the risks of war. Invader after barbarian invader - his own ancestors in fact - had been turned away from Byzantine territory, loaded down with gifts, and with the suggestion that they look further west. Charles did not fear war with the Bulgars, but such a war would tie up his forces just when he was on the brink of destroying the power of the German pagans, bringing them into the Christian fold under his own rule.

Would Irene keep the peace on her Arab frontier and join him in confronting the Bulgar enemy, or would the empire be so involved with the Saracen threat that it would bribe the Bulgar khan on its northern frontier? Worse, there were rumors that the empress-regent might change her mind about the marriage of their children; might make common cause with the Bulgars against him instead. Every Byzantine ruler since the great Justinian and his brilliant general Belisarius had harbored fantasies of reestablishing their rule in all Italy and perhaps even in Gaul again. It would be better that the marriage of their children be hastened. "Besides," Charles had confided to Ricolf with amusement, "they seem to have developed quite a fondness for each other." Then he had scowled. "I trust you have not misrepresented the young emperor to Rotrud, Ricolf." In another man a tear might have moistened the king's eye. "I can deal with the Bulgars alone if I must, but I will not have Rotrud unhappy."

The knights made haste. Several weeks later Bertmund entered the chapel of a small palace in Constantinople which had been assigned to them. He found Ricolf already there.

"You are praying, mi-lord I did not mean to disturb you."

"Oh, It is just as well, Bertmund. I do not feel the connection that these Greeks do through icons."

"Who do you pray to, Our Lady?"

"Sometimes, but sometimes to Belisarius."

"The general you admire? Do you pray to a soldier?"

"To a man, Bertmund. We have need of his wisdom ....and of his goodness. What is the use if this whole thing with the emperor and Rotrud is not for good?"

"You have not told me what it is we must do."

"Because I do not know, myself, lad. This we do know, Great Charles wishes good relations with the empire. My hope is to get the princess Rotrud and the basilios together, not just as pawns of state, but in happiness. If they are to truly love each other as we hope for, then they must know each other and choose each other for themselves, not just out of duty. I'm sure that Constantine has studied the campaigns of Belisarius, but perhaps I should remind the emperor of Belisarius' love for his wife, Antonina, and see how he reacts."

"Tell me, mi-lord"

"She'd been a whore." Bertmund looked shocked. "Yes, and the general knew it and married her anyway. Now few men would do that no matter how much they might love the girl. Oh, the less pious ones might keep her as a mistress, but Belisarius married her because he was righteous; and he was faithful to her always. He took her on campaign with him and would not touch any of the girls his army captured. But Antonina had at least one affair; with a man that Belisarius had adopted as a godson to please her. He's often been derided as a cuckold for not divorcing her but I see it differently. Antonina probably just didn't share the horror of infidelity that the righteous pretend to. Prostitutes know human nature very well. I think he did too and was so great a man - not the general, but the man - that he didn't care a bit what other people thought of him. It may have been a strange love, lad, but a true friendship. Despite her wantonness they loved each other dearly their whole lives together. That is the kind of love I would have the basilios and Rotrud bear for each other ... without Antonina's history or infidelity of course. Rotrud is not that type, pray God. But she is just the type for him. She has been studying more military science than most of Great Charles' barons put together. She will support her man mightily. I can imagine her going on campaign too and I think Constantine won't care what anyone thinks of her just because she is from the woods.

The two Franks were happy to be back in Constantinople. It was May and a fine time to be in Greece. Certainly the city had its unattractive elements: It was dangerous at night despite the best efforts of the city prefect and his troops. The streets, though often straight and wide, were overcrowded with carts and vendors. It stank in summer, but it wasn't summer yet, and Constantinople was *The City*. There was nothing to compare with it in the Christian world on a sunny day. Ricolf and Bertmund, honored by being granted a company of Vigla guards for escort, strolled the its side streets. There was so much to entertain them. They stopped for noon services and to pray another hour before the famous relics of the Virgin in the church of the Panagia of Blachernae near the great walls. There were kept her mantle and robe which had been brought to the city from Jerusalem.

When Ricolf indicated that it was time to do some sightseeing among the more secular objects in the city, Bertmund felt that he would be in trouble with the Lord if he were to hurry his prayers. "It is not right that we should go so soon. These monks have devoted their lives to Our Lady. They spend days in fasting and meditation before her relics." Ricolf reassured him with a blessing of holy water and reminded him that it was not the hours before a relic which mattered to the Lord, but a man's intention. In their case that was to close the gap that was widening between two Christian states. How could that be better done than for Bertmund to see, speak with, and understand all the Christians of the city and their work, creations, and pleasures?

Outside, the streets of Constantine's City were loud with activity. It was the feast of Saint John the Evangelist. There were festivals and fairs before the many churches and in the many forums. They stopped in the Forum of Bovis to listen to some street musicians, distribute a few coins among the needy, and stroll about nibbling fresh fruit and a little fried fish wrapped in bread.

The street crowds showed some interest in the Frankish visitors. While it was far from unusual for some Roman general or dignitary to pass by, enveloped by a huge number of guards, he would normally travel by horse, in a carriage, or on a palanquin. Foreigners on foot were usually merchants and too common (and dirty) to be noted. But Frankish knights strolling afoot escorted by the empress' own guards in full dress uniform were a bit unusual and another festive sight. Fathers took a few minutes from business to share it with their children. Wives and young women watched from the seclusion of roofs and balconies. Even the city's many slaves, who seemed not to be any more oppressed than the peasantry, relaxed a few minutes from their chores to view the passing parade apparently without fear of the whip. The ambassadors were not in their formal dress, which might have interested even the jaded populace of the world capital. They were wearing simple Frankish breeches and cloaks. Long Frankish broadswords did hang from their belts however. These were marks of rank among barbarians, though unnecessary here as weapons with a company of Vigla guards around them.

In late afternoon they relaxed in one of the city's public gardens and then began wandering back to their quarters by way of the forums of Theodosius and Constantine the Great. There a tall column stood surmounted by a fine statue of the city's founder. Ricolf began to wax ecstatic about him, praising the emperor who had ended persecution and brought the light of Christendom to the Roman world. He lectured on Saint Helena, that emperor's mother, and the many relics she had brought from the Holy land to Rome and Constantinople, where the millions of Christians living in those cities could see and venerate them. It was nearing sunset when they reached their quarters overlooking the Bosphorus. Some rays from the west dyed the sails of fishing boats that rose as they put to sea for the night's work. Villas and churches on the Asian shore glowed. The evening star shone high in the western sky. Ricolf dismissed their guards and directed them to a nearby wine shop with enough coins to get pleasantly drunk. It had been a good day for visitors and guards alike.

Not far from the palace where the ambassadors were watching the Bosphorus fall into evening shadow, the eunuch Aetius entered the sleeping chamber of the empress-regent, or rather the bedroom of a still-beautiful woman who for awhile had descended from her imperial heights. Most of the rules which would normally circumscribe the relationship of empress and minister were suspended at moments like this when the widowed ruler of the world needed a bit of tenderness. When Aetius answered the great lady's summons he could not know if it were for a matter of state or personal. But he knew the clues, and before even entering he had relaxed and put his official mind to rest. There were no guards within many yards of the chamber. Irene would have dismissed them with some thin excuse. They would certainly have understood her real reason. They would take an enormous time carrying out whatever mission Irene had set them. In the room itself, hung round with tapestries of woven silk, the centerpiece was a huge bed of porphyry and white marble set with highlights of gold and gold braid. Nearer the walls carved tables, likewise of marble and gold, held lamps of alabaster and books illuminated by the finest hands. First among these had to be a Psalter in the Celtic style from the scriptorium at Aachen, sent six years before by Charles of the Franks.

There was no subtlety whatsoever about the next clue. The empress sat on the edge of her great bed. She had removed every trace of imperial finery and wore only an embroidered tunica that she had raised to well above her knees. Her feet were bare. She had released her hair which flowed over each shoulder, across her breasts, and to her waist. The empress of the Roman world might have been some simple bride, or - they both smiled as the thought struck each at the same moment - a brazen hussy.

"Aetius, sit by me." The minister bowed and began to move one of the room's lighter chairs to beside the great bed.

"No, my dear friend, here. Sit here." Irene patted the silken coverlet of the bed and Aetius sat beside his mistress, who handed him a comb of ivory decorated with images of holy virgins to warn the user of the vanity such a device could bring forth in a woman.

Neither said a word for quite some time as Aetius set about one of his lighter and more pleasant duties. There was indeed much that was still manly about the beardless aide and he enjoyed stroking his empress' hair, sometimes allowing a hand to stray immodestly. Irene made no gesture of annoyance at this. She had, after all, been a wife and had long ago lost any excessive sense of modesty. If she feared sin she comforted her conscience with the thought that Aetius was not really a man. *Besides, I cannot be perfect. I do my best for the saints. Christ will forgive me an indiscretion with a eunuch. I am only a weak woman, I am cursed with a woman's body and lusts, the monks would say.*

"I am not handsome, Empress," Aetius finally said, "I am told that some demon has cursed me as a lizard."

"What do you mean, dearest friend?" the empress gently asked. Aetius bowed his head and as discreetly as such a thing could be done, stuck out his tongue which was indeed quite long. He only flicked it out lest he appear gauche, fearing to overstep himself in a radical attempt to please his mistress. She, however, only laughed a great laugh and said very quietly: "Hush, my friend." The lady paused, grinned, and added: "You can be my pet lizard." Then she moved as though to place a chaste kiss on Aetius' lips. A moment later her own lips parted.*

Eventually Irene gently pushed Aetius to his feet. "Please bring me the clothes laid out there. I don't wish to be fussed over by aides at the moment." She looked as though to blush and pointed to a long marble table by a window that overlooked the Bosphorus. The night breeze was sweeping the city clean and for a moment the minister was distracted by the fresh air, and by the melodious chant of sailors from outside the palace who were raising sail on warships setting out, even at night, for some far quarter or Irene's empire.

"Now deep in ocean sank the lamp of light, and drew behind the cloudy vale of night." Silently Aetius thanked his tutor of many years past

---

* See note on eunuchs, pg 218.

for forcing him to memorize Homer.

Irene brought his attention back to her. "I will not need that tiara. I can simply cover my head with my palla."

Aetius begged to be permitted to clothe his empress and this was permitted. There would be no court or public appearances for some hours and Irene was able to take this rare opportunity to relax in only a fairly simple, if beautifully made, stola and embroidered tunica. Aetius placed her feet in the red slippers that only the rulers of the world were permitted to wear.

"What of Constantine?" Irene spoke matter-of-factly. "He will soon be a man."

"Yes, Augusta." Aetius deemed it wise to retreat to his role as minister and advisor, trusted and respected to be sure, but not overly familiar. "He has quite a crush on his fiancé, you know. I hope she does not disappoint him."

"Does he? How sweet. But I'm afraid we'll have to disappoint his puppy-love. It was a mistake to get involved with the Franks just to regain the Ravenna exarchate. It is gone to the Franks now anyway and we would have to cede real authority over all Italy to Charles if the children wed. No, our concern must be for the eastern frontiers. We cannot be engaging the Bulgars in the north at the same time, and an alliance with Charles would surely bring war in the north. Khardam cannot take this city and sooner or later he will turn west. We will not want an alliance then."

Aetius sighed but only to himself. *There goes the plan,* he thought, but he only said: "Probably yes, Your Serenity. But it may not be so easy to disengage. Ambassadors from Charles have recently arrived in the city. What can I tell them?"

"Nothing for now. Stall them. I am quite willing to salve Charles in other ways. We could cede Sicily. Stauratius thinks the navy cannot hold it. Either Charles or the Arabs will grab it sooner or later anyway. Stauratius was right five years ago; we must try to buy off the Bulgars. Charles can have his war with them, but the empire must not help either side."

"And Constantine, Your Serenity?"

"He will simply have to get over it. I suppose someday he'll rule, but not in my lifetime. By then he may have developed some iron in his backbone. Disappointment builds character. Meanwhile, do try, friend, to find him a distraction." The empress took her minister's hand with a sweet smile. She knew how beautiful she was. She was beautiful, and even a eunuch could appreciate that. "These ambassadors: are they not the same men who came when Constantine was betrothed? They seemed quite nice for Franks; especially the younger one; he must be a handsome young man by now."

The following week, at Irene's order Aetius appeared before some monks of a closely cloistered monastery to be flogged far from the Sacred Palace. She, herself, spent more time than ever in prayer and was not seen to touch meat before the next feast of the Nativity.

The Patriarch Paul was in conference with a young monk of Studion. That in itself was unusual. The monks considered the clergy as little more than minions of the state, ever ready to compromise holiness for expediency. In their turn, priests and bishops barely tolerated the monks who seemed to believe that the empire should be nothing but a monastery on a grand scale and be governed as such. In his heart Paul suspected that given the monks' way, all men would be aesthetics and all women virgins. Today however, Paul was listening intently to the rather unkempt man in a patched habit who stood defiantly rigid before him as though to show he was neither impressed nor cowed by the leader of all Christendom east of Italy.

"Tell me the dream, Brother." Paul was trying to ease the uneasiness that lay behind the monk Cyril's demeanor. Obviously, Cyril would have preferred his cell and chapel to the rich palace of the patriarch.

"All Holiness ..." In his turn, Cyril tried to show the respect due the man who sat before him in a study of fine wood paneling, marble, and polished brass fixtures. The patriarch sat on a finely worked chair, if not a throne, and Cyril did admit to himself that he felt a bit intimidated by the riches of the world about him in this room. "All Holiness, at first it was a battle between two serpents. There were two great snakes such as were said by the pagans to have crushed Laocoon with his sons, and they were twining about each other, trying to crush each other, and even taking into their mouths each other's heads to crush them."

"What did you think of this?"

"There was more. At last I realized that what I saw was not two snakes but one great beast with two heads and no tail, trying with all its might to devour itself. Holiness, I hate the iconoclasts and they hate us. I will say no more; but you bishops must find a way, without confirming the evil of the iconoclasts, to end our warring before Christ's Church devours itself." The monk paused as though in fear of the next thing he would say. "Christ forgive me; I know my brothers won't; but peace is more important to the Lord than victory when it is his children who are fighting each other. The holy icons must not again be desecrated but we must have peace."

The patriarch rose and placed his hand on the monk's shoulder to ease his worry and pain. "You are right, Brother, and your dream was certainly a vision from God. In our zeal for the holy icons we have forgotten charity. But do not be distressed. We will try to lead your brethren - not force them - to see that peace, not victory, is the will of God. The icons are victorious, thanks to the holy augusta; but we shall not gloat about it." He blessed the monk who received the blessing with a far better spirit than that in which he had come to the palace of the patriarch.

Afterwards Paul thought upon what had transpired that day. He was hated in the Sacred Palace for he had opposed the icons when that was the wise thing to do. He supported them now only because to oppose Irene's will would certainly mean his losing the patriarchate. Monks were a pain in the ass but surely this humble man from Studion was far holier than he.

———————

The next meeting of the three who ruled the world was tense. After some discussion of the Arab threat - the troublesome Harun al-Rashid had succeeded to the throne in Baghdad - the delicate subject of the basilios' engagement to Rotrud and her replacement had to be explored.

Stauratius offered a solution. "We will allow the basilios some recreation for awhile. Then we can simply follow a provincial tradition, Basilia. The provinces will send the most lovely and talented girls of the empire here, and His Serenity can choose which most pleases him. I think that his crush on the Frankish girl is but a fantasy. He is surrounded by too many older women who are always telling him what is best for him; and the girls of his own age are children of courtiers. Their fathers want them to be on the throne for their own honor and profit. He has known these girls all his life; some are quite jaded little *princesses*." The eunuch hissed the word. "Perhaps a girl not from the capital would please him. He would like a little innocence and daring and he fantasizes that in Rotrud."

"Not entirely a fantasy, Stauratius. According to Elissaeus she really is adventurous and quite sweet. If the boy were not emperor I might like to see them married." The empress paused a long moment as though about to reverse her decision but then hardened her heart. "But the Bulgars may well attack her father's land; and besides, Charles has iconoclast sympathies. I cannot bring that family into mine. For the sake of the empire we don't want that and we do want peace in the north."

After the meeting the ministers withdrew together. Stauratius drew Aetius into an anteroom and surprised him with his candor. His words reflected those of Irene herself. "Aetius, I need your help. You know and I know that Her Serenity does not wish that Constantine succeed her next year, if ever. Believe me, I am not trying to trap you. You have always been closer to the emperor than I have. ... I'm not sure quite how to say this but he must not show too much interest in affairs of state. We must interest him in other things: ceremony, history, art. He has always had a taste for the arts. Perhaps women too. ... It were best that I not go into detail. Her Serenity does not trust her son to rule well and has turned her mind against a Frankish connection because of his weakness and Charles' sympathy with the iconoclasts. …Christ forgive me; I called the basilios weak. But I must be candid. Our interests here are alike, whatever our differences elsewhere.

Aetius looked at the other ranking eunuch of the empire. This was no trap. What he was saying was on everyone's mind as Constantine approached manhood. "I rather like the boy, if I may call him that. Let me try to keep him a boy. It would be for his own good." Both dignitaries knew what that meant. He would be allowed to reign but one way or another Constantine would not be permitted to actually rule. It wasn't just the icon issue which so preoccupied Irene either; if he were to rule there was much good reason to believe that Constantine would replace both of them with academics, Franks, and strategoi who still harbored sympathy for iconoclasm. They preferred not to dwell on the fate that usually befell fallen ministers.

CHAPTER 15

Beth was walking to the Hudson Tubes after work; work having been a long session posing for a guy she didn't much like. She didn't mind being cold in a bikini in an under-heated studio on a winter day, or even posing for kinky stuff if the photographer was nice, even with those who got a bit unprofessionally hot. In fact, she kind of liked those who were men and showed it. But this jerk was cold as ice. He wasn't queer; that would have been okay. He was one of those completely passionless men who probably worked math problems for the pleasure of it and that was scary. Now the day was drawing down. Beth had eaten a hot dog - just one - and was looking forward to getting home and into bed with a big mug of hot cocoa. She'd probably read some more of *Dalton's Byzantine Art and Archeology* and fall asleep early.

When she got home Beth did make the cocoa. She did get under the warm covers with her book. In her bureau were the leather undies she sometimes posed in. She would need them for the young man who was waiting and dreaming of her. The lovely lady in thong and boots removed a corset and a collar. She fastened each device to herself; first the collar which closed with the thud of a hasp, then the corset which was difficult to lace up by herself. For a moment she fussed over her braids, then she stepped into her mirror.

"Good morning, Your Serenity. Did you sleep well?"

Startled, Constantine sprang to a sitting position and swung his feet to the ground. He could barely see the figure before him for the blaze of sunlight behind her in the doorway. What he did see was puzzling and strange, a demon certainly, for though it took a female form it wore no tunic.

"Holy Mother of Jesus!" – a manly expletive.

"I am Beth of Newark."

The demon glided toward the far wall. Now, without the sun behind her, Constantine could see that it wore the tiniest of leather garments with just a strip of leather extending back between its buttocks as the demon turned round and round in the sun. The light flashed on its corset and two large and naked breasts which swung from side to side. Its legs were encased in boots. They laced up to the knees but the heels of its feet did not touch the ground at all. They were held a hand's-breadth off the floor by thin wooden soles which themselves curved like a woman's curves. The morning air was brisk and Beth of Newark tried to cover her big breasts with her arms, not, it seemed, out of modesty, but only to warm them.

Constantine noted all these things yet his eyes were fixed upon the demon's head which seemed to float upon a black leather neck. Beth threw out her arms and spun again to show the cords that tightly laced her corset.

"Am I pretty? Now don't pretend you aren't aroused."

Aroused Constantine was, but terrified too.

You? I saw you when I fell. Are you not Rotrud?"

"Perhaps Rotrud, perhaps Beth. Should it matter, *My Gracious Lord*?

Constantine awoke with a headache and with much to fear on his mind.

"Seigneur Ricolf, I just had the strangest dream." Young Constantine was speaking to the tall Frank in buckskin who had arisen from his cot at a pretty little monastery on one of the islands just south of the capital. The monastery was hardly a place of self-denial and penance. Because of their fine climate these islands were sometimes used as places of honored exile for princes who might seek the imperial purple. Ricolf stifled a yawn and tried to be as attentive as a rude Frank could be to the emperor of the world, far from the usual trappings of that office at five in the morning. But sleep was still in his eyes. Constantine had tried to speak in Cicero's classical Latin. Ricolf struggled with a Gaulish Latin patois.

"Dream? A good one I trust; a pretty lass with a big chest I hope? Only a foreigner such as Ricolf would dare speak thusly to the emperor and he only in private.

"Actually yes; and not much clothes either."

"How so, mi-lord?" Ricolf was consciously using the western form of address to a superior. Had the emperor wished to be treated as nearly godlike they could have stayed in Constantinople.

"She was dressed in the strangest manner, all leather - what there was - and her heels were higher than her toes."

"Ah, the whores of Rome do that." The older man was now giving serious attention, and thinking of the forms that demons had been known to take. "Down, boy. I mean: Down, Your Serenity." They shared a smile but both knew that there must be limits and the ambassador was testing them.

This is scary. Maybe the priests are right about devils being all about us.

Constantine had the same concern. "I hope she's not a demon. She

106

had long blonde braids like Rotrud. At first I thought she might be Rotrud in a dream again. But she called herself Beth of Newark - wherever that is - and she had a rump like a horse .... but no hooves like a devil. She could also walk like a horse. She was prancing around when I woke up."

"Did that excite you, Your Serenity?"

"Yes. Everything about her excited me. It is very difficult to think chastely when I dream."

Ricolf roared a great rolling laugh despite the seriousness of the matter under discussion. "A demon? Ah, Your Serenity, I'd send you to the monks for penance except that they see devils everywhere. We need a more objective view. Tell me, does this apparition love God?"

"I don't know, Ricolf. I hope so. We did not speak of it."

For a moment Ricolf considered what the lad and his vision did discuss but then blocked the image from his mind.

"You have dreamed of Charles' daughter before tonight?"

"Yes, often."

"And you dreamed that she dresses like that? I don't want to disappoint you, mi-lord emperor, but she's not that way … although of late she has been doing some strange things ... studying military history, tactics... It does seem that she is trying hard to interest you. Ah, but I think it is just a young man's imagination at work. Don't fret too much about devils, mi-lord; a dream is usually just a dream; no more."

"She knows my mind. I am emperor of the world, Seigneur Ricolf, but that is a duty. For myself, all I really want is some good sex – married sex but exciting – and for the Lord to tell me that I made it through life as a good Christian when I die."

That might be a problem. The church taught that sex was just to make babies for Christ. Truly, love was good but sex should not be any more exciting than necessary.

Nicephorus had to be careful. He was not known for spending much time on his estates. He did not much care for the rural life but now he had let it be known that he would be visiting his villa near Trebizond in Anatolia. He had actually made it a point to cackle about it to *the idiot emperor and his superstitious mom,* and jest about his vacation: "Too bad that duty must keep you here, Your Sacred Majesties. But the cares of state et cetera ...." The estate that he would visit was near Trebizond but not so near as to invite visitors, nor yet so far as to arouse suspicion. It was summer again and the grapes would soon be maturing. New wine flowing was as good an excuse as any to spend some weeks, even a couple of months in the fresh Black Sea air. God knows no one but the '*idiot*' wanted to be in steamy Constantinople in summer. If required, the scheduled weeks could easily be prolonged without raising suspicion.

Thus a few days after celebrating Pentecost with the emperor's household and the patriarch, the prince, with his wife, was carried by servants through the crowded streets to the imperial harbor of Boucoleonm which his exalted titles permitted him to use. This was important. It was of utmost importance that he not seem to be skulking off. The day was bright; the breeze fresh. The sailors actually seemed happy to see him approaching. *Probably looking forward to sailing away from the city's stench*, Nicephorus thought. *They are right. It will be a pleasant journey and there is no reason not to enjoy it too.* He did not even curse the servant carrying one of the poles of his litter when he briefly stumbled. Of course, Nicephorus did not ever actually curse, or at least rarely. He was too much an aristocrat to indulge in base vulgarities or misuse the names of saints. A curse from him was likely to be a mere remark like "clumsy fool", or "dumb farmer" if he was very angry. Nonetheless, the words carried as much force or more than some drover's more colorful vocabulary and the object of his expletive must worry whether the remark was the end of the matter.

Getting out of his palace and to the quay had been the usual hassle that even nobility are not immune to. Anna, his wife, felt she had to add a few things that they would surely not need at their villa, and Nicephorus double-checked that the rich and appropriate gifts he had personally hidden in their baggage were safe from Stauratius' spies. There was a robe of fine Chinese silk which the Bulgar khan could have acquired from a tribe further east. There was an exquisitely decorated Damascus spathion from before that city was lost to the Arabs; a sword that he could have acquired in many ways. Most useful was a set of silver jars that held Indian spices to improve the Bulgar menu: pepper, cinnamon, cloves, nutmeg, and ginger. Hopefully Irene would be glad to have him out of the city, and the imperial hierarchy too occupied with their petty squabbles to pay his departure much attention. *Fools! We'll be thinning your ranks quite a bit*, he thought. *Ah, but the day is lovely. There is no rush until after I drop off Anna.*

After a boring week of looking at grapes, Nicephorus would leave Anna at the villa. The trip into Bulgar country would be made as quickly as possible lest he be missed. While Anna oversaw a great flurry of activity at the estate he would feign illness, but set sail by night across the inland sea to where the empire's adversary waited.

CHAPTER 16

Whatever Nicephorus might think, the young prince and his mother endured the hot and humid summer air of Constantinople for good reasons. For an emperor to be away except when at war was to invite intrigue and treason, for the capital was the heart and soul of the empire in a way not true of any great state today. The city stank in summer, yes; but it was also an open-air museum in which the greatest of ancient Greek art was publicly displayed in city squares. The relics of innumerable saints sanctified its golden domed churches. There were feuds and frequent riots but there was also an active theater. There were both amateur and professional sporting events. There was nightlife with dining and dancing, music and infidelity. There were constant theological discussions which could end in fist fights or knife fights. No other place, rural or urban, was so exciting; courtiers felt exiled if required to live even a little distance outside its great walls. On more than a few occasions, rebels had been permitted to enter unopposed when the monarch was not at home.

Besides, there were things to be done. The Patriarch Paul had just been replaced by a layman of great prestige who was quickly ordained priest and consecrated bishop. In Tarasios Irene expected to find a grateful and malleable minion to reinforce her extreme beliefs. Instead, Tarasios, while a devoted supporter of the icons, was also a realist. He insisted as a condition of accepting the patriarchate that the rulers call a great synod so that the iconodules of Constantinople and the iconoclasts of Asia might come to speak with a single voice.

Tarasios had been picked by Irene and Aetius when the ailing Patriarch Paul resigned because of poor health. He was holy. As a layman he had been suspected of wearing a hair shirt. He told Aetius of the single monk of Studion who had visited his predecessor, seemingly the only monk more concerned with charity than with victory.

"The holy monks!" he complained with some anger. "Right belief is important and sometimes it must be fought for; but not everywhere. Christ rules us all, orthodox and heretic alike, and He is most patient. We must emulate that. Only one monk in all the city seems to have understood that.

"The monks mean well but they hate sex more than the blessed John Chrysostom did. They distrust women and would consider them satanic had not women been the only disciples to remain loyal to Christ Jesus at the crucifixion. They never think where the next generation of monks will come from if not from pretty God-fearing mothers. And they think the clergy are too worldly, too political. Perhaps sometimes they are; but that is our calling as it is yours also. We are in the world, you and I; the monks ought not to be, but they are too. They do not leave it to the clergy and statesmen to direct the affairs of this world but intrude their radicalism. Noble as their intentions are, the monks - even those of Studion here in the capital - tend to be a bit, shall I say intolerant. They know the scriptures and the saints and fathers very well - perhaps too well. But you and I must live in this world and know much more; and be tolerant of others' wrong beliefs. Elsewise the demons lead us into hate and violence against our brothers."

There was doubt about his predecessor's poor health. Paul had left the patriarchate for a monastery without informing anyone. When Irene sought him out he had claimed great physical and mental pain brought on, he feared, by his support of iconoclasm while Leo had reigned. His last words to them had been a plea that the icons be a bond between Christians, not a source of discord. Obviously, the iconodule Tarasios agreed.

Aetius liked the forthrightness of Tarasios, but he warned him that not everyone in the Sacred Palace would be so understanding. Charity made an excellent sermon but dangerous policy. The monasteries were powerful, and if they were to challenge his authority, they would win. The new patriarch had been picked to be the velvet glove but Irene was closer to the monks of Saccudion and Studion in spirit, and theirs was an iron fist

---

My Rotrud:

I read your latest letter with delight. There are few people here who can ignore the fact that I will be their master, and speak or write to me in so friendly - so endearing - a way. The only one around here who I am still in both sufficient awe and regard of that we can speak like brothers is my old tutor, John Pikridios.

I've enjoyed the visit of your barons: Ricolf of Bacheim and Bertmund of Loutern. Of course we'd met when they brought your father's agreement to our betrothal, but I was only a boy then. Even so, from what they told me of your wonderful good humor and your regard for learning, I knew then I was destined to care deeply for my blonde princess in braids. I too enjoy books, though not always the ones that my tutors assign..

Do not trouble yourself about your language skills and I will try not to trouble myself too much. I'm sure we will always be able to understand each other, even if your Greek and my Latin are a bit rough. When you are by my side you will pick up our spoken language easily enough, and I have learned that you are already reading in it.

110

I have your portrait before me as I write this letter.

"To the steeds of Pharaoh's chariots would I liken you, my beloved:
    Your cheeks lovely in pendants, your neck in jewels.
    We will make pendants of gold for you, and silver ornaments."

How much I yearn to see my betrothed with my own eyes. I have dreamt of you. Truly the face of the Lord shines upon me.

Constantine put down his pen. That was enough. He could quote Solomon but he dared not write exactly what his dreams had been. But truly, Ricolf and Bertmund had again dwelt on his fiancé's high humor and playfulness at least as much as they had emphasized her piety and intelligence. Perhaps - just possibly - when they were wed, she might dress for him as she - or Beth - did in his dreams; and there was no reason he could not direct that a special riding crop be made for her use; one with emeralds and gold and scenes of valkyries from the northern legends instead of some saint on the handle. How beautiful his bride would be in thong and braids and holding that sparkling crop. He could have the boots made too, just for the bedroom. Whore boots, Seigneur Ricolf called them; but then hadn't Ricolf himself told him that the Illustrious Belisarius had married a prostitute? Had they not lived a long and happy life together?

—————————————

"Ah Prince Nicephorus!" Khardam greeted the Byzantine grandee warmly. Like Nicephorus, he was an exceptionally strong man, though not as tall as the Roman; and his hug was so firm as to stop just short of being painful. The forest clearing was warm and grass covered. Obviously someone had scythed it in recent days, but with the warm weather it was already becoming studded with wild flowers again. "I have heard much of you and long hoped to make your acquaintance. You must be hungry after so long a journey and it is past midday. Relax … Relax. There is plenty of meat ready over by the fires, but I'm afraid these woods cannot provide much fresh fruit to make you feel at home. We do have apples and berries though and we do quite wonderful things with nuts and honey. Come, join me at that table away from the crowd." Under his breath the khan added: "Sometimes there is more privacy in the open than there is between walls."

For a time Khardam had ceased his incursions into Roman territory and had come near to a small village on the northwestern shore of the Black Sea - called the Euxinus by the Romans - but not so near as to make the meeting a public affair. It had been put about that he had come to bathe and indulge his taste for salmon. A rumor that he was also interested in the wife of one of his war-captains had explained with a wink why he was accompanied only by a very few chiefs, some necessary aides, and several hundred guards from his own family. The Bulgar army waited in Moesia where it still threatened Thrace. His greeting had been warm but informal, as Nicephorus was certainly not in these godforsaken woods as an emissary. If Irene were to discover that he was not in Asia but across the Euxine Sea in the great khan's embrace, it would mean his death or at least the loss of his eyes. *Irene would enjoy that,* Nicephorus mused. *I wonder: Do I hate her more than she hates me, or does she hate me more?* A futile question; there was enough hate between the two to satisfy Satan himself.

Nuts and honey. Does this khan think to appear humble or does he think that I look down upon the Bulgars? Well I shall not do that so long as they serve my purpose. Afterwards? Well, we'll see. Now is for diplomacy. Nicephorus had educated himself well in the Bulgar language and the khan had spoken in fairly good Greek. This was not unusual or suspicious, for Nicephorus was a diplomat and the khan's people were neighbors, like it or not.

"Great Khan, we are not so proud... " It was Nicephorus's turn to play the humble courtier. "Even in the city we have Bulgar food. There are taverns which specialize in northern dishes ... and not just for your people. Quite a few of us have taken a liking to your fare." The few trusted men who had escorted the caesar across the sea took seats together and began to eat heartily as Nicephorus had instructed. He could not afford even a suspicion of slight in the camp of the empire's enemy and his potential ally. Both men understood his purpose here and the others at the simple log tables in the forest clearing could guess. Nicephorus had dressed-down enough for the occasion not to appear haughty or insolent before the barbarians; he was merely neat. He had decided that riding clothes would be rustic enough; leather and rough fabric well-fit for traveling without looking deliberately rude; and they need bear no obvious religious symbols to offend the pagans or make them suspicious of his true intention. Certainly Nicephorus had no intention to be a missionary. *That day will come in God's time,* he thought. *It is God's purpose that they be made firm allies first. Christ is patient. He will wait. When I am emperor I shall repay my debt to the Lord... and my debt to the idiot boy and his icon-smooching mother too.*

The afternoon passed. As evening came on the two men moved into the relative warmth of the great khan's tent. A trusted servant tended the brazier, being sure that what smoke the hardwood produced went out a roof hole. Still, it was an insecure place for making life or death deals - neither in an open field nor behind thick walls - and Nicephorus was glad when the khan had made his last demands and he his own. He had begun by reminding the khan of the universal child's game: "You may have some of the marbles, but not all." Khardam had agreed. The negotiations had not

112

been as difficult as Nicephorus had feared. They were not one-sided. True, Nicephorus was the suppliant and he played the part well, yet not so humbly as to seem powerless. He might well become emperor even without Bulgar help and they would not want to have refused him. Even if he did not, the Roman court held little love for the Bulgar tribes, and a friend there would be valuable to Khardam. Then too, if Bulgar help did bring this man to the throne, then they would have free access to the rich Adriatic lands and perhaps to Italy itself. In name the Khan would have to rule over the local population as the representative of the future basilios in Constantinople, Nicephorus himself, but that was a detail. Probably he would be expected to confront King Charles of the Franks but that was in the stars anyway. There could not be two such great powers in the west and Khan Khardam did not fear the Franks, but was secure in the strength of his arms. Secure but not foolish. Charles and his father Pepin before him, and his grandfather, known as the hammer, had all been strong and aggressive kings in their time. He did not underestimate the Franks.

At last the negotiations were done and the two men relaxed, comfortable in each others company, or at least as comfortable as a traitor and his master can be. Neither quite trusted the other not to betray him for, of course, either would; but they felt secure that for now they had a deal.

"Bring more beer!" Khardam had drunk little until then and Nicephorus even less. Nor had this passed unnoticed by either man. They had evaluated each other and come to favorable conclusions about their potential success in working together. Both men were more reticent about important things than their apparent openness revealed, and both knew and appreciated this fact. Drink is well-said to loosen tongues and there were those matters which neither man wished to reveal to the other. Both also understood that, and neither wanted to give away more in negotiation than was necessary just because he had lost his sobriety. Both were also glad of the other's restraint; one does not wish to be in life and death negotiations with a drunkard. Now however, with the negotiation ended, though Nicephorus continued to drink in moderation, not particularly caring for beer or the Bulgars' fermented mare's milk, the khan began to indulge himself just a bit more.

"Do you not like our beer?"

"Ah, it is an unusual taste for me, Great Khan."

"Then you shall have wine. The locals produce quite decent wines here. Please ... try some, and if it does not please you, say so. I have some good Roman wine in the baggage."

The evening watches passed pleasantly; the conspirators enjoying the party together with Khardam's closest friends and whatever Bulgar chieftains and shamans had been invited to accompany him to the coast. Such important men had to be watched closely for signs of undue ambition, but so long as Khardam continued to win battles he had little fear of this. No single chief could confront him and an alliance between several was far less likely than that each would continue his present profitable allegiance. The toasts between pagan and Christian were discreet with such minimal and generic reference to deities as religious orthodoxy permitted. A goat had been sacrificed but blood sacrifices were also common among the Christian peasants of Anatolia. Like most of the Greek intelligentsia, Nicephorus openly abhorred such blood sacrifices but dared not ban the rites on his rural estates. One could never be sure if they were merely superstitious or demonic, and he knew himself not to be saintly enough to dare provoke devils.

All in all, Nicephorus was pleased to confirm Byzantine secret service reports that the Bulgar chieftain appeared somewhat cultivated, and Khardam watched his tongue as carefully as did the Byzantine prince. But at last, relaxed and mellow, Nicephorus felt he could drop discretion in a purely personal matter which would also show his humanity.

"Most excellent Khan, if you will permit me to indulge a secret that few men know: I prefer my women to be unwilling. That's frowned upon in my circle but maybe here... You may have a captive?"

"Ah, of course; but may I suggest one of my own slaves. I've been wondering how to discipline Lucia. She thinks that she is here only for me and expects me to make her a great lady. She even took that Latin name ... Well I just might do that for her if she's good. You see, she's done things with her mouth that I'd not dare ask of one of our Bulgar women if I want to keep my head. Even the khan's authority has limits when it comes to angry kin. But right now she needs to have her opinion of herself reduced somewhat. ... I do like the girl, but she is a slave and mustn't forget it.

"Her mouth? A flute job? That's hardly unusual." The prince thought it appropriate to speak in a vulgar manner here, though he rarely spoke of such things at all. To do so at court would compromise his image.

The khan wrapped his arm around Nicephorus' shoulder and spoke *sotto voce*. "You do not understand. I have no need for a jug at night. She swallows piss. If I drink too much beer I just call for her to spend the night in my bed. She thinks it's love." He laughed then resumed a conspiratorial attitude. "If I loan her to you she'll be pissed as an Avar demon with me. I think you'll find her quite unaccommodating and I believe she'll put up quite a fight unless I order her not to ... and I won't. There's nothing like a good fuck from some stranger to put a slave in her place."

Nicephorus laughed a roar of a laugh. Beneath his cultured veneer the Khan of the Bulgars was a boor at heart just as Nicephorus would have liked to be at that moment. "If you're certain that you won't be needing her services tonight, great Khan; yes, I'd like to borrow this woman for a little rape?"

114

"Yes, yes, and perhaps a little whipping, but I'd appreciate it if you'd not maim her. I need my jug and I don't want to have an angry slave biting my cock off. ... And don't pass up the piss drinking." The conspirators toasted the coming night, clashing mugs together loudly. Outside, the guards knew that negotiation had ended and drinking had begun. They hoped that the night would not end in a knife fight as could easily happen. What was the temperament of the Greek? How much blood money does the life of a Greek prince demand? The guards were solemn, but the remainder of the evening went well inside the tent. A very few of the khan's close relatives and high officials were invited to speak openly with their new ally. More beer and wine were brought in but Nicephorus continued to drink in relative moderation. Girls entertained, first with songs and dances and then with teasing until, quite late, Nicephorus retired to a pavilion that had been prepared for him.

Tallow torches lit the place, their smoky light falling on a young girl who stood tied naked to a post by ropes and prickly vines which stuck her at every movement. Nicephorus was now quite mellow and strangely relaxed despite having just agreed to betray his country to the Bulgars. He wondered why. *Perhaps it is because the thing is finally afoot. Ah, when I am basilios I can bring this girl's special service to the Sacred Palace if Anna lets me.* He drew out one of her breasts by its long nipple and twisted hard, appreciating the good grip that he could get on it. Judging by her jet black eyes and hair Nicephorus concluded that she was of Mongol stock. *Normal enough among the khan's suzerain peoples.* He had studied quite a bit about not only the Bulgars but also their predecessors, the Avars and Huns, who had ruled before them here in previous centuries. Avar and Hun were now too closely intermarried with the original stock of the land to be clearly distinguishable any longer, but further east the racial differences were apparent. *Yes, Mongol, but not entirely;* for her eyelids were open quite wide. That frightened animal look was uncommon in the eyes of Mongols which usually did not open so wide and round. Nicephorus spoke to the girl in Bulgar, hoping that she would understand. "I like the vines. A nice primitive touch. Was that Khardam's idea?" She did not answer. "We have some things in common, he and I. I'm to teach you a lesson, slave. You seem to think that you are something special. No, you are just a very pretty latrine." Nicephorus showed her his whip.

He put on his gloves. It was a delight to very carefully begin unwrapping the vines; carefully to avoid pricking himself, not because he cared about a slave's pain. Nicephorus discovered that she had been standing on thorns. *Ugh, that must hurt*, he thought; *nice touch though.* After removing a few windings he stopped. "You'll be moving quite a bit when I whip you, slave. I think I'll leave the thorns till later." He raised the whip but her features revealed nothing more than the fear they had shown before. *It is hard for us Romans to read Mongol faces*. He struck her many times, hard enough to draw a little blood but not so viciously as to leave permanent scars. That had been Khardam's instruction and it would be enough to satisfy him. He was only to humiliate the girl, not cripple or kill her. Anyway, if Nicephorus was a cruel man there was at least some limit to what he would inflict on an innocent plaything. Perhaps it was Christian conscience, or perhaps fear of damnation, or concern lest he offend his host; but though he was sadistic, he would not inflict a serious injury on this girl. After all, she had not offended him. His soul could take some comfort in this restraint. Though the girl would spend a most unpleasant night, she was not further tortured. Nicephorus excused the beating to himself, and the thorns too. They had been inflicted at the khan's order. He really did like rape however, and felt a good deal less guilty about that. He repeatedly stuffed the teenage girl, who a few hours before had envisioned herself the khan's favorite and a great lady. Nicephorus just considered that this was the usual thing in a world where many towns were sacked at least once in a female's lifetime, where bandits were an everyday concern, and where even friendly armies often took whatever pleasures they wished from the countryside they passed through. The girl felt wonderful to Nicephorus. It is one of the pleasures of fidelity that when one does cheat the feel of another woman is as fresh as when he was very young.

After raping the girl Nicephorus stood thinking of all that had passed between himself and the Bulgar leader that night; then he added one more humiliation to satisfy the wish of Lucia's master. He made her kneel and required that she swallow him just as she would Khardam. He held her head rigid by her earrings. She expected semen but instead Nicephorus voided a flood of hot urine down her throat. After that he left her to try to sleep on the ground while he passed the night alone on a bed of furs, thinking for awhile of his wife across the sea and their future as emperor and empress. Just before falling asleep his mind turned again to the girl. *She will be a pleasant sight to see, tied like a dog to a stake first thing in the morning; and I'll no doubt need to piss again.*

The Byzantine prince and his small retinue were gone almost with the dawn. Nicephorus made some apologies for his necessary haste. To have been ill or be gone from his estate for a few days of hunting was understandable; to be missing much longer was likely to arouse suspicion. Besides, he missed his wife. The slavegirl Lucia was more than happy to see him go. Khan Khardam had some explaining and soothing to do, but he had made his point with her. Still, as he stroked her hair that night and admired her wounds he allowed that he might one day rule Italy with the help of the Greek bastard - as Lucia would ever after call Nicephorus. If so, he promised he would free her from slavery and make her the great lady she wished to be. *The lady Lucia*, he though smiling. *By then you'll be too old for me anyway.* Khardam broke open the dried blood of a cut and began to lick the salty juice that trickled out.

CHAPTER 17

"Beth, with those long legs you should have been a dancer." Eddy Miller was posing his favorite model.

"Oh, I did take a few lessons in school, but I didn't like the teacher. 'First position ... second position ... *en pointe.*' Not a lot of fun."

"Do you think you could still pose those positions?"

"Not on my toes. I never really got *en pointe* for more than a few seconds before I quit; and I haven't the ankle muscles."

"It would make a nice spread. You could wear something long with those stems peeking out when you spin."

"It wouldn't be much of a pinup. I can't see guys who look at *Titter* being turned on by ballet."

"I'd like to see you dance, Beth."

They looked at each other for a long moment. Beth was smiling her famous smile, but Eddy seemed lost in thought. It was time for Beth to leave. When she had gone Eddy walked into the night in search of relief.

It was evening in Constantinople. Constantine with a few disguised guards had slipped away from the palace. The teenager wanted to see the city, the real city which had not been prepared for a visit by the Anointed of God: swept, decorated and perfumed, and strewn with flowers.

It was evening but not yet night. There was still light on the streets lined with stucco and terra cotta houses. Some of the houses also served as shops or workspace for their tenants but others were just dwellings. Those who did not work in their houses but on small farms, or were merchants, or were employed in the city's many workshops were headed to their homes. Many looked tired from the hard work of their day but others were walking together in pairs or small groups, sometimes talking quietly and seriously but sometimes laughing too. *God told Adam: "By your sweat you shall earn your bread" and so they do.* It was not an unhappy populace just a weary one. Soon they would be with their wives and children. There would be food enough. Even those who could not afford much meat would still have plenty of bread and vegetables. Bread was free for the poorest and anyone could grow a few vegetables in the fine Constantinoplian climate. Good water was brought from the mountains by the city's aqueducts and was free at the fountains. Simple table-wine was inexpensive.

Constantine stumbled on a paving stone that stood up too high. He recovered just as one of the guards rushed to support his emperor. Together they entered a small square where an unimpressive fountain took the last gleams of twilight. It was not one of the great forums but a simple crossing of streets with a fountain. Some merchant who might have been busy a few moments before with a last minute sale was still closing his stall and rolling his awning. An hour ago the little square would have been very busy and noisy. Now it was quiet and pretty in a simple way that Constantine noticed more than those who spent their days there would have. It was nice to just look around at the things that generations of plain folk had produced. Simple things like paint on wooden window sills instead of the marble-work that was polished daily at the palace. He noted the roofs of red clay and the tastefulness of arches and vaults about him. There were no trees, only stone and stucco and a few plants in pots for their color. This was the city. It felt almost enclosed, and every sound was loud. Some reverberated. There was enough of nature not far away, olive groves and orchards even within the walls. People here were happy to be clustered one family upon another where they could chat together without even leaving their windows. Besides, the summer had been unusually cool so the stench was tolerable and nothing more than Constantine was used to. At night the mule dung would be collected for monastery farms. Gutters beside the traveled way removed much of the other wastes when it rained. His people lived in this scene and were so accustomed to it and so busy with their routine chores that they hardly noticed it was pretty; except maybe sometimes, when the seasons changed and the breeze was fresh, and there was nothing of importance for one of them to deal with. Then he might take a moment to rest by the fountain and sip a little water before heading home to dinner, children, and finally bed with the wife he loved.

The last rays of the sun gilded the simplest things. Constantine was totally relaxed and without a care. Far down a street with a view of the sea behind her, a dancer pranced from one doorway to another. Her steps and clothing were not of his century. Back-lit by the sunset her whole long legs flashed beneath a full-length skirt. For just a brief moment she stood *en pointe*. Constantine was amazed. It was the most beautiful pose he had ever seen, in its way more erotic than when Beth wore boots and a thong.

Constantine was at last of age to rule. He had been raised to the title of basilios years before when his father had associated the boy with himself on the throne. Now there should have been a ceremony in the great church to confirm this, yet the weak council of regents did not arrange it and dissolve. Instead it just faded away leaving Irene still in power. Irene put off imparting real authority to her son by reason after reason; reasons confirmed by all the high authorities of state - her men.

To an extent Nicephorus had tried to take the place of Constantine's dead father. That had seemed self-serving and suspicious but not evil. From Nicephorus Constantine learned that not everything about being ruler of the world was a tiresome chore. By stages as his skill with lance and bow increased, his uncle had introduced the emperor to more and more dangerous sports, hunting particularly. Since he'd been an eight year-old boy Constantine had been skilled in catching birds with nets; by twelve he'd learned to kill pheasants with an arrow. He learned falconry, often called the royal sport. (For which reason he had to do it like he had to do everything else that was "royal.") Now there was hunting boar with the lance and there was hunting deer with the palace cheetahs though he actually preferred just watching the great cats. They lounged about his throne room to impress visitors and for the pleasure he derived from seeing their pretty faces. Furface always kept her distance; cat or not, she would be nothing but a snack to one of her cousins.

An attack on the young emperor was always possible. Constantine had enemies and he knew it. The woods between the capital and Adrianople were a fine place for an ambush but possibly no less safe than the palace itself. The usual precautions had been taken. There was a half regiment of guards. But were they loyal? There were the tall and brutal ax-men from the far north. Could they be bought? There were friends and relatives. Uncle 'Foros had proposed the trip, a chance for the emperor to try his hunting skills against real adult game and risk real adult pain and even death if the boar turned against him as he was momentarily unprotected by the other hunters. *Perhaps*, Constantine thought, *I am the hunted. If so I must learn to respond like the hunted with strength, cunning, and bravery.*

There was no way of knowing what motivated the Armenian monk who shot the arrow. He had been quickly dispatched with an ax. He was identified but had not been seen for months at his monastery near Trebizond. No one in Constantinople seemed to know him. There was no one to torture for information. He seemed an unlikely candidate for a palace intrigue. More likely just a disgruntled iconoclast. *Of what use*, thought Constantine, *are strength and cunning and bravery? The priests are right: Trust in the Lord and be prepared to meet Him.*

Now the emperor was not only the pride of the city but the darling of the masses outside its walls. Mother, usually popular among the women of the city, was rumored to have shown insufficient sympathy when her heroic son returned to the palace seemingly unshaken by the experience of having an archer place an arrow beside his head.

"Until now, such dangers have only been academic to you, Constantine. Now you know what it is to rule. But put your faith in our Lord and His saints and you will be as invulnerable as I. I would like you to take some vacation. Make a tour of the provinces and let the people see you. Do not be concerned with affairs of state for a few more years yet. I can take care of that and you can continue your studies so that you will be better prepared to rule when the Lord takes me to his bosom."

That speech, which was spread by word of mouth from servants to shopkeepers, had seemed cold, unfeeling, and definitely self-serving even to the women of Constantinople. It was rumored that Irene's piety and ambition had so enveloped her that even her maternal instincts were subsumed in them. The country folk had another explanation: The royal lady had been in much too much of a hurry to return to affairs of state after giving birth for Irene to nurse and tend a babe herself. She had only seen him clean and diapered by his nurse, Flacilla; more like a pet than her own infant.

There was worse. The only city west of Cathay which could rival Constantinople in the beauty of its architecture, its wealth, and the commerce which crowded its streets and markets, was Baghdad during the reign of Harun al-Rashid. Located on the banks of the Tigris River, it was the capital of the Abbasid caliphate, the most dangerous enemy of Christendom. The Abbasid dynasty had revived the fortunes of Islam which a few decades before had been declining in the face of Roman counterattacks. Now the west was confronted by a vigorous and talented commander and one who did not wish peace with the infidel.

The Saracens were increasing their incursions into Byzantine-controlled Anatolia. There were almost monthly raids and the number of men in the raiding parties was steadily increasing. To contain the enemy meant committing large forces along the border at all potential invasion sites. That was expensive, draining, and in the end nonproductive. To wage serious war would be even more expensive and the risk of defeat very real. Stauratius was cautious. Constantine would have dared the counterattack; Irene would not.

The empire is a mess and mother seems unable to straighten it out. We're sending tribute to Harun. The Anatolian armies hate her. Only the monks are happy, but she wants me to tour the countryside.

Fortunately for Constantine's peace of mind Furface took this moment to enter his study and announce by jumping onto his desk that it was bedtime.

———————————

Constantine awoke, his ass still screaming. He had not been

122

spanked since he'd outgrown Flacilla's rather mild chastisements. He had been dreaming again; but what a strange dream it had been. The fair lady had been as fair as ever.... slim waist, long legs - long legs clad in heavy boots almost up to... Oooh! He tried to hold onto the image. He really wanted to preserve it in his mind but, as is usual with dreams, it faded even as he tried to pin it to earth. His rear didn't hurt either; but he wished it did though he could not imagine why he wished for such a strange thing except that the thought made him feel very good. At least that would be better than the headache he did feel.

The council to formalize reintroduction of icons was called when Constantine had just turned seventeen. Despite the patriarch's hopes for reconciliation it was a shambles from the beginning. Armeniac troops opposing the restoration of the icons intimidated the prelates in the great cathedral at Constantinople. The council had to be adjourned. Stauratius sent these iconoclastic troops away by a stratagem that had them believing that they were required for renewed hostilities with the Arabs, and the council resumed in the town of Nicea.

On the iconodule side, the monk Platon led the representatives of the monasteries who had never wavered in their loyalty to the icons. He was abbot of the monastery of Saccudion and well known and respected at the Great Palace. Platon was a pious man but also an independent-minded and fanatical supporter of the icons. For that he had been exiled by Leo. Now Platon and the monks insisted that public renunciation of their errors by formerly iconoclast priests and bishops was insufficient, and that they must also be humiliated and anathematized. Despite this muttering of the monks, the realistic and worldly bishops, under the guidance of Tarasios, finally settled on humiliation alone.

The council concluded that: "We keep unchanged all the ecclesiastical traditions handed down to us, whether in writing or verbally, one of which is the making of pictorial representations, agreeable to the history of the preaching of the Gospel, a tradition useful in many respects, but especially in this, that so the incarnation of the Word of God is shown forth as real and not merely fantasy … We define with all certitude and accuracy that just as the figure of the precious and life-giving Cross, so also the venerable and holy images, as well in painting and mosaic as of other fit materials, should be set forth in the holy churches of God, and on the sacred vessels and on the vestments and on hangings and in pictures both in houses and by the wayside, to wit, the figure of our Lord God and Savior Jesus Christ, of our spotless Lady, the Mother of God, of the honorable

Angels, of all Saints and of all pious people. For by so much more frequently as they are seen in artistic representation, by so much more readily are men lifted up to the memory of their prototypes, and to a longing after them; and to these should be given due salutation and honorable reverence, not indeed that true worship of faith which pertains alone to the divine nature; but to these, as to the figure of the precious and life-giving Cross and to the Book of the Gospels and to the other holy objects, incense and lights may be offered according to ancient pious custom. For the honor which is paid to the image passes on to that which the image represents, and he who reveres the image reveres in it the subject represented."

Constantine signed the decrees of the council. It was almost his first public duty now that he had come of age. But his mother also signed.

———————————

It wasn't long afterward that Khan Khardam showed his friendship to Nicephorus; or perhaps it were better to say he put a down payment with Nicephorus against future cooperation.

Pamphilus, the double agent, spoke to Eustathius of Dalmatia. Eustathius spoke to Nicephorus. Early on a Monday evening after drinking a quantity of beer - most unusual for him - the caesar left his palace alone. He left without any guards or hangers-on about him - also most unusual. But then, as a high dignitary he might be about some business requiring discretion.

Indeed he was. Dressed in the simplest attire in his wardrobe, Nicephorus hurried with many turnings into a residential part of the city he did not often visit. Being careful that he was not observed, he slipped into a small but neat and attractive house. He was greeted by the only servant of the house, a Balkan slave, and led to where Lucia waited for him. The girl did not smile at the "Greek bastard", but neither did she cower before him until her servant had left the house. She was the down payment to Nicephorus as a house in the great and exciting metropolis was a payment to her. Khardam had sent his jug to the caesar and Lucia was about to earn the high status she had been promised. When they were alone Lucia's eyes became truly fearful and she began to back away from the nobleman. He followed her into a thick-walled storeroom with an oaken door. There were no windows and only a common oil lamp in one corner gave a bit of light to show that Lucia had spread a thick layer of cushions against one wall. No one would hear her protests and pleas to the sun and moon - or to the mother of God whom Khardam had instructed her to include in her prayers.

124

Her complaints would not be play-acting. On the cushions Lucia had left some rope and a whip such as that used to chastise young slaves. Nicephorus kicked the door shut. No one would hear her screaming; at least it would be no louder than some drunken man's wife might make. No one would hear the final weeping just before he left.

As instructed, Lucia tried to fight off her attacker, unsuccessfully of course; consoling herself with the thought that tomorrow, or whenever her ass healed, she'd go shopping with the gold solodai that he would leave as appropriate payment for a barbarian peasant's service.

CHAPTER 18

Beth was posing for Edward. Eddy had decided to do something different with her today. Instead of the usual bikini poses he'd asked her to bring a flouncy dress to his studio, if she owned one. She did. Her parents had bought it for her high school prom and she'd kept it as a keepsake. It was all velvet and satin with quite a bit of décolleté. The shots as she bent over would have turned on almost any man she knew except Edward. He was her friend but he always affected a warm yet professional attitude when they were working. The poses were pinups so the skirt went up and she showed a lot of warm stockinged leg too. She suspected why Edward could be so detached but said nothing. Edward did like to see Beth looking pretty though, even if that was as far as it ever went.

When the last roll of 35 mm Ektachrome was finished - and a few plates too - Beth changed into street clothes and they went out together into the winter grubbiness of city streets looking for Chianti and pizza. That was easily found just down the block; a nice quiet place where couples could talk without being either overheard or drowned out by the chatter of others. Beth was twenty-seven and Edward thirty. Beth's modeling days were nearing their end and Edward had never had the business or artistic success he'd expected eight years before. Oh, it had been fun for both; there was no self pity or regrets. Still, as the evening turned into night, talk turned to what exactly constituted success, and even nobility in failure. They weren't going to shake up the artistic world any more than their beatnik friends would. They would settle into a routine. Beth would get a job. Edward would probably work as a staffer for some newspaper or magazine. But it had been fun; and the fun wasn't all over, just what they could expect from life was changing. It was Beth who finally brought herself to use the cliché: "Happiness is in running the race. One doesn't have to finish first. So many people never even try. Nobility can come with success and fame but it can come with failure too. Nobility is who, not what, you have become."

Neither of them was entirely satisfied, but then, neither of them was really disappointed either. Beth had earned a share of fame, though pinup fame was fleeting. Edward had at least made a living doing what he liked to do and would continue to.

After they had parted with a chaste kiss, Beth wandered back to the bookstore where she's gotten Dalton's *Byzantine Art and Archeology*. *If I'm gonna get into this stuff I should know the history behind the art*. She found a history book; one with plenty of nice pictures and maps.

At home that night, she tried to shake off the mild depression she felt, not so much for herself - she'd had her fun - but for Edward who had nothing but his art, and that was turning into a trade. Then she did the weirdest thing. From her drawer she took the leather thong she so often posed in. She put it on though it was tight and uncomfortable. Then she put on the gown she'd been wearing for him earlier, got into bed, and fell asleep.

She curtsied low with the deliberate delicacy of a prom queen as she grasped her long velvet skirt with each hand and bent her unseen knees. Her gown spread wide on the mosaic floor. Constantine had never seen such a bow but he liked it ... a lot. Beth's head bent toward the floor for a moment before she stood upright once again, all six feet of beauty. *I might introduce that bow for the ladies of the court*, he considered. The sight of several hundred women curtsying would be charming, especially if he were to also introduce the apparition's dress style. *It is more dignified by far for women than prostration, yet demure. The clergy shouldn't object so long as they wear a wrap 'round their shoulders.*

Other men would have seen a young lady obviously strong of heart and just submissive enough not to offend their manly pride. Constantine saw Beth, the same girl who had first come to him in much less clothing and with no such modest demeanor.

"Hi, girl."

"Hi, Your Serenity. You summoned me?"

"No; I was having a perfectly nice dream when you just happened into it."

"Hah; you were having a perfectly boring dream."

"Until now. ...Beth, should I fear you? Everyone says that I should, but I don't."

The apparition, which had been in front of Constantine, was now beside him, holding the teen emperor's arm with both hands and looking into his sleeping eyes with her own dark eyes.

"No, Constantine. No. Never." Beth looked at the emperor as though lost in thought but said no more. Then her great smile broke out. She danced around his bedroom, that velvet skirt flying and her arms outstretched. "Do you like these shoes? I got them just for you."

"They look so different. I've never seen shoes like that." They were different. The soles were mere pads that were strapped to Beth's feet with thongs of leather; but not the raw leather that held Roman sandals to the foot. The thongs were polished black patent leather unknown before the nineteenth century. They were worked with silver fittings and glass "jewels" to take the light. The thin black thongs crossed and recrossed her calves until they disappeared under the velvet skirt. Like all the footwear she came wearing, these raised her heels high, very high. She had to walk on tiptoe but showed no difficulty in doing so.

The apparition was grinning her big grin and Constantine could not feel anything but safe and comfortable. She did not have her whip.

"Are you Rotrud?"

"Perhaps."

"Are you Rotrud?"

"Should I be?" The apparition pranced around the room again letting her skirt fly high around her legs. Constantine was in his bed looking up at her.

"Perhaps I am Rotrud of Newark."

Then she was gone. Constantine lay awake, trying without success to hold onto the fading image. But it was gone.

So this is what real happiness is, he thought, knowing it was just a dream but somehow hoping it was a beginning. *I'll see you again. Not just for a moment. We'll rule the empire together, you and I.* It was a fantasy and he knew it; but it was also a hope and a prayer of sorts; something of his own to hold onto, more precious than all the ornaments that were daily thrust upon him. *Christ help me.* He almost spoke it aloud. *To live with her would be to live. Could that be heaven? Could it be everlasting? Lord, let her be Rotrud, or at least let Rotrud be like her. It would be no sin. Rotrud will be my wife.*

But the engagement with Rotrud was broken by Irene. Constantine was not even consulted but only advised that affairs of state had forced an "unfortunate reappraisal, et cetera." Aetius was deputized to bring the news to Ricolf and Bertmund. It was not necessary to request that the Franks leave the city as soon as possible; that was understood. At least it was Aetius who told them - his own anguish plainly evident - and not Nicephorus or one of the lesser palace eunuchs who would have been filled with glee to at last show his true feelings toward "barbarians".

"I am sorry, Your Lordships." Aetius chose the most respectful term he could think of. "I am sorry not only for the loss of a valued ally of the empire and two true friends; but I am sorry for the princess and His Serenity. They would have been happy together. I doubt that the emperor will ever feel the same toward another woman as he does for Rotrud, no matter who he marries."

Aetius went to the door so as to leave but was stopped by a hand on each shoulder. It was Bertmund who spoke wisdom beyond his years: "The world changes; our lives are what our thoughts make them. I'm sure they will always think fondly of each other and that can not be bad for the future of the world."

Charles broke the word to Rotrud in as gentle a manner as the old chieftain could, speaking softly to his daughter beneath the gold dome of his new church, and reminding her that the affairs of men are often in the hands of fate. In the following months he did his best to distract her with songsters and picnics, and with parties at which the flower of young Frankish manhood were required to appear. Rotrud's sorrow was real. She never mentioned that she had lost the crown of empire, only that she had lost a boy whom she had never met but had come to care for. For years to come her thoughts would often dwell on Ricolf's tales of Constantine's faraway court and the fond letters she had received from him. She never knew, nor could have understood, the feelings that the boy had not dared put on paper.

Charles did his best to console his daughter while in his heart he harbored disgust for the perfidious Greeks. He did not blame Constantine, for he had heard the facts; but neither could he show any respect for the young man. In fury and to protect his daughter's name the lord of the Franks had it rumored that it was he who had broken the engagement in anger at the restoration of idolatry in Constantinople. Yet Charles was too much a realist to ban images even within his own frontiers. There was the pope to contend with; and besides, many of his recently adopted peoples were fresh from paganism and could not understand a faith entirely free of images. In fact it was the great beauty of the Christian churches with their mosaics, icons, and fresco depictions of an army of Christ's saints and angels, which had won their hearts for Christ and their souls from Satan.

It was just as difficult for Constantine as for Rotrud. He was titular ruler of most of the Christian world. He had grown old enough to believe he had a voice in his own future but Irene soon disabused him of the notion. Constantine was furious. He ranted at times like a tyrant and at times like a child. He would have nothing of breaking his betrothal to Rotrud and tried to enlist what aid he might. But he had been surrounded since an early age by minions of his mother. Only John Pikridios tried to help his former student and he was gruffly told to mind his books.

Constantine considered abandoning the capital and taking camp among friendly troops in the Armeniac theme. *Then mother will see that she cannot tell me what to do.* But the patriarch intervened. He strongly insisted against such a move. Tarasios explained that it would split the loyalty of the army at a most grievous time since a Roman force had just been defeated by Bulgars in the Struma valley. But there was worse, he counseled; there were his dreams to be considered: "My son," he advised in a frightening way,

"Are you sure it is Rotrud whom you have never met that you love, and not the demon of your dreams?"

Aetius tried to soften the blow but Aetius was no saint. Ambition, ability, and cunning, without much regard for the harm he was doing, had raised him to the highest office of the empire after Stauratius and the augusta herself. At one point he had even hoped that one of his own family might marry into the imperial household; but now he was realist enough to know his enemies would frustrate any such ambition. Possibly that was why he sympathized with the emperor, or perhaps it was because he too could never choose a wife to sit by him and share his cares. Whatever the reason, he did his utmost to console the lad and arranged distractions. He and Stauratius had agreed that the best way to preserve Constantine's life was to distract him with pleasures. Even aside from Irene's religious concerns, for the sake of the state Constantine might reign, but he must not rule. The Armeniacs must be prevented from gaining power through him. Almost reluctantly Aetius began to introduce Constantine to young friends of a dissolute sort, for he rather admired the emperor's idealism if he most certainly did not share it. *Youth*, he thought wistfully, *He'll have to suspect everyone and care for no one if he hopes to stay alive and on the throne at all.* Constantine learned drinking and wenching though he never did them without guilt. Nothing was reported to Irene. She would not have wanted to know. Irene, in fact, showed remarkably little concern for her son's hurt. She stopped just short of suggesting that if Constantine could not be pious, he would, at least, be a more effective ruler if he occupied himself with the needs of his body instead of his heart.

Soon it was too late for Constantine and Rotrud anyway. Stauratius sent an harassing expedition into Italy in an attempt to destabilize Charles' recent acquisitions by fomenting rebellion among the Lombards against their Frankish overlords. The Franks were once again called barbarians. Perhaps they were, for the leader of the Byzantine expedition was captured and put to death by torture. Henceforth there might not be major war between the empire and the Franks but neither would there be unbroken peace. Then too, Harun al-Rashid, in Baghdad, was not only a superb strategist and an effective commander, he was also crafty. To further split the Christians and foster suspicion on Irene's western border he began sending precious gifts of friendship to Charles. Quietly, however, Charles' daughter urged Lord Bertmund to love and be a true friend to Constantine whatever the differences between her father and his mother.

Irene agreed with Stauratius that it was in the best interests of the empire that Constantine marry a simple Greek girl from the provinces. To that end there was a beauty and refinement contest, as was the curious way brides were sometimes chosen for the greatest ruler of the western world. Among the finalists was a young girl, Maria of Amnia. Lovely of face, she was also pious and courteous, educated in theology, art, and literature; and most important, not interested in advancing a husband's ambition. She would be a beautiful gem for Constantine to display to the people and to distract him from the cares of state. She would be grateful to have been raised from the obscurity of a provincial family to the greatest estate in the world empire. Most important, she knew to whom she owed her good fortune.

Finally Constantine relented, telling himself as his mother had told him, that the ruler of the world had greater duties than to follow his heart as some priest or shepherd might. On his bed John Pikridios left the book of the emperor Marcus Aurelius and a note which only said: *Duty. All of life is duty.* Constantine knew it to be true. Had not his father and grandfather followed their beliefs dutifully when they endangered their own lives by destroying the sacred images? He began to hate being emperor. It was the way of fools to seek the purple for only the evil had ever profited by it.

As the marriage date approached Constantine did his best to hide his feelings. Maria was indeed pretty. It was said that she was even more beautiful than the empress had been at her age. This embarrassed Maria for she had no desire to be compared to the empress; much less to some naked statue by Phidias as some courtier had said in an attempt to please his future mistress. She might, in fact, have been the most beautiful young lady in the empire with long dark hair that hung in loose waves when she let it. She was religious, which pleased Irene, favoring images of the sainted monks of the desert. Such piety was quite disarming when combined with the girl's quiet disposition and natural beauty. However, her education. while broad, was restricted to what she had learned from priests, and she preferred hearing Saint John Chrysostom to listening to the complexities of state affairs. In short, Maria was lovely to look at and simple whilst Constantine was like a stag bounding across the hills. Even after their wedding he could sometimes not help but drift into his dream world and think of what life might have been like with the bright Rotrud:

"She walks in beauty, like the night ..." to borrow a phrase from a poet familiar to the apparition but not to Constantine who was watching through closed eyelids, asleep, dreaming.

She was dressed in what would become known as a body stocking or leotard: all black and covering her figure tightly from neck to toes. When she walked she did so with grace but powerfully, on her toes and the balls of her feet like a dancer, so that those tightly encased legs seemed even longer than they were, and they were long. First one leg would thrust far ahead like a show horse's, then the other, then a pose.

Beautiful as she was there was nothing dreamlike about the girl, though there was about everything else. She pranced on those long legs through a fantasy of thin white mist and greenery with the sun penetrating here and there, its rays dotting the landscape around her.

Her face: It was her face, her eyes, her hair, her smile – particularly that smile. The light of it competed with the sun's rays so that she seemed more on than in the scene.

The emperor was dreaming. He knew it but pretended to himself that he did not. After all, his dreams were certainly more than normal dreaming, whatever normal dreams might be. Did not scripture itself describe her:

> *"Who is this arising like the dawn,*
> *Fair as the moon,*
> *Resplendent as the sun,*
> *And terrible as an army with banners?"*

Rotrud or Beth? It mattered not. Neither could be his.

After Eucharist, breakfast, and a reception, Constantine was able to escape the Great Palace for a short time almost alone. Wearing nondescript clothing and accompanied by a minimum of guards, he rode to the sea of Marmara and the Church of Saints Sergius and Bacchus. He tried to pray but was lost in thought. He hoped his thoughts would be acceptable to Christ Jesus as the best prayers he could manage at the moment. *If there is such a thing as fate, then the fates have opposed me all my life. Or is my life opposed to the will of Christ? I've lost Rotrud forever. In her distress, she is said to have born someone else a child. Mother's made an enemy of the Franks. She's ruled for eight years now. In eight years she's surrounded me with her friends. She has appointed all the high officials and they can never be removed except by a rebellion. The only ones who want that are the iconoclast troops of Anatolia. If I accept their support just to gain power I am as bad as those who rule now. Is there no middle ground on icons? And what's the use of finding it if there is any? Both sides want victory for their theology far more than they want peace. Besides, who would I replace her eunuchs with? Armeniacs? They would be as hated here as Stauratius and Aetius and the rest of mother's men are in Asia... and they know a lot less about running the state.*

CHAPTER 19

"Men seek retreats for themselves, houses in the country, seashores, and mountains; and you too are wont to desire such things very much. But this is altogether a mark of the most common sort of men, for it is in your power whenever you choose to retire into yourself. For nowhere either with more quiet or more freedom from trouble does a man retire than into his own soul, particularly when he has within him such thoughts that by looking into them he is immediately in perfect tranquility; and I affirm that tranquility is nothing else than the good ordering of the mind. Constantly then give to yourself this retreat, and renew yourself; and let your principles be brief and fundamental, which, as soon as you return to them, will be sufficient to cleanse the soul completely, and to send you back free from all discontent with the things to which you return. For with what are you discontented? With the badness of men? Recall to mind this conclusion, that rational animals exist for one another, and that to endure is a part of justice, and that men do wrong involuntarily; and consider how many already, after mutual enmity, suspicion, hatred, and fighting, have been stretched dead, reduced to ashes. Then be quiet at last. But perhaps you are dissatisfied with that which is assigned to you out of all the universe. Recall to your recollection this alternative: either there is providence or atoms, fortuitous concurrence of things; or remember the arguments by which it has been proved that the world is a kind of political community, and be quiet at last. But perhaps corporeal things will still fasten upon you. Consider then further that the mind does not mingle with breath, whether moving gently or violently, when it has once drawn itself apart and discovered its own power. Think also of all that you have heard and assented to about pain and pleasure, and be quiet at last. But perhaps the desire of the thing called fame will torment you. See how soon everything is forgotten, and look at the chaos of infinite time on each side of the present, and the emptiness of applause, and the changeableness and want of judgment in those who pretend to give praise, and the narrowness of the space within which it is circumscribed, and be quiet at last. For the whole earth is a point, and how small a nook in it is this your dwelling, and how few are there in it, and what kind of people are they who will praise thee."

Marcus Antonius Aurelius – The Meditations

Constantine grew in age and became the basilios in fact as he had been in name since he was a boy, though his advisors answered first to

Irene. Now his every hour was circumscribed by religious and imperial ritual since he represented Christ on earth, the true ruler of the world. The young man could hardly move without doing so in procession, accompanied by musicians, courtiers, eunuch-angels, and priests. He moved amid incense and icons several times a day to different chapels within the palace complex, and several times a week to various churches where he would celebrate feasts and festivals to commemorate the miracles the saints had wrought throughout the city. He was robed by eunuchs; all others were required to cover their eyes in the presence of the basilios except when an emperor was on military campaign as Autocrator and Imperator of Rome's armies. His clothing was heavy with jewels and gold brocades. Nearly everything he touched must be of gold whether it was a dinner plate or a tiny implement to remove the imperial ear wax. Some close advisors and old friends might simply stand in his presence, if behind closed doors, but all others addressed him from a prostrate position and heard his answers not from the emperor's own mouth but relayed by a subordinate to whom Constantine was required to whisper in court Greek. Every week he presided over a great dinner in the Triclinium for dignitaries, sometimes high and sometimes low, and once a year for the poorest citizens to be found. There were dances and plays after eating, but these affairs were as much religious as secular. Guests reclined on couches in the ancient Roman way. The emperor, presiding as the Isapostle, broke bread and poured wine in imitation of Christ.

Maria bore two children, both girls, and looked on them as gifts from God more than as her husband's offspring. When Constantine tried to play with his daughters Maria would hand them to him as she might to a guest. She became so preoccupied with the two babes that the husband and wife drifted further apart as their first years of marriage passed.

Unfortunately for Constantine, all the ranking officials owed everything to his mother. They would prostrate themselves and humbly wait upon their emperor, but Constantine's only true support were a few weak courtiers and his old tutors - Pikridios particularly - and those stratagoi from the Asiatic themes who had always opposed Irene and icons. These officers favored the basilios by default rather than from regard or friendship. Although the commanders of the Asiatic troops did not know the emperor well, they saw him as their hope against his mother's plans.

For a time Constantine tried to distract himself from at least part of the politics of his office as Aetius had urged. As God's representative it was necessary that he attend and sometimes officiate at religious services which were often in churches far from the palace precinct. This took up much of his time. When otherwise free, he would summon a famous professor or one of the chamberlains well-versed in ceremony to consult with on matters which did not threaten Irene and her eunuchs. Constantine was not so dull as to think that any of this was of greater importance than those matters which he was encouraged to leave to his ministers: appointments, diplomacy, and finances; but duty aside, it was hard for him to assert himself in politics because Stauratius, Aetius, and the other eunuchs close to Irene really were far more expert than he, and because his mother had been supervising these things for many years already. Constantine knew he was not good at the details of finance and taxation. Besides, ever since his fall at age fourteen his head often bothered him, forcing him to his bed. The doctors had done little to help. His physicians only prescribed a willow bark infusion and that the emperor lie in the darkened sanctuary of the church of Holy Acacius.

Anyway, it really was as important in Byzantium that the emperor be seen in pious ritual as it was that he be knowledgeable in secular affairs.

The following several years were ones of turmoil within the imperial family. For a time Constantine even thought to desert his post and let his mother have the empire. Yet God had put him in this place and, like Marcus Aurelius, duty required that he act as emperor. That, not her beauty, meekness, nor piety, was the only reason he had married Maria of Amnia who had been chosen for him instead of the distant Rotrud whom he loved.

There was, however, one important area where an emperor not only could, but must assert himself and demonstrate leadership before the people; one where he need not fear competition from his mother. By steps that would not seem to threaten Stauratius, Constantine began to concentrate such time and wit as he could muster to study military science so that eventually he would be able to lead his armies himself against the Arabs and Bulgars. That might be seen as threatening the primacy of Stauratius in councils of war, but he determined to demonstrate his worthiness to his mother and put the unpleasant old man in his place. As the months passed he doubled his efforts, querying those stratagoi who had actual experience about the ways of war of Bulgar and Arab. The general organization of Byzantine forces was set, but he began to supervise in person the details of logistics, training, and troop distribution. This did not please the more combat-cautious Stauratius but he dared not challenge his basilios directly. Much as Irene might wish to rule, her interest was in religion, not war, and she seemed willing enough to allow her son to occupy himself with such matters.

In 789 circumstances briefly changed. Stauratius almost missed a plot of the Armeniac troops to demand that Constantine exercise his rights and duties alone. He was alerted to the danger only when Constantine defended the rebels. Still thinking it possible to love his mother as a dutiful son must, he planned to arrest Stauratius on whom he blamed his impotence but to allow her to still sit beside him. Now their authority would be reversed. He would rule and she merely reign and advise. For a few days

Irene seemed to yield, probably feeling that Constantine himself was her best protection from the riotous troops who supported him. Unfortunately for Constantine, just when he tried to arrest the logothete of the dromos the Armeniac plot fell apart. There was an earthquake in the city and although damage was fairly moderate, Stauratius convinced the superstitious Irene that God was displeased that she would take second place to her son in contravention of a vision imparted to a monk of Studion. Stauratius had Constantine placed under close guard "for his own protection from the rebellious generals who would destroy all that we have achieved together for Christ and his saints." Stauratius also arrested the emperor's few true friends. John Pikridios was flogged and sent to a monastery. Constantine then had to face his mother.

Out of the realization of how fragile her hold on the throne was, Irene dealt leniently with the conspirators, punishing them only by exile or by forcing them into monasteries. Her son was another matter. She ordered him to appear before her and ranted her scorn: "Impudent, unappreciative child" was the mildest thing she said as she struck him again and again, just as she might have when he was a small boy and not the strapping twenty year-old who flinched from her blows. "You're a little dreamer; just a child," she snarled disdainfully. "Grow up! What do you know of ruling an empire? You would be nothing but a pawn for those traitorous generals. Don't you see how they wanted to use you, stupid boy?" The blows continued. Irene picked up a strap and went after the emperor who fled around the room ashamed that he felt very much a child now, where yesterday he had imagined himself master of his own house as well as master of the empire. "It will not happen again. You will never grow up and you will never rule so long as I live. Saint Michael preserve us from idiots on the throne. How long do you think it would be before the wretched image-breakers were in arms against a weakling figurehead like you? If it weren't that I am strong we'd both of us been killed long ago and some heretic would be wearing this crown." She threw the royal diadem at her son and departed the room with her anger not yet spent, yelling to whatever advisor was within hearing. "Beat him! Teach the big brat a lesson. He will never rule and he will never dare attack his mother again so long as the holy saints protect my throne and this empire. Beat him. Beat him hard. If he were anyone else I'd have him dead and his head on a picket." Her orders were carried out as though her son were not emperor.

"Aetius, my dearest friend in this earthly life, I fear for the empire if Constantine shall ever reign alone. We have only just restored the sacred images and our work must not be undone by an impressionable boy. Those rebellious dogs have clearly shown how easily he can be influenced. For the

138

sake of Christ and the unity of the Church it is best that he never rule alone."

"Empress, he has been of age for three years now."

"Which is why I am requiring that all our troops take a new oath of loyalty; that my name should always take precedence over his ... That I reign no longer as augusta or even basilia, but in my own right. For that reason I intend to be regarded and addressed as the basilios – as though I were a man. If this is a coup against my own son, then it is for his own good and that of the empire... and, I suppose for your health too. He bears you and Stauratius little fondness. He is a foolish boy. He has a beautiful and compliant wife yet I know he still moons over that Frankish girl."

Constantine did soon manage the return from exile of John Pikridios. He could arrange that much but little more, nor could his friend be of much assistance against the powerful eunuchs. Even within the Constantinoplian guard where the emperor was making his mark on the technical level, his life would be at risk were he to try to use it to affect political change.

"I am troubled, Your Holiness." The emperor was confiding in the one man that he knew must keep a secret. "It is three years today since I came of age and still I do not really rule. Oh, I can issue orders and they are obeyed in less important things but if I try to change anything of substance, it just doesn't happen."

"I know, Your Serenity; but try to understand. Though God has put you on the throne he wishes you to consult with others. The Lord works though men. He rarely gives a direct revelation even to the Isapostle. Concentrate on holiness, Your Serenity. I have always supported the holy icons as firmly as any priest or monk, but I have seen how some of the clergy are more interested in victory for their side than in love of the neighbor who opposes him. This is not Christian. You must be holy in yourself, Sovereignty. Your example will do more to bring Christian peace than anything that I can do. That is your most important task as basilios and no one can take it from you. For the rest, the augusta's advisors are wise and experienced counselors and you are still young. I think that you should listen to them."

The two men spoke some more but it was a waste. It was now clear to Constantine that though the patriarch showed true Christian love, otherwise he was as much his mother's man as Stauratius, Aetius, and those stratagoi residing in the city. Long before the death of his father, his mother had surrounded herself with like-minded men and loyal eunuchs. After Leo's death they had quickly replaced any ministers of an independent mind. Those few whole men of importance still at the palace owed their jobs to the sufferance of the eunuchs and knew it. After almost ten years of Irene's rule the only opposition to the cabal in Constantinople were the commanders of troops in the Asiatic themes. But Constantine did not want to be beholden to a king-maker there any more than he wished to be a puppet of Irene's clique. He had no other supporters with any power. He was emperor but with no more power for change than some teacher like John Pikridios. When Constantine had tried to assert himself he had met defeat. His mother had sided with Stauratius and Aetius and the rest of the old guard. Besides, he wanted religious peace and the Asiatic strategoi would no more follow him if he opposed their strict iconoclasm than the main army in the capital did when he suggested compromise to the strategoi there. However much he might regret it, the patriarch was right. All looked for power by associating themselves with extremists. None cared to build a Christian edifice that would house all of Christ's people.

It was a conundrum that Constantine could not escape. There seemed no answer. If Irene continued to rule then the icons would have total victory but there would not be true peace. Maybe that was the will of God, after all. Constantine wondered and prayed. He knew that he should be decisive, but that should not mean replacing the tyranny of the iconodules with that of the iconoclasts, though that might tempt some men. Then he would be able to rule in fact as well as in name, but over what? An empire still divided and factious, having simply replaced one cult with another in order to satisfy his own ambition.

Even if he could somehow handle his mother, it was clear he would never fully rule with the cadre that ran the empire now. And should he take the throne alone with the support of the Anatolian garrisons he would need continued armed support to stand against the monks and the old guard. Surely that was not what Christ wanted. Constantine wanted sectarian peace and to get on with the business of facing the Arabs and Bulgars in decisive battle. But to what avail if no others wanted peace? He did know that simply to rule for the glory and power was not a worthy pursuit. It was not even an honest pursuit. Though young, Constantine knew that he could only do what could be done. Neither side wanted peace and he was in the middle and a target for both even if he supported neither. Mother was the darling of the monks. If overthrown they would connive for her restoration even if Constantine supported the icons since his heart was not so one-sided as was hers. He had to consider the facts of the situation.

There never was, either then or in any age past, room for two strong leaders on the throne; nor would Constantine sin to force religious enemies together. Irene must rule and he must accept what opportunities to serve Christ and the empire might present themselves. Or so he convinced himself. *How different it would be if Rotrud and I had been allowed to wed, and she sat beside me instead of mother. Then her father and I would quickly put an end to the Bulgars. I'd be free to face Harun, and everyone could venerate the holy icons or ignore them as he liked, just so long as all respected all others who are trying to serve Christ in their own way. "As you judge, so shall you be judged; as you are kind, so shall kindness be shown to you."*

Beth took the items she would need for the young prince who was dreaming of her. The items that the lovely lady in thong and boots removed from the drawer were such as would excite him; first a leather mini and a brass and leather corset. The heavy corset and a wide and thick collar would serve for armor. She slung a dagger in a sheath of gold and silver from a strap which parted her armored breasts. Lastly she took up a riding crop. Slowly, in the way the dreamer enjoyed she fastened each device while Wagner played on the phonograph and Kirstan Flagstad chanted a valkyrie war cry.

Constantine awoke. *If only life were that simple.* He covered his head with a pillow and tried to be happy with Maria.

Beth and Eddy Miller were at a coffee shop in the Village. They were watching the passing parade outside the window by their booth. Beth was also watching Eddy. Beth liked that her friend always dressed nicely. She also liked that she didn't have to when she was with him. Edward wasn't the suit kind, but he wasn't the T-shirt type either. He knew better than to wear anything that would show off his skinny arms. He did favor the outlandish: wide cravats and French berets in an age that considered "dull" and "charcoal" the height of men's fashion. *He should be a matador in a suit of lights*, she thought. *No, He hasn't the figure and he isn't machismo. Maybe a courtier to the sun king, rouged and with knee breeches. Nah, his legs are scrawny. Maybe Bohemian artist is best for him after all.*

"I'm worried, Edward; and I don't even know why."

"Not so unusual, milady. It's called the blues. What you need is some excitement in your life."

"No; it's not that."

"Is it those dreams? Are you still having them? Maybe you should see a doctor."

"No. It is the dreams, I think; but I don't want them to stop and I don't want happy pills. Funny thing though, it's like I know things will happen and I can't do anything about them. Maybe that's why I'm so down."

The photographer and the model talked some more. In fact they talked until it was late into the night. When at last the coffee shop closed,

Edward invited friend to his apartment for a drink. They did that sometimes. Eddy could be trusted not to get fresh. This time was different however. It was as though he wanted to say something but wouldn't. Beth chanced the first move.

Edward had never dared hope it. He'd thought himself too mediocre. Cuddling with Beth was a pleasure he should not have denied himself all these past years; and Beth learned that though her friend was really shy and as frightened for his soul as she for hers, he liked girls. That was really good. All these years she had wondered about her friend. *"As you judge, so shall you be judged; as you are kind, so shall kindness be shown to you."*

Constantine had no sooner reconciled himself to being powerless than, to his surprise, the Roman world was turned upside down. It seemed the depressed ruler might actually be able to create peace in his realm. Fearful of her son's growing popularity in the army, Irene had implemented her plan to have the entire military - both the main body troops in Constantinople and the provincial garrisons in each theme - take an oath that she should have precedence over him. She sent dignitaries to all the units to impose it. Despite grumblings that soldiers ought not to be ruled by a woman, each regiment in turn swore it until at last Alexios Mousoulem, the drungarios of the watch, attempted to impose the oath on the ever-dissident Armeniacs. Alexios had been sent to Asia specifically because he was not an extremist supporter of images. Irene and Stauratius thought he might persuade the troops there. Instead they persuaded him and arrested their previous commander. They pronounced him their new strategos. Soon other armies joined them. The troops of the Thrakesion theme of western Anatolia were still under the strategos Lachanodrakon who had ruthlessly carried out Leo's orders to rid his theme of icons and crush the monks. Irene never felt strong enough to remove him from command. There was as yet no armed rebellion against the throne but there was loud objection to Irene. Several of the provincial armies gathered near Atroa in Asia Minor and demanded that Constantine exercise his responsibilities as God had intended. Friends of Alexios imparted to the emperor their master's new found horror that a woman and her eunuchs ruled the empire instead of Christ's anointed. "We know how much you love your mother," they would say to him; adding that the poor woman was ill-advised by eunuchs who thought only of themselves and the influence of their families at court. "You have loyal subjects across the Bosphorus, Your Sovereignty; men like our master who command the troops of the Armeniac, Thrakesion, and Anatolian themes. They regard the empress for her piety and wish her no harm; have no fear of that. But she is taken in by ambitious ministers who would have her believe that were you to rule, you would destroy the icons once again. We know that is not so, nor is our master so concerned with pictures as he is that you should rule the empire as Christ intends."

This was a new tack by the Asiatics, a more conciliatory approach. In fact the very moderation he longed for. Constantine did not trust them; no, but they might go forth against Irene, Aetius, and Stauratius even without his support and then the dynasty itself would be in jeopardy. Constantine who had so recently been cowed by his mother listened and acted, for he was no longer a child without knowledge or understanding whatever the empress might believe. The Bithynian regiments of northern Anatolia hated not only the oath, but the heavy-handed enforcement of Irene's religious convictions. Their ranks were infected with the dualist heresy of Paul of Samosota so like the Armeniacs, they detested having images forced upon them. When Irene ordered the image-bearing banners restored to the head of their columns instead of Christ's simple cross of victory, they joined the other dissidents and there was a coup. No blood was shed but a frightened Irene was persuaded to entrust rulership to her son.

Now merely the queen-mother and no longer empress, Irene spent one long year in honored internal exile at her new palace in the Eleutherian district of Constantinople; away from the daily affairs of state, amid fields of fruit trees and vegetables, but safely within the city walls. "I think you need a rest, mother," her son had said, and personally accompanied her in regal procession there. "Pray that the saints shall aid me in the work I must now shoulder as emperor in my own right. I have never really thanked you for all you have done to raise me to be a fit emperor." With this and similar babble the son put away his mother for his own good and the good of the realm. "I will visit you when you have rested, mother.... You'll like the chapel here. It is solemn yet pretty, a fine place to be alone with the saints. Of course this palace is not so large as we are used to but it is very comfortable and quiet. Every window on the south and east sides overlooks the sea. You always liked a quiet retreat. There is still some decorating to be done. You might enjoy overseeing that..."

Stauratius was not so lucky. He was whipped and sent to a lonely village in Armenia where iconoclast troops could watch him and he could think upon his sins. The rest of the high eunuchs who had surrounded Irene, including Aetius, were likewise barred from the palace but not flogged.

For a year Irene would spend a part of each day with her confessor or prostrate before the icons she had brought with her, worrying for the empire under the rule of Constantine. *Will he learn*, she wondered? *It is necessary that he not impede the return of the holy images throughout the empire. Surely our constant warring with the Arabs will end if only they can see the efficacy of our worship so near them. At least Constantine has a good Greek girl for a wife. That barbarian Rotrud was nice, I'm sure, but entirely unfit. He needs a wife who thinks more like me. I can advise Maria in all things and she will understand the needs of the empire far more than Charles' daughter would have .... Oh, I must get back to Constantine before he does the empire damage. He is still too young and foolish to rule. Much too young, too foolish. What does he want? Just unity with the western provinces? Ahhh, I must get back to the Great Palace. The boy has even sent poor Aetius and Stauratius away. They were the only people upon whom I could always rely. The only one there now with a brain is Nicephorus. Nicephorus may be a pompous ass but he is family and remains near to the throne. They say that the Bulgars are making trouble again. Maybe he can persuade the fool boy that there are more important things for an emperor to consider than what he himself desires. Besides Nicephorus has friends among our Bulgar enemies. He can be a great help to Constantine.*

The year of Irene's exile from the Great Palace saw Constantine's first attempt to show military ability and bring his enemies to battle. War clouds were gathering in the north and his new advisors from the Armeniac theme were more than troubled. They had all had plenty of practice fighting Arab light cavalry, but had little - or in many cases no - experience against Slavic infantry. They sought advice where it could be found. They recalled experienced lieutenants from the northern frontier, but not senior strategoi. It was said these could not be spared to visit the capital; in fact, the Asian generals feared that they might be superseded in Constantine's estimation.

There were other sources of information. Most of these were legitimate enough if of questionable worth. Traders and priests brought rumors to Constantinople but could hardly be expected to give accurate estimations of enemy strength, much less any reliable information about internal squabbles among Khardam's clans which might be exploited to Byzantium's benefit.

There were also less trustworthy sources. For the peasant of the East - and for peasant and most noblemen alike in the West - the centuries after the loss of Rome were a time without history. He saw little of change and had but a weak grasp that times past were very different from the world of his own day. He lacked a sense of progress and would, in fact, not have understood progress. So he readily placed persons of very different times and places together in his stories, and extrapolated morals and laws which seemed appropriate to him from the verbiage of Our Lord, heroes, and the prophets, without regard to intent or context. Scientific truth, which was uncertain, was less important than either revealed or intuitive truth. It was a time of much faith and little science. If a relic was not, in fact, the bone of a saint, or if the saint had not done what was attributed to him, it didn't matter. What mattered was the unchanging now, and the myths that supported the now were themselves a part of the now. Stories of omens were mixed with sacred visions; real facts were mixed with prejudice; and the whole interpreted in the light of holy and unholy prophesies. A popular astrologer assured both ruler and ruled that a great winter thunder they had heard was the gathering of an angelic host that would ride with the emperor's army against his enemies.

But Constantine was neither a peasant nor a barbarian. He would never have been seduced by such predictions of heavenly assistance except they seemed to confirm the opinions of the priests and the unfounded boasts of certain of his Asiatic strategoi.

But Patriarch Taisios was troubled. Not by piety alone had he risen from layman to the most important place in Christendom after the pope. Though he was pious, he was also one of Byzantium's most intelligent and learned men. He was not only concerned that Constantine might listen to soothsayers and thereby lose Christ's blessing, but that he might be listening to demons and imagining them to be the young princess he had loved and lost. What might the devils' unholy purpose be? Were they set upon destroying the emperor's mind or on bringing down the whole of Christendom through him?

Constantine consulted with his eldest stratagoi and with the more successful of the Armeniacs who crowded to the palace seeking places of influence for themselves. He probed Alexios about strategy, and questioned the caesar Nicephorus for his knowledge of Bulgar ways. He also prayed for bravery and ability. He consulted Christian astrologers who might read God's purpose from the heavens, but crossing himself and asking Divine forgiveness, he also allowed a superstitious minister to speak with the soothsayer who claimed to read the future in thunder and lightning.

Then he went forth against Bulgar forces that were probing near the fortress of Probaton some twelve miles from Adrianople. At Adrianople, centuries before, Roman legions had met their first defeat by Germanic invaders. It was April and Constantine hoped to overlay a happier history on the place.

As evening was falling scouts clashed and were soon reinforced by main body troops. They fought against enemies and shadows alike in the night until at last both sides fled the field of confusion and gore. The emperor was angered by such cowardice in his troops. Had the enemy not faded into the forest, the shamed troopers might have redeemed themselves before their basilios at dawn; instead Constantine could only upbraid the Asiatic stratagoi in whose leadership he had trusted; charging them with having cared more about removing his mother from the palace than about instilling discipline in their soldiers.

Then a great fire destroyed the Quaestorium of the Great Palace and large parts of the Patriarch's palace too. It seemed an evil omen.

In September, Constantine again tried to bring the empire's foes to battle; this time going against Arab forces on the Anatolian frontier. At least his Armeniac stratagoi knew the enemy there. He nearly met his death. Arab raiders had seized the fortress town of Silifke in Cilicia. If reinforced they could ride north through the Cilician gates and into Cappadocia. That would put the frontier far too close to the capital. Worse, it would cut the silk road to China and probably give Harun al-Rashid a harbor on the Euxine Sea. He might even capture the port cities of Sinope and Trebizond. To cut the silk road would do extensive damage to Byzantium's finances. To have Arabs on the Euxine Sea would mean contending with pirates there as the empire already had to on the Mediterranean. It would also make an alliance between Baghdad and the Bulgars probable. With five thousand main body cataphracts from Constantinople Constantine rode to the Waterless Towers, near modern Karaman, where traders from the eastern Mediterranean met the caravans of the silk road.

At the Waterless Towers he was joined by the army of the Armeniac theme commanded, Alexios Mousoulem. Their combined cavalry moved east to confront the raiders. Constantine's Constantinoplian troopers were a highly-trained and elite force, quite used to being lauded, fussed over, and feared; however, the army of the Armeniac theme were the more battle hardened troopers. Sometimes their armor was rusty and their manner was usually rude, but they were experienced in the ways of border warfare. They knew that Arabs could not be brought to pitched battle. Arabs preferred feints, maneuver, and quick raids into Roman territory which forced their enemy to expend energy and resources in defense of his cities and towns.

Constantine hated such warfare. He did not wish to fight endless frontier skirmishes with the Moslems as Stauratius had been doing on and off since the basilios had been a boy. He was impatient for decisive battle but that was not the Arab way of war. Harun would pick at his enemy like a blackbird on carrion until it was thoroughly weakened and tired. Then luck - or the will of Allah, he would say - would present him with an opportunity to roll up Roman resistance. Islam would gain and Christianity would lose another province. That had happened again and again since the time of the Prophet Mohammed himself, from Egypt to Baghdad. Now Harun's light cavalry was at the old game again. The main body of the Roman armies might have impressed another foe but they were unable to even engage Arabs. Cataphracts were too heavily armored to catch light cavalry. The raiders just fled east.

At least Silifke had been liberated and the Cilician Gates secured. Stauratius would have been satisfied. Constantine, however, ordered his forces in pursuit. Alexios with the Roman heavy cavalry kept to the coast road intent on getting ahead of the enemy who was riding cross country toward the safety of Tarsus. There Saint Paul had been born but it was now in Abbasid hands and had been heavily fortified by Harun. They failed.

Constantine and a detachment of five hundred Khazar horse archers cut inland to pursue the enemy on his own terms and slow his progress across the Cilician plain. When Irene received word that her son had joined battle with Arab scouting forces and was chasing them into enemy controlled territory, she merely noted it with a nod which revealed nothing. It was good but not overly important. She returned to her prayers.

In Baghdad, however, the caliph was most interested. He spoke at length with his military advisors. It was not unusual for an emperor to lead the Roman armies in person, but it was unknown for him to be with so small a detachment so near the caliph's fortified frontier.

From his throne of gold and pearls Harun listened intently. The ministers, prostrate before him, spoke guardedly. They would not risk giving poor advice no matter how confident they might feel at the moment; for though Harun al-Rashid is justly remembered for the wealth and luxury of his court, and for the libraries and centers of learning which he established in Baghdad, he was an iron man, quick even to have friends executed. He listened to soothsayers in contravention of his own prophet's warning.

"If we can capture Constantine, how much do you think Irene would pay to get her son back: the whole of Cilicia and half the gold in her coffers?"

"Yes, Commander of the Faithful, but not so much as she would pay to receive him back maimed so that he cannot rule."

"Ah, an evil woman, an idolater even among idolaters. But let it be so. She will answer to Allah for her sins and the faithful will profit by them. Send cavalry to Cilicia. Reinforce Tarsus!"

There was no battle with the fleeing raiders and Constantine did not fall to an enemy. But he did fall. It was a simple accident. Like Absalom of old he failed to negotiate a tree branch. Fortunately for him, he did not meet Absalom's fate; but the emperor was *hors de combat* long enough for the raiders to escape. Nor was he caught by the Saracen reinforcements dispatched by the caliph.

"The fool escaped us, oh Commander of the Faithful. Some demon struck him down before he reached our lines."

"Do not be so sure it was not for his own good the demon struck him down. He is rash. That is good. But do not think him a fool because he hates us more than he fears for his safety."

CHAPTER 20

My Beloved Emperor:

I must write to you with sad news. Your dear friend and mine, Ricolf of Bacheim, has fallen in battle against the pagans. Our lords are still in combat and I do not know any more, except I am told he died well, if dying can ever be said to be well. I can also assure you that my father will avenge the loss of the finest knight I know, and my father's best and noblest friend since Count Hruodland died defending our army in the Pyrenees when I was but a child.

I will ask his friend Bertmund, whom you know, to send you further details when he can. Now is not the time to say more, save that I will miss Ricolf more than I can say. He was not only my father's loyal advisor but my great friend. Ricolf told me so much about you. He loved you. It was from him, as much as from my Greek tutors, that I learned of your court and city. He admired you and did all he could to support you in council even after our betrothal was broken. I know that we will both miss him. I know too that his soul rests with the Lord.

Ever Your Dearest Friend,
Rotrud

———————————

Constantine was never to love his wife though he tried to. As their first years of marriage passed he felt increasing guilt that he could not. He treated her with kindness and a sort of formal affection but the marriage had not been of his choosing. Though Maria tried at first to win his love - and he to return it - she had no concept of how to do it. What she did was out of books and songs, not out of heat. Nor was the advice of the ladies of the court of any use. A whore might have been able to educate her but the lady would never have spoken with one. That was her problem. Though she came from a modest provincial family, she was a lady. She tried to be all that the aristocratic wives told her to be: kind, obedient, pious, and understanding; they did not say exciting and aggressive. Her husband was the emperor. He had more power than other men could ever want. He had no need to lord it over his wife like some merchant or farmer. The two began to live their own lives. What Constantine could not help but long for was his Beth-Rotrud fantasy, a woman who would treat him as an equal and a playmate and not an emperor; one who would attack him in the night, perhaps shove a knotted silk cord up his regal ass and wail like a demon while she massaged his prostate. A whore would have understood that.

So their lovemaking was inadequate save to make babies and stave off sexual stress. Maria believed it sin to seek her own gratification, and that she need only sate her husband's animal urges. That too was what was wrong. The young augusta - she was never crowned basilia - did not like descending from piety just to perform a chore that Constantine could have enjoyed as much with some slut of the palace. She had been raised to expect love to be a spiritual joy intended by God only for procreation. Any great variance from that ideal was sin or at best crude and unnecessary between sophisticated people. Mere physical sex was not her joy. Maria was everything that the devout Irene had looked for in a bride for her son, and the emperor of the world was left unsatisfied.

It was while brooding alone in his wife's chambers late one morning that Theodote, a lady-in-waiting, approached him brightly and carrying a goblet of mild wine. Her emperor was in need of cheer and some vivacious female banter might drive his melancholy away. The girl was pretty though not conventionally so, nor in any specifically erotic way. She was pretty in the way his cheetahs were pretty. Her face was quiet and as playful as a cheetah kitten's. Perhaps she had sensed something of the frustration that Constantine tried to meet with stoicism. Here in the empress' apartments, where the formality outside was laid aside, the cat looked at her downhearted ruler with the kind of gentle face with which a mother might look upon a child who had been very good all day. She approached brightly, even swaying a little. That alone was an affront, for the ruler of the world was usually addressed by men from a prostrate position if at all. Women had some dispensation in this and, as noted, formalities were relaxed in the empress' quarters – but only by so much. Still she knew that Constantine would not be offended today. In fact, it was what the emperor wanted and needed.

She curtsied low - a strange bow which Constantine had introduced within the women's quarters - then dropping to her knees before him, the girl presented the goblet but did not avert her eyes. The cheetah dared to look him in the face and meet him gaze to gaze. She could not know that until this moment he had been thinking of his Rotrud – not the Rotrud of Frankland but Beth the saucy valkyrie of his fantasies. Now he was seeing something of her before him..

Constantine's marriage would not last long; nor would the exile of his mother. Irene whined to anyone who would listen until, the next January, her son re-associated her with himself on the throne. Why? Possibly out of love, or guilt, or just as possibly because he wanted her experienced hand nearby. Irene had not been entirely mistaken when she had harangued her son about generals who would try to use him for their own ends. After all, they had forced her from the throne for their own purposes.

The Armeniacs would not accept her return however. Nor had Irene forgiven Alexios Mousoulem's support of Constantine which had driven her from power. She summoned Alexios to court where she could watch him. When the Armeniac regiments asked his return to command of them she suspected a plot and tried to persuade Constantine that he was conspiring against them: "If we allow him to return to the Armeniac theme he will have an army at his back," she warned.

Certainly Constantine by then understood the intricacies and dangers of imperial politics. He had been taught from youth not to trust anyone. There were rumblings aplenty among the Asiatics against Irene and her anti iconoclast policies, but to many of these iconoclasts even Constantine's religious moderation was insufficient; they wanted victory for their cause as much as Irene did for hers. They feared Irene's extremism and had little faith that her son's protestations of love and toleration were anything more than tactical maneuvers. They were probably right; Constantine seemed vacillating to have brought his mother back to the palace and they saw Alexios' removal to Constantinople as little better than house arrest.

Would Alexios have seized the crown if he could? Quite possibly. Eventually Irene and Stauratius convinced Constantine that the strategos had only supported him to weaken both him and her in expectation of one day taking the throne to "save the empire," a common theme in Roman history. Then Constantine grew angry and might have ordered Alexios' execution except for some lingering doubt that his former supporter's actions had been entirely self-seeking. Instead he had the strategos flogged, tonsured, and confined at the praetorian barracks within the palace grounds.

In her own quarters Irene smiled a thin smile. *Silly boy; but it is for our own good. The Armeniacs are traitors and iconoclasts at heart and Alexios shuffles between them and support of the crown. The man cannot be trusted.*

For the emperor, even more trying days were to follow. A monk of Studion again pleased Irene with a vision that was just what she wanted to hear, though it would have grieved another mother: An angel of God had told him that it was ordained that her son would not rule. By one excuse or another Irene persuaded her son to replace his Asian military advisors with men more experienced in civil affairs. One by one, first less, then more senior offices fell again into the hands of her eunuchs.

Stauratius, still brooding in a far-off village, was surprised when he was permitted a visitor; more surprised when he recognized the disguised visitor as the caesar Nicephorus; more surprised still when he was released into the custody of his unexpected visitor; most surprised when together that evening in a quiet inn Nicephorus ordered him to bed with a young Bulgar woman. *Does he mock me?*, the eunuch thought; but the woman smiled a knowing smile that said *wait*. The night was cold. She cuddled. Stauratius found he was pleased to have his back warmed. He had not felt warm breath on his neck since his mother had caressed him as a child. He had never before felt his ear being tickled. When the former Logothete of the Dromos stirred in his sleep and started up to go to the latrine she held his penis with her lips and mumbled: "Empty yourself here. A eunuch can play games too." Thus Lucia, who was prepared to do anything to be a great lady, would be a bond between Stauratius and the hated Nicephorus. Unbeknown to Stauratius she was also a channel to Khardam.*

Stauratius, Aetius, and Irene's other advisors soon returned to the palace and Stauratius determined on the same purpose as Irene; to displace Constantine. He knew that without Irene in charge, he, who again wielded great power under the augusta, would have none; would, in fact, be fortunate if he only lost his eyes.

---

* See afterward, pg. 202, and note on eunuchs: pg. 218.

CHAPTER 21

The Bulgars used axes to break arms or separate them from the torsos of militiamen who stumbled in flight. The screams of mutilated men lasted into the night till death took them. Others, gone mad with pain, dragged themselves with their knees into a nearby stream to die.

Those who were taken uninjured were greased and they served as torches for the Bulgars, now drunk on captured Roman wine. Intoxicated with wine and blood and lust they raped both aged peasant women from a nearby village and girls not yet old enough to have breasts. Then they slit their bellies open. The only thing that the less hardy regretted in the morning was having pinned crying children to trees with arrows through their arms and legs.

Most officials in Constantinople thought it to not be much more than a raid in force or minor land grab; but it was not a raid. Neither was it a battle for some land and livestock. In frontier war a wise leader looks to having peace someday, wedding or watching his children marry into the local population. Such cruelty as this could only be the beginning of a war of conquest with terror as a weapon.

There followed the usual insults of that age. The Bulgar khan sent a sheep in imperial red boots to the capital with a note demanding tribute.

"The Bulgars are the immediate threat, mother. The Arabs must be dealt with too. But for now, if we can beat back the Bulgars so that they will not trouble us again we'll secure the northern frontier and then be free to take on the Arabs with our whole armies. We must punish Khardam, not send tribute or just mess about with him in Moesia."

"But my boy, while we are waging war in the north the Arabs will threaten Asia. Even when, with Christ's help, we do drive them back, they will leave remnants of their belief. They are the first priority. The Monophysite heresy is strong enough without being reinforced by the Arabs' hostility to sacred images. What we need is not offensive war against either but a strong defensive line against the Arabs and to turn the Bulgars west. We need to send missionaries among the Armenian and Anatolian peasantry still under our power to persuade them away from iconoclasm. When they are truly free of that doctrine and love Christ's holy saints they will joyously throw back the Moslems."

"But the Bulgars, mother. We've seen before what their type can do. It would be a mistake to appease them. It is more important than ever that we confront Khardam with all our power, not try to turn him west. We have angered Charles enough, and Harun is trying to court him. It would be most politic that we show our friendship by standing strong against Khardam."

This was as much as Constantine dared say. He could not challenge Irene directly for since the arrest of Axexios Mousoulem he had lost the regard of most of the Armeniacs, his one-time supporters; and the rest of the staff owed their positions to Stauratius. Besides, this much was clearly true. For the rest? His mother might guess but it would not be said.

The "sacred images," the "holy icons," sometimes I think you've been infected with the holy madness, mother. There are other things to be concerned with than some pictures. Christ will protect them. We must protect the empire.

But actually, Irene relented. Constantine was now twenty-two and five years married to Maria of Amnia. Even Irene admitted that he had some administrative ability. He might again attempt her exile if he felt powerless.

"If the boy wants to prove himself a great battle leader I must allow it," she told Stauratius. She may also have hoped that the activity would make him more mature and help him to get over a Frankish girl whose picture he still kept in his desk. Hopefully - as at Probaton - his attack on the Bulgars would be indecisive. That would secure her own power on the throne even among the hotheads who would prefer that her "foolish boy" reign alone.

Constantine sent their answer to Khardam. It was a "tribute" of horse shit.

To Stauratius she said:

"How can Constantine be expected to comprehend the plots of the iconoclasts and the devil? He does have some knowledge of warfare though. I have largely avoided war at great expense to the state. At a time when proper worship itself is endangered we cannot afford idle adventures. But perhaps if he cannot be content with his toys here in the city, we shall allow him some martial exercise against those troublesome Bulgars. That might actually encourage Khardam to look further west. You, my friend, have served me well in campaigns when we have had to fight. Assist the boy. Do not let him lose our armies but it is best he not shine too brightly either. You have friends to be his advisors, don't you? I have spoken with that insect Nicephorus. He is quite knowledgeable about the Bulgars. The three of you might consult together in these matters. Nicephorus may finally be of some use to the throne, but do not trust him."

Stauratius and Nicephorus had not often been found together and of

154

like mind before Stauratius's exile. The two could not have been more different. Stauratius was absolutely loyal to his empress while Nicephorus was loyal to no one, dwelling instead on the gloom of his own political impotence. Since the return of Stauratius to power that had changed. Today they were alone together. Stauratius had actually invited the caesar to dine with him in his country villa, or rather palace, in the Blachernae district on the outskirts of the city far from the urban stench. From its windows they could enjoy the breeze that lessened the oppressive heat and humidity of late summer. They could also view the unscalable walls of Theodosius which had - together with the protection of Our Lady - always preserved the city from attack. Only a few decades before they had once again proved their invulnerability when an Arab army had besieged the city early in the reign of Constantine's father. They were Constantinople's strong defense. On such a lovely day they were also beautiful.

Conversation started out with chat far more amiable than had been usual between them. In the past Stauratius had showed only formal diffidence to the rank of Nicephorus and the caesar had begrudged the real power of the eunuch. But that was before Nicephorus introduced the logothete to Lucia. Mid-afternoon passed slowly into twilight. The two men gossiped cheerily about things and persons on whom they could agree. It was actually pleasant. Nicephorus quoted Homer as the sunlight failed: "Now deep in ocean sank the lamp of light, and drew behind the cloudy vale of night." It was a charade and they both knew it. Both were classically educated and neither cared a whit about it.

Little by little Stauratius dared to hint at the danger which might befall the empire if Constantine were to again attempt to rule alone. In time he confided the empress' insecurities about her son's ability and particularly her concern that iconoclasm might reemerge even in the city itself. She had again suggested that it would be best if she were to be given preference in all affairs. This was insurrection, certainly, though not in the name of overturning the government but of securing it in its strongest form. Stauratius easily led Nicephorus to admit that this was hardly a treasonable offense.

And admit it he freely did. Nicephorus was happy to drive the wedge deeper between the hated mother and son. His Bulgar friends could hold their own against the combat-timid Stauratius, but Nicephorus felt far less certain that barbarians would be a match for an aggressive Roman emperor. Constantine was learning fast. He no longer trusted anyone: not him certainly, and not even his Armeniac supporters now that he had imprisoned Alexios Mousoulem. The emperor had failed in his first attempt to rule alone, but he was a quick study.

"Do you think that it is possible for the empress to retain first place with Constantine beside her?" Stauratius asked.

"No."

Even Irene had not suggested that. The accomplices did not dare to look at each other but Nicephorus rose from his chair and began to pace while Stauratius seemed lost in worry ... perhaps for his soul.

By the time Nicephorus left, the old enemies were friends, if only fair-weather friends. Each for his own very different reasons had determined to do whatever might be necessary to preserve the empress in power ... anything that might be necessary.

In the weeks that followed Nicephorus insisted that Lucia work hard at improving her Greek and Stauratius took a liking to this barbarian girl who did not disdain him as a man for his disability, nor think of him as a queer sort of woman. Men knew better than to do either - aloud at least - for Stauratius was powerful and vindictive; but women often did. The great man requested of his friend that Lucia join his household staff. Nicephorus only asked that she be allowed to retain her own small home where he might from time-to-time see her privately.

Soon Stauratius would be seen with Lucia by his side and were it not for his beardless face one might have thought them married. In private, she would take his arm and sit as close to him as a bride. Nor did Stauratius seem to mind but relished this sort of companion marriage. Few people, man or woman, had ever before cared a whit for his comfort. But he was deceived. He would talk freely with ministers and army officers while Lucia was in the room, and sometimes to her alone as he thrashed out affairs of state at home. Lucia made Nicephorus aware of the deepest thoughts of the first minister. These, with other intelligence, he fed to Pamphilus to be forwarded to other agents of Khardam. The Roman Empire was betrayed on a flood of urine.

The women's quarters of the Great Palace were really like a palace of itself. Ancient Athens, so highly regarded by the Byzantines, had allowed women little freedom; but in Rome aristocratic ladies had not been so fully segregated and Byzantium's heritage was from both. Furthermore, the empire was located half in Asia where the traditions were far more restrictive. Proper ladies did walk the streets unveiled but were always escorted. Women of the lower classes were as untroubled by such conventions as fishwives or simple housewives anywhere. Having to work in public beside one's husband breeds equality.

For the upper classes: though as in Rome they might attend parties or the theater or the Eucharist with their husbands and brothers; wives and daughters and sisters would sit separately, together with only the younger male children. So it also was at the palace. Women and men mixed socially but as evening fell the ladies would retire to the women's quarters to discuss among themselves the day's events and doubtless the most attractive of the males.

The ladies in the imperial quarters were either relatives of Constantine - his wife, babies, and mother - or their clouds of female attendants and servants; so the emperor was as welcome in that harem as any husband with his family. There were just more of them. Most of the ladies could judge his mood and would make themselves available or scarce accordingly. Maria did not seem to care if some Cubicularia chatted up her husband while she and Irene listened to a visiting monk or scholar, or a reading from one of the church fathers. Constantine would sit with the girls - sometimes with a baby on his knee - drink a bit of spiced wine, and for a few hours forget the cares that wore him down. No one took any special notice when one of the Cubicularia was missing, except Constantine. When the vivacious Theodote was absent the emperor would soon cut short the chatter with some comment that he had some studying to do, or was tired and needed to arise early in the morning.

But if Theodote was present he was happy. He tried not to give her any more attention than he did to the others, but he longed to. Theodote was easy to watch. She sparkled like a diamond among pretty pearls. She did not chatter but when she did add to the conversation what she said was always worth hearing. More than once Constantine was reminded of another lady, one that the sun itself walked beside. If Theodote was not as beautiful he didn't notice; he was smitten. There was not a meanness nor an anxiety about the girl. Surely, she could not always feel as cheerful as she appeared, but of all a Cubicularia's duties helping the emperor to relax was of the most importance. Sometimes the others forgot. Theodote never did. She suspected his heartaches, knew his troubles, and thought the world of him.

However the emperor was a married man. He had taken an oath and he took it seriously. He forced himself to be content with chaste companionship amid the chattering women about him, pretending to himself that he actually cared about the play or singer under discussion.

Then one day Constantine was disturbed in his work by a loud dragging sound and rising from the couch where he was reading a dispatch, walked out onto a balcony of the palace which looked down on a sunlit interior courtyard. As he watched, a tall female figure entered directly below him and proceeded quickly across the yard. He could only see her back. She wore a long black cloak - not from his century - which fell to just below her knees. Her calves were encased in familiarly tight high boots; boots that laced from toe to knee and hugged her calves like leather skin. As in a dream it did not seem at all odd to the emperor that she was dressed so strangely; the thought of crossing himself several times did not even occur to him. What should have been most startling was an overlong chain hanging from her wrists. It was so long that instead of hampering her it simply dragged behind her like the iron train on some regal gown. Her feet were not chained and the woman swept rapidly across the courtyard as though she were in charge of the palace rather than a prisoner. Even her guards kept a discreet distance as though she were mistress of the place. Then she turned and brightly raised a manacled hand in impish salutation to her master and lord, the ruler of the world. Constantine awoke knowing his desire and his sin. He had been dreaming his old fantasy but the girl's features were those of the Theodote.

Later that day he asked a minor but trusted and ambitious courtier to have a woolen cloak made, dyed deep black with sleeves that would be long and wide. The lining of the cape and its hood would be of precious lime green silk from the palace workshops. It was to be held closed by large and ornate golden hasps at the neck only, so that the wearer's figure could be clearly seen when walking briskly as in his dream. Constantine was clearly excited as he spoke, flushed in the face. The open cloak was unlike any the courtier had seen, more a thing of fashion than for warmth despite its great weight from the heaviness of thick wool. Constantine ordered the aide to sketch the garment while still in his presence and fussed over it until it exactly matched the image of his dream. Then after swearing the man to absolute silence upon pain of mutilation and a promise of promotion beyond his highest expectation, the emperor ordered the whore-boots, a leather thong like Beth's, cuffs, and the chain.

Yet when the items were delivered, he put them away.

Rotrud took the veil at the convent of Chelles. Her last request before the doors closed behind her was that her friend Bertmund of Loutern so inform the Emperor of the East and bring to him her prayers for a long and happy life. Her father did not object.

"Thank you, my friend." Constantine sat quietly for a long time and Bertmund understood why.

"I loved ... No, I love her dearly. Seigneur Ricolf always spoke so well of Rotrud. He described her so fondly that had he not been so honorable a man I'd have been jealous. I think that fate has not seen fit that we be too happy, Rotrud and I. But, my friend, an emperor has more to concern himself with than happiness." Again Constantine sat in quiet thought for several minutes. Than he rose and gestured for Bertmund to follow him outside.

"My father always said that walls have ears. I expect you have a similar saying. Bertmund, you are only six years older than me but that is long when one is young. You studied the Illustrious Belisarius from Ricolf, did you not?"

Ricolf had died under the ax of a Saxon chieftain but like Ricolf, Bertmund had actually studied not only the career of the great general, but Roman treatises on strategy and tactics and had grown into a man of honor and ability. Constantine sensed that he should be listened to and he could be trusted.

They sat together near a tall cypress in one of the smaller and very private imperial gardens. Here there was no place to hide eavesdroppers and Constantine could forgo formalities with this foreigner. It was summer and the scent of flowers made the garden almost too peaceful for a discussion of war plans against an unwashed barbaric enemy who was burning and raping a path along the northern frontier.

"This will not be another skirmish. I will throw Khan Khardam back to the steppes of Asia. I will go forward with my troops as my father would have."

Bertmund hesitated. The young monarch was bearing the burden of office as well as many an older man might, but still he was young and had not entirely lost the feeling of invulnerability that curses the young and causes them to do foolish things. *Urge on your troops, Your Serenity, but do not charge into battle. The soldiers will only think you foolish and worry that you will get them all killed.* That is what Bertmund wanted to tell the emperor but one does not speak in such a way to an imperial host when said host can have your head removed on a whim.

"Your Serenity, may I offer another plan. Send your master of horse in your stead. You are needed here. The Arabs threaten in the east. It would be unwise for you to be so far from the capital." The emperor would not be persuaded. For Bertmund to press the matter would only discredit him in Constantine's sight. "You are brave, Serenity." Bertmund meant what he said; Constantine was brave and generally levelheaded. He turned their conversation to logistics and matters of strategy against the Bulgars. "They have developed a strong Mongolian cavalry arm but still rely mainly on foot soldiers. These are good but like our own German enemies more concerned with personal honor on the field of battle than with battlefield tactics. They will stop to take hostages or loot. That is their weakness."

"And ours, Bertmund?"

They outnumber you badly. Too many of your troops have never seen combat – chased a few bandits and marauders here and there, but not fought a pitched battle against hundreds of men wielding axes."

"I want Christophorus, and Photus; and Bardas if he can be spared." Constantine reeled off the names of the three best generals who could be released from the Arab front with the familiarity of an experienced war plans expert. "I *will* lead my troops in battle. The emperor owes that to men who will die in his name. But I am not a fool."

Not a fool, Bertmund thought, *but still young enough to be foolish.*

In July Constantine led a large force from Constantinople northward along the Thracian coast.

Still early, the army had prayed its prayer for victory:

"Lord, Jesus Christ, our God, have mercy on us. Come to the aid of Christians and make us worthy to fight to the death for our faith and our brothers. Strengthen our souls and our hearts and our whole body. We pray for this oh mighty Lord of Battles, through the intercession of the Immaculate Mother of God, Thy Mother, and of all the saints. Amen"

After being blessed by the patriarch, Constantine's cavalry led the way out through the Golden Gate of the city. The army arrayed itself on the hills outside the bright white triple wall. The emperor halted his charger and faced Constantinople which behind the walls glowed pink and gold in the early morning sun. Three times as Imperator and Autocrator of the army he made the sign of the cross over the city and prayed:

"Lord Jesus, I leave this city in Thy hands. Shield it from all misfortunes and calamities. Protect it from civil war and from attack by the barbarians. Make it impregnable, that no one may harm it, for it is in Thee that we put our trust. Thou art the Lord of pity, the Father of compassion, the God of all consolations. Have pity on us. Shield us from temptation now and forever. Amen."

Battalions of cavalry moved out from the city followed by a thousand pack animals, caparisoned in exotic harness, draped in red blankets, and with their legs protected from insect bites by leggings. As ruler of all Christendom, Constantine could not travel light. He must make a show. Besides food and wine and medical supplies, weapons and armor, the baggage train had to include a great pavilion for the emperor and another to serve as his private chapel. There was even a portable steam bath for the emperor, to impress barbarians and to refresh the monarch after a day's march through enemy or half-loyal countryside, knowing every moment that his person was the principal target of the enemy. He carried the wages of the troops. He also had gifts packed for authorities in the towns through which the army must pass and, of course, for any lords of the enemy tempted to make a private peace. Most important of all, the train of mules carried Byzantium's great secret weapon: barrels of fire liquid, and the machines to spit it at an enemy stockade or any barbarians stupid enough to

160

directly charge the Roman line.

It was a two-week march along the Thracian coast and then inland. The army was confident. It had been drawn from European themes and was secure in the belief that God would give it victory. The holy images had now been returned to the churches, and were being carried before the army into battle again. The young emperor himself was only vaguely aware that victory was uncertain. His purpose was not just to punish Khardam who had seized several frontier forts the year before, but to destroy the barbarian before he might dare attack toward the Thracian wall, Byzantium's last strong defensive position before the city itself. It was the summer of 796 by Gregorian reckoning.

Despite his own religious and practical misgivings and warnings of damnation from the priests, Constantine again listened to those who divined the course of wars from entrails and thunder. He intended to meet the enemy west of the fortress of Markella but the spies that informed him of the enemy's preparations were as loyal to Nicephorus as to him.

Two days after the Christian army left the security of Markella the first troop of cataphracts were riding the Roman road shortly after dawn. Their path was through the forests of the Struma valley. Constantine boldly rode in the van amid banners and horns and surrounded by men in chain armor that could mask even their faces in battle. The camp where they had spent the night was not yet entirely struck. The imperial tent still stood and the pack animals to carry the imperial paraphernalia were not yet fully loaded. These would be the last animals ready this morning and the last units in the procession save for a rear guard of light cavalry archers.

"Bulgars!" was all the first horseman to sight the enemy yelled before he fell gurgling blood. The enemy was far sharper than the Roman cavalry expected, though they should have known. They were well-directed and the next Roman to take an arrow in the throat was the patrician Bardas. Other high officers soon passed from this earth, including Constantine's firm friend and advisor, the iconoclast strategos from the Thrakesion theme, Michael Lachanodrakon. Of the first five hundred armored men on the old road through the woods of modern Bulgaria only a disheartened remnant, many wounded and mutilated, survived to bring news of Khan Khardam's battle skill to Markella. Behind them other troops of cataphracts, unable to maneuver their armored horses in the close confines of the forest, likewise fell to the barbarian infantry and the mounted Mongolian light archers who would pursue the defeated Byzantines throughout the day.

Aside from a few light archers, the bulk of the Roman army were Irene's favorite garrison troopers and iconodules from European themes. They rode behind their sacred images. The Bulgar infantry ran into battle behind their horsehair standards. They disdained organization but attacked in waves of ax-wielding demons, each clan competing for glory and loot with its neighbor. Rude as this tactic was it worked in the dense forest. The cataphracts tried to maintain some order to protect the more lightly armed auxiliaries and the holy icons. One after another trooper would take hold of a falling icon or the battle standard emblazoned with the Chi-Rho, Christ's monogram. One after another they died as the horsehairs advanced against the Christian army. Horses fell and cataphracts tried to fight afoot with the infantry, or else run as character and circumstances gave them to. For a time the Romans fought with the desperation of impending defeat far from home, until finally there could no longer be any hope of retreating as a unit. Finally they were too scattered for Constantine and his generals to rally. They destroyed their own fire-weapons which had not even been brought into play. Behind the smoke the soldiers tried to extract themselves from the battle, usually in small groups of comrades. A few, including Constantine and his guards, succeeded; many failed. When the barbarians pursued the Romans back through their camp some began to loot and plunder the emperor's pavilions even before the battle was done. One even dared to appear before his comrades in the imperial purple still stinking of sweat and gore and holding some poor troopers guts up before his comrades in mockery of the consecration of Christ's body. The fleeing troops still tried to protect the images that they had relied upon for protection. Whatever Constantine's doubts about their efficacy, he would not see these desecrated if he were able to prevent it. But the attempt failed. Christ's sacred standard was taken to Khan Khardam who mocked it and would have crushed it under foot save for fear of the Christian God.

It was a wasted battle. The wealth of the defeated army's camp might alone have been sufficient to purchase the friendship of the Bulgar khan. Now he was rich as well as feared. Now little stood between the Bulgars and conquest of the entire northern provinces.

"For the great weight of our sins God turned away from the Romans on the field of battle and the heathen horde was victorious; just as of old the Philistines mastered Israel before at last, a repentant king David threw off the Philistine yoke and destroyed God's enemies. This the Lord did, that chastised, we might turn unto Christ Jesus for safety from the tempest. Nor were the shields and armor of our cataphracts proof against the barbarians for God permitted the enemy - mounted archers and even infantry - to route our heavy cavalry. Even three of our most highly esteemed strategoi and magistros died that day, and the holy emperor himself barely escaped by the intercession of the saints before God's heavenly throne. Then were Christ's people ravaged by wolves and those who fled to monasteries died under torture together with the monks. Horses were stabled in the churches; holy relics were thrown into the dung heap; and sacred vessels that ought only to hold Christ's precious blood, became

drinking cups for beer and mead. It was an evil day. Indeed it seemed that Christ had forsaken us. God preserve us from such another."

... Theogenius, the monk

Had he not lost the imperial baggage train to the barbarians Constantine would have burned the astrologers' damned books. *My Lord Jesus, forgive me that sin and the losses it has caused your holy people.*

Had he also been betrayed?

The news brought by imperial agents to the city was even worse than the rumors which preceded Constantine's arrival. Usually the peasants' terror exaggerated fact but in this case their reports were confirmed and extended, filled out with details of how many small forts along the old frontier had fallen. Not all to be sure, and not the new fortress of Markella. The Bulgars were neither equipped for nor disposed to besiege such a strong point. That put at least some Roman cavalry at their back; not enough - there were never cnough - but hopefully enough to keep them from consolidating their gains before the defeated European force could rally and link up with those troops which could be spared from the Asian front.

Fortunately for Byzantium, the barbarians paused again.

"Is Nicephorus loyal?" The empress put the question bluntly and it was impossible for her First Minister to answer diplomatically. Besides, Stauratius was not only the chief minister of the empire, logothete of the dromos, but also Irene's best friend after the protospatharius Aetius. He was one of those whose loyalty she held absolutely.

"Nicephorus, Your Serenity? Let me remind you: with your late husband's death he lost any real power. He is a bit of a joke in the foreign office."

"As he is in the women's quarters; but a rather dangerous joke. Nicephorus is a vindictive man. One would not want to have him learn that you had joked about him. He is still a caesar and not without friends. The question is: has he the belly to attempt to overthrow my throne?"

"Nicephorus may be a pompous and disappointed man, Your Serenity, but he is no fool."

"All the more reason not to trust the man. He can be dangerous. He is aging and may feel that he has not many years ahead in which to enjoy sitting on this throne and hurting you and me and Constantine. How did the Bulgar dogs know the route my son would take? Spies? Of course spies, but they would have needed Romans willing and able to give information."

"I'd swear that no high officer would have betrayed us to dirty Bulgars, Your Serenity. Some few might support an iconoclast rebel but never the Bulgars." Stauratius was blithely unaware of the part that he himself had played in the betrayal: Lucia.

"Perhaps no one would have informed the Bulgars. But any one of dozens might have leaked information to someone like Nicephorus or his stupid brothers to gain his friendship. It could not hurt some rising officer and ... Mother of God help us ... some might want to play both sides .... Nicephorus still has fantasies of taking this throne some day. He would say otherwise but don't trust the man. Find out, and if he is disloyal, prove it. I want proof so no one will defend him."

With the betrayed emperor without much of his army, the danger to him, and to Irene too, was great. But soon Nicephorus himself revealed his treason to the throne, though not his part in advising Khardam. As he had planned, his own name was on the lips of the city's worst rabble, many of their gang-bosses being suddenly made wealthy by gifts from his brothers. As custom required, he professed not to be seeking the imperial diadem yet prepared to be forced to the hippodrome by the crowd where he would be raised on a shield to take the throne from Constantine.

Now proof was unnecessary. Nicephorus had shown his hand too soon. Irene only had to watch as her son acted decisively, arresting Nicephorus, his brothers, and the agents who had misled him in the attack against the Bulgars. To merely imprison the conspirators would invite further treason on their behalf. The sentence for treason against the emperor who held a mandate from heaven to rule the Christian world was death, but His Clemency reduced the sentence. He even prayed for his unworthy uncle and cousins: *May Christ have mercy upon them.* A heated blade took the sight of the caesar, and his brothers lost their tongues so that rather than face Christ Pantocrator, the Ruler of All, with the sins of treason and sacrilege fresh upon their souls they might find in reflection and penance remorse for their sins and Divine forgiveness. They were soon after released from prison with the expectation that they would retire to monasteries or their estates to consider their wickedness. Instead the brothers remained troublesome, roaming the streets of the city and fomenting discord.

By now Constantine was no longer the immature emperor of Byzantium who had fled from his mother's beating but a young man with a wife, two daughters, and bearing the weight of the western world - sometimes sharing, usually disputing real authority with Irene. His wife despised that her husband was human with human needs, instead of a priest as she supposed priests to be. He loved his daughters but army command often kept him from them, nor was his wife desirous that he should intrude on her rearing of the two young girls.

"There is no guile in your son, Your Sovereignty." Irene was still frightened and angry that she had nearly lost her throne, and probably her life, when Nicephorus attempted the coup. Now Stauratius was prostrate before her. She had not bid him rise and, anyway, he did not want to meet her eyes. What they were discussing was treason.

"How do you mean that, Stauratius?"

"If I may be candid, it is not entirely a compliment. The basilios is likable and he is good. But a ruler must be as devious as his enemies."

"Yes. I think Constantine will never learn. But he is my son. What shall we do? He and I feud like adversaries. We have little in common in the way we think. He still has support among the Armeniacs because they know his heart is not truly with the holy images. I cannot have God's work undone by a dreamer who can be used by the iconoclast fools."

"Then the Armeniacs must be turned against him, and he against them, so that you alone are regarded by the army. I am sure he will listen to you, Serenity. There is friction between you but you are still his mother and that is sacred to him. He does not know all that you would do for the sake of the empire and the saints." The logothete had said more than was politic. He could lose his eyes for the implication of his words. But he gambled correctly that the augusta's thoughts were already far ahead of his words and that Irene would welcome the knowledge that she was not alone in them.

Constantine confessed his sins before the patriarch. They spoke of the lost battle against Khardam.

"You should not feel guilty, Your Sovereignty. It was your first major engagement. There will be others. For now, perhaps it were best you entrusted command to Stauratius. He has experience. Besides, Your Sovereignty, you must concentrate on keeping the fanatics among my clergy from killing each other. That is the most important thing. I am not saying this to distract you from our outside enemies. Christ will deal with them if we love each other. It is most important that you devote yourself to bringing peace here at home."

"But All-Holiness, how am I to do that when the empress and all around her do not wish peace?" Constantine's gesture swept the room and walls. It seemed to indicate the whole palace and the city itself. The "Ruler of the World" was frustrated. "Besides, I am unfit to heal Christ's church. I have sinned."

"So have we all."

"No; that is not what I mean. Those troops ... those men's lives. ... I lost them."

"Men die in war, Your Sovereignty."

"I listened to soothsayers."

"I know; and other men paid with their lives for your sin. Carrying that burden will be a greater penance than any I could require of you."

While Constantine's blood still boiled with anger at his betrayal by Uncle 'Foros and his shame at losing so many men to Khardam's barbarians while himself escaping uninjured, his mother took the opportunity to further weaken him and at the same time wreak revenge on Alexios, still imprisoned in the praetorian barracks.

"Do you understand now? There are many men who would grasp the throne if we ever showed weakness. Your friend Mousoulem is like those other traitors. Mousoulem was never your friend. He only wanted to use you against your mother. If he remained free he would have turned rebel again at his first opportunity. I have spoken with the saints, Constantine, and asked God's mercy on him. Do not take his life but it must be that he cannot be emperor."

The empress retired to a private chapel. *Mousoulem is mine now.* Irene prostrated herself in prayer. *You would not have me happy at his falling low, Lord. But, Lord, surely you wish him fallen. The man almost cost me the throne when he tried to use Constantine two years ago. Then who knows what might have happened to your empire on earth. My boy would not be a strong emperor and Constantine believed him a friend. Constantine only wanted to exile him but it is better we be rid of the snake forever.*

Had Alexios been loyal to the emperor or a traitor as Irene insisted? If so he paid the price for treason. At Irene's urging Constantine ordered the much respected former leader of the Armeniac army blinded, but Irene kept her own hands clean.

When word of Alexios' blinding reached the Armeniacs they rebelled against the imperial treachery as they saw it. They defeated the first troops sent against them and blinded the commander in retribution.

It was not just Constantine's error in blinding Alexios which had set off the rebellion. Theological argument leading to political sedition was the poison of the empire. It is difficult to understand today why the Asiatic troops of Armenia and Bithynia who had always supported Constantine against the intrigues of Irene and her advisors now chose to desert him. It would not seem to have been to their religious advantage, for they rejected the image-worship of Constantinople. But Constantine would not entirely eliminate image-worship; and for them, as for Irene and the monks they opposed, tolerance of false belief was not a Christian virtue. It no longer mattered weather Irene or Constantine ruled. It was a pox on both of them.

In the dispute Constantine and Irene had common cause. Stauratius placed agents among the rebels and several of their leaders were turned.

Some other officers were unwilling to disavow their sacred oaths of loyalty to Constantine. With their reluctant aid Constantine, leading his troops himself, broke the rebellion. Later Irene spoke to him in as fond a manner as she ever had. "You have shown strength, my son. You have shown strength against rebellion. I am proud of you. Our reign together will be as glorious as any in history. We have saved Christ's church; and you, my brave boy, will yet send that cur Khardam slinking back to his filthy lair."

Covering her head the lady knelt on her chapel floor, her head bowed to her hands, and prayed a prayer of thanksgiving. *The troops who supported Alexios must also be punished. It would be best that were done in my son's name so that they know he is not their friend.*

On her unctuous advice Constantine severely punished the rebellious cataphracts. This last act made him more unpopular, even among those troops who still felt duty-bound to him. They had to watch a thousand veteran comrades tattooed as traitors. As intended by Stauratious, the "Armeniac fools" had been turned against the emperor, and he against them. He lost what remained of loyalty in his Armeniac and Bithnian regiments.

ˋˋˋˋˋ

CHAPTER 22

The weight of the world. Constantine would willingly have shouldered that whole burden had he been permitted to; but in fact, most often he could only take the responsibility for the decisions of his mother's appointees, perfunctorily put before him for approval. He devoted himself to the defense of his realm; working, as was necessary, with Stauratius. In the several years following his humiliating defeat by Khardam, Constantine fought battle after battle, winning some minor engagements and losing others. He skirmished several times with Bulgar forces and tried to bring Harun al-Rashid's armies to decisive battle without success. The Arabs would raid Roman territory and withdraw before the empire's heavy cavalry could outmatch their lighter forces in the field. Khardam, too, refused decisive battle when the emperor advanced against him near Adrianople. His army faded away to where the Roman cataphracts could not follow. Constantine began to think about emphasizing light cavalry such as the Arabs and Bulgars employed but that would be politically unwise. Many junior officers of the Constantinoplian guard of cataphracti were the excess progeny of rich and powerful families. They had influence and they valued their prestige as the empire's main defense.

Constantine did not love his wife. He loved his cheetah. *I'm sure that she would dress sexy for me and we could have a lot of fun together.* But he was a husband and father. *Or do I just like pretty girls in tight boots and leather underwear?*

He had tried to live chastely as the priests said he should, though as emperor he could do whatever he wanted ... could have whatever he wanted. His aides would be discreet.

The eunuchs would rather I was a lecher anyway, and stayed out of their way. Even the priests didn't really care what he did in private. Though Byzantine society was constantly concerned with religion, prostitution was legal and mistresses common. As emperor he was the Isapostle, but as Constantine he was a sinner like everyone else. *Damn, I want sex to be fun but it's not just sex. Theo's sweet and cheerful, and smart; and she cares*

169

about me for myself. I'd love Theo with or without the boots. It would be a joy to make her really happy. For a long time he sat alone considering a future better than any he had imagined since he'd put aside all hope of a life with Rotrud. He had his fantasies but that was all. He also had his duty. He summoned the handmaiden.

"Theodote. You must go away."

The cheetah's eyes dropped. She bowed but said nothing. She began to withdraw for Constantine was lord of all her world and she was simply a handmaiden.

"Wait, Theo. You are good. You deserve an explanation." No one "deserved" an explanation from the basilios, and few received one. "If you remain here I know I will sin against Maria."

Theodote stood looking at the mosaic floor but seeing nothing. A figure of the huntress Diana returned her look with its own unseeing eyes. Theodote hated that pagan figure from before the Christ, the God who had become human like her. She would have wished it gone but had no strength to do more than control her tears. Though of noble birth she was young and only of minor service in the Great Palace. Still, to be a servant who daily waited upon the augusta was no small position in the greater world. That was over now. She would have to leave. There would be talk among the aristocratic ladies of the city. Had she displeased her ladyship? Was she inelegant or prone to offend, or stupid? Had she been sent away because of a lover? Worse yet, would the truth slip out and the affection the basilios felt for her be a subject of bawdy humor among the meanest citizens and household slaves? That would be bad for her; but it would be more wretched and shameful yet to embarrass the troubled lord that she loved despite herself.

Constantine sensed it all. "You will not go in disgrace, Theo. You have not wronged my wife or tried to tempt me. But I care far too much for you. I can arrange a fine marriage for you. You are very young and you are pleasing. You will make a fine young nobilissimus a very happy husband. Or is there some young man that you already admire?" It was a speech that Constantine forced himself to make. He wanted to see to the girl's happiness yet he did not really want that she admire some other man instead of him.

"No. Your Serenity. I am yours if that should be your desire. But it will not be that I sought to tempt you or that I betrayed my lady."

The emperor's next words were a request as to an equal. "Will you do something for me while you are here, Theo? In my chambers is a cape. I would see you wearing it."

A few minutes later Theodote reentered the room where Constantine sat. She was holding the black cloak closed with one hand and brushing back some strands of her hair with the other. She was tall - not an Amazon

170

like Beth - but tall for a Greek. The tailor had not allowed for that. The hem of the cloak did not reach her knees.

"Will you take off your sandals?

She did.

"And let your hair fall?"

She did.

Now the cheetah's eyes were fixed upon the floor and the emperor could not read them. Theodote released her hold upon the cloak so that it fell open. She wore no tunic beneath. Still she did not raise her eyes but spoke in a low and submissive voice.

"There were curious looking boots with it, and cuffs and a long chain too. Shall I ..."

Constantine cut her off in mid-sentence.

"No. Just stand there for me awhile." The girl had misunderstood. He had not required her naked much less chained like some prisoner; and she herself had just said that she would not tempt him. Still, she was young and lovely to look at and he could not force himself to look away. For a full five minutes they stood there contemplating infidelity but then the emperor just took her hand and turned her around. He allowed himself one hard pat then closed the door and went out into his garden alone.

Some weeks passed. Constantine and Theodote avoided each other as much as possible but he made no further move to send her away in a gracious manner. Theodote twice reminded him while hoping he would take no action. Constantine would not be unfaithful in body but he could not help his spirit nor again raise the subject. He could not send the cheetah to another, so they put off the parting day by day and pretended to themselves that they were not in love.

While Constantine devoted his efforts toward ending the Bulgar threat, Harun al Rashid in Baghdad was not resting. He wished history to remember him: yes. as a supporter of the arts, and certainly as the Bulwark of Islam, but also as a conqueror in the tradition of other califs. His harrying assaults on Byzantium's eastern frontier convinced the monk Theodore, who had replaced Platton as abbot at the Saccudion monastery, that he must remove his monks from the Asiatic shore to the safety of Constantinople. There they would be welcomed by their brother monks of Studion.

Now he was visiting Studion. He would be made abbot here too and he prayed that those monks already there would not resent him. Insects droned in the little suburban orchard outside his window for spring was again upon the city. In his cell he had hung a simple cross over his cot and on the wall a painting he himself had made of the Holy Mother. Now he sat on the straw mattress to eat the meal he had prepared for himself. It was simple, of course, as demanded by the order; just a few vegetables and water and a bit of bread; no oil. At Saccudion it had not always been possible for the monks to prepare their own meals as St. Basil had wanted. When the monastery had been large that had been impractical; but most of the monks had later been exiled by the iconoclastic emperors. Others had won the crown of martyrdom. Many others had not really belonged in the holy life. These had simply been retiring from civil life and wives and responsibility. They had too-readily shed their robes when faced with persecution by the evil Lachanodrakon and others who served the false emperor Leo. Theodore prayed that the Lord would forgive their grave sin.

As he ate he considered a hymn he was composing in his mind in memory of a departed friend, a monk of great virtue:

As a son of the day you have gone afar,
But as for us, we cry for our loss as we think of the grace that
adorned thee.
All thy love and zeal and sweetness we keep in memory as we do the
cross you bore
When you followed the Lord. Alleluia.

Theodore was considering a modified rule for Studion, one appropriate for the reduced population. It would be easy by the standards of those monks and hermits who still sought places to be alone in the desert, but harsh enough for the repentant urbanites soon to come under his care. It would be difficult enough for them to concentrate on their prayers, particularly since he intended to introduce night-long vigils; he dare not require too much more. But at least he would make aristocrats forgo having personal slaves and work the monastery's fields themselves. They would certainly not be permitted any female association except for mothers and sisters.

Theodore looked out the window. It was good to be in the city. True, the life was not that much different from Saccudion. The icons were being set up again and talented monks were copying badly damaged holy pictures. That was of immense importance. The life of prayer here was much the same. Why then was Studion better than Saccudion? Was it because the countryside was boring in a way life in the city was not, even in a cloister? Maybe so; a troop of soldiers were riding past; that might not be exciting but at least it was a change from the monotony outside his cell in Asia. There was news to be had here too. He could do more to effect the life of the empire from Studion. He was certain that was the will of God, no matter how unworthy the servant. Otherwise, why had he been denied the crown of martyrdom?

He took his bowl to wash it in the refectory. Soon it would be vespers. He should have concentrated on that but other matters intruded on Theodore's thoughts. He understood that not everyone wanted the life he had chosen - his cousin Theodote, for one. He had been able to get her a position as a cubicularia to the holy Irene. He'd hoped Irene's piety would be an example to her. After all, the empress was able to combine the fullness of a secular life with her duty to Christ and the saints. Theodote was young, and she was good, certainly; but not yet holy. He had heard troubling reports about her vivaciousness. He had heard that the emperor found her company pleasant. Theodore was unsure of Constantine too. His ambitions seemed to be military. *Well, that is necessary in the nation's leader.* He was also a married man, again something necessary; *a virtue actually for one who must provide a son to rule after him. But by Maria*, he hoped, not by his cousin for whose soul he worried and prayed.

That concern was personal. What most troubled the saint was Constantine's apparent willingness to compromise with the iconoclasts who had murdered his brother and sister monks and nearly destroyed Christ's empire. Constantine was not at all like his dear mother ... *Unfortunate. Unfortunate for the empire and for his soul.*

Khardam sent a messenger to Constantine. He carried with him the rotting hands of a missionary priest.

"The Great Khan of the Bulgars sends greetings to the king of the Greeks." Insulting enough: for to be basilios was far superior to any mere kingship. He was also the Roman emperor of all Christendom, not a mere Greek. "You are bid to appear before our lord to surrender Macedonia which you hold weakly. You cannot win in battle. To save the lives of the Macedonians I suggest that you do not dawdle.

"Oh yes, your spy still lives. Have no fear for his soul; he has not abandoned his god, though it seems his god has abandoned him. He does look humorous though, eating scraps from the Great Khan's table with his mouth, just like the other dogs. You might like to make a nice reliquary for these."

Constantine did not whisper his reply to a eunuch, nor did he allow Stauratius or Aetius to frame an answer in his name. Neither did he raise his voice: "Tell Khardam that I shall indeed appear before him, but with fire, and with an army that will cover the land to the horizon." Then he spoke to Aetius: "Have someone write a full reply in something the Bulgars can understand: pictures perhaps," and to the envoy: "Can the great pig at least understand pictures?"

Constantine began to plan another campaign. This time he would not underestimate his enemy, nor would he trust in soothsayers; but only in the Lord of Hosts and in the council of his generals. *I will be very busy. At least I will not have to send Theo away now, not just yet.* The thought gladdened his heart.

That evening Constantine summoned Bertmund of Loutern. At Charles' wish he had assumed a role in Constantinople not unlike that of a foreign military observer today. He alone among barbarians was allowed to stand in the emperor's presence. Ricolf, were he still alive, would have been pleased that Constantine received the Frank as a friend, even if Charles' larger plan had been frustrated.

"Remember, Your Serenity, that Belisarius won his battles more by deception than confrontation. Make the Bulgars believe that you are doing one thing, then do another."

"I only have limited forces; never enough cataphracts. I can't make a believable diversion and still have a large force to do the real fighting."

"The Bulgars are lightly armed. It does not take cataphracts to defeat them. In fact cataphracts slow you down with their servants and baggage. Besides, Belisarius would remind us that a few cataphracts attacking at a decisive moment are of more worth than thousands trying to engage infantry in the woods. He would not hesitate to use those thousands in other ways than combat."

The emperor knew the truth of that. He had lost his heavy cavalry in the forests of Moesia because they had been useless there. "Explain yourself, Bertmund."

There was no one else present but a few guards outside the door. Were they trustworthy? Even if they were, they might let slip something that they'd overheard. Bertmund thought it best to stretch protocol and moved close to Constantine so that they could speak in whispers.

CHAPTER 23

Before Constantine could take on the Bulgar enemy he was betrayed at home. Constantine felt hurt as much as betrayed when Stauratius told him of Maria's participation. Although he and his wife had not been close, he'd been faithful to her. He'd avoided Theodote, just as in his younger years he had put aside his infatuation with Rotrud whom he had never met save in dreams. None of this was because he had found love in the wife he slept with. Maria had been chosen for him, not by him. Yet husbands and wives share much beside their bed. He had not thought her his enemy. He hated to believe that she had not at least felt the same loyalty to him that he did to her.

Stauratius only informed the emperor that his wife "may well have joined" a plot against him. He supplied no reason why, nor details of how he knew, and had left Constantine to consider what reasons he might. Constantine did not aggressively pursue the reason for Maria's betrayal. If he suspected the truth, in his heart he did not want to be told.

In the weeks before the treason was discovered, Irene had seemed to turn against Maria. As she had given insidious advice to Constantine to punish his once faithful Asian troops, Irene was now encouraging his infatuation with Theodote. She knew a divorce and remarriage would alienate the people, the clergy, and particularly the troublesome monks. There would be trouble and the troublemakers would have the support of at least part of the army. Of course Irene would not have condoned her own son's murder, but then, she may not have thought through the logical outcome of a plot against her son. She probably only intended that he be intimidated to lessen his power once again and force him to call on her for aid. That she had turned against Maria and encouraged her son's affair was just another effort to weaken his fragile grasp on power.

For his part, Constantine could not understand why his mother's chief advisor had informed him of the plot and forestalled it. They had never been friends. Stauratius was capable to be sure, but entirely Irene's man. But the scheme had involved not only the disgruntled Maria but the emperor's own formerly loyal supporters in the Armeniac theme and it was getting out of hand. The fact is that Stauratius foresaw its excesses and feared that he himself would be associated with it. He knew that the emperor felt him capable of murder and treason.

Constantine was not heart-broken to divorce his wife. There was no proof against Maria but none was needed. Suspicion was more than enough when the life of God's representative on earth was endangered. He even suspected that Maria might be innocent. If so she was still no friend. She would not be punished, but she would be put away and their marriage dissolved. *"What God has joined together let no man put asunder."* He reminded himself that it was his mother, not God, who had joined him to his wife. *What had any of this to do with God? I loved Rotrud.* Yes, they had two daughters, and Maria might still bear him an heir but she might also murder him in his sleep if the charge was true. That would not only be a crime against his person but also against God's holy will, for which she would have to answer to Christ at the judgment. Even if, as seemed likely, her treason would not rise to the level of murder, and if she did one day bear a son she would no doubt poison the child's mind against him, as his own mother had likely poisoned hers. Fortunately the evidence of her treason was weak: basically the word of Stauratius and paid informers, her suspicion of a comely handmaiden, and a few unexplained meetings with suspected dissidents. Constantine was not forced to take any more severe action than to require her to take the veil at a pleasant convent. The pious lady was not displeased and retired, taking her daughters with her to raise as nuns. Constantine directed that they be well-educated when older. He loved the toddlers and continued to visit them nightly when not on campaign. In years to come one of them was easily persuaded to leave her convent and wed an emperor.

None of the talk about a plot mattered to the populace. Word that he loved a cubicularia was enough to discredit the weak charge against Maria. Constantine failed to consider that the people, and particularly the monks, would not believe his pious wife a would-be traitor simply on his word. Mobs protested that under church law Constantine could only divorce his wife for adultery or treason and that certainly she could not be guilty of either. Ignoring how he had protected them by warring on Arabs and Bulgars while Irene connived against him at home, they declared him simply a foolish son and ungrateful husband; an adulterous sinner enamored of a handmaiden.

Now Constantine lost the respect of the people and any remaining fear of his power among the monks; as well as the support of most of the army, iconoclast as well as iconodule. None considered that Maria had failed in her first duty to the dynasty. There had never been anything to keep the lonely Constantine and prudish Maria together, save the hope of a male heir. Physicians thought it a medical defect in a woman if she could not

176

produce boys.

Irene summoned the monk Theodore. He walked alone to the Great Palace and was led to a chapel where Irene waited prostrate before a reliquary containing a nail from the crucifixion. The monk also prostrated before the holy shrine for some minutes, before indicating by a more relaxed demeanor that he was ready when the empress should care to address him.

"It is Constantine," she finally said, not at all to the monk's surprise. "He sent poor Maria to a convent just so that he could be free to sin with that slut Theodote."

Theodore was not surprised that Constantine loved someone other than his wife. Though it saddened him to know his cousin had become a slut, she was still young. Age would often bring repentance to the worst of sinners. That Constantine and Maria had not been greatly in love was well known in court circles, and Theodore was well aware of the goings on at court. In itself, it did not matter. He had kept his peace so long as the emperor sinned in private; but for the Isapostle to have divorced his wife and the mother of his daughters was a serious matter, certainly not a step to take simply because he lusted after another woman.

"He intends to wed Theodote and raise her to the purple," Irene added after a moment.

They talked together for awhile before Theodore returned to his monastery, walking more slowly, lost in thought and praying. The next day he visited the patriarch who assured him that he would not perform the wedding ceremony. To the two men it was settled. They were sure that between them they could dissuade Constantine from the wretched path he was pursuing. Neither knew that Irene herself was even at that moment encouraging her son's remarriage. Even though she had also picked Maria to be the emperor's wife, she had not promoted either woman for her son's happiness. That did not so much matter. For the good of the state what mattered was not his happiness, nor even the martial strength of the empire which seemed to preoccupy Constantine and many of her own advisors, including even Stauratius. What mattered was that her "fool boy" not rule. The hated Nicephorus had at least understood that. Irene's attempts to rule while her son only reigned were failing. He had proven himself a brave and competent commander. Despite the loss of his first major battle against the Bulgars he did have ability. But to Irene the Bulgars and the Arabs were not the first concern of a ruler. The spiritual life of the Christian world was what would bring Christ's reign to earth, and only she seemed to appreciate this. Others gave it lip service but put little behind their words. She would win over the pagan enemies for she was firm in fidelity to the images, her single-minded solution to all the realm's problems. She would do what she must to end heresy and win Christ's blessing. Surely, He would approve.

Had He not said that He had come to bring a sword, to set son against father and daughter against mother?

Maria preferred life in a convent to that of wife to the basilios. In the Christian Roman Empire it was common for married couples to retire separately from the world, albeit, most often at a later age. Byzantium suffered greatly from a loss of many talented officials to the monasteries, some even while they were at the height of their usefulness. Nor was religious life always a hardship. Not only in the east but also in the west, it could be quite pleasant. In a stratified society such a life could be a career or lifestyle choice for tired courtiers and excess progeny, one which had little to do with spirituality.

But Maria was spiritual, so with her contentedly in a convent Constantine raised the woman he did love to be his augusta. This he did in the month of August in a ceremony amid the marbles of the Augustaeum, the forecourt and first hall of the palace precinct. All the high officials of the state and many Church dignitaries - though not the Patriarch Tarasios - attended as he placed upon Theodote's head the crown of empire adorned with cloisonné images and pendant strings of diamonds. After her coronation the new empress passed in grand procession down a colonnaded passage before the senators and patricians of the empire and from a balcony greeted the city's fickle populace while guards paraded before her. Priests blessed the occasion and grandees and populace alike prostrated before her. Theodote reverently bowed before the cross of Christ with a candle in each hand. With disarming and honest modesty she spread her arms wide before her husband's subjects and heard the cry of all: "God save the augusta."

On that same day the emperor and his empress were formally betrothed.* They were married the following month. The wedding was celebrated in St. Stephen's chapel within the palace complex. There were, however, sour notes. Theodore, Theodote's cousin, refused to attend and damned the couple. He echoed Irene's epithet of "slut." The patriarch - more fearful of the power of the monks than of Constantine - would not celebrate the wedding. Instead wedding crowns were placed upon the heads of the emperor and his bride by a priest of no great status.

Theodote herself had warned Constantine that their marriage would be unacceptable to the populace and the monks: "It is not necessary, Your Serenity, my love," she had said. "There is the hidden door and to have your love is more than I could ever wish for. You should not risk upsetting the clergy."

---

* This is not an error. Curiously, an emperor could raise his fiancée to the dignity of basilia before their marriage.

But as Constantine would not be an adulterer wed to Maria, he would also not live an unmarried fornicator. Nor would he jeopardize the soul of the handmaiden he had come to love despite himself. For her own reasons his mother had minimized the discontent which would be stirred up by his divorce and remarriage and assured her son that he and Theodote would soon win over the hearts of the people. Then the monks would have to accept their marriage.

"After all," she'd said, "even if Maria herself might not have killed you while you slept, she might have stood apart and allowed an assassin in. She was not to be trusted. You had no choice but to divorce her and, of course, you must have a male heir. Besides, any shopkeeper can divorce his wife and remarry under the civil law whatever the clergy might wish. Why not the basilios with the good of Christ's empire at stake?"

This serious problem aside, Constantine was happy on his wedding day. As was the custom, the gentlemen and ladies of the court escorted the couple to the bridal chamber while the palace staff divided before them shouting: "Welcome, God-chosen augusta! Welcome, God-protected augusta! Welcome, wearer of the purple! Welcome, thou whom all desire!" In the bridal chamber there was more happy clamor before a golden bed perfumed and strewn with summer flowers. It was a tribute to his cheetah and Constantine relished every moment of her glory. That evening a feast was held in the triclinium of the nineteen couches for the greatest magnates of the empire while Theodote entertained their wives separately; and so it went for forty days with feasting and dancing and music as the whole city celebrated. The populace enjoyed the festivities whether they approved of the marriage or not. As happy stories spread, Constantine hoped that people would indeed come to think fondly of Theodote, despite their scruples.

Even as a young boy Constantine had been fascinated by the many exotic items brought from far away. By his century, brocaded silk, though expensive, was too common at court to attract his attention; but the arms of Persia and Arabia were the best to be had, and the most beautiful. Beautiful too, and functional, were items of clothing knitted of wool or cotton and shrunk to hug the body. A knitted woolen cap was a godsend in the wet and cold of winter, but he had learned when whoring that the stretchable fabrics were even more delightful hugging the hips of a pretty round bottomed lass like Theodote. He ordered some less functional garments made.

So Constantine lived happily with Theodote but was troubled that he still feuded with his mother. One day he was in a palace garden looking at the ground. His head hurt as it often had since his fall from a horse as a teenager. The palace physicians had been of little help; neither had his mother's icons and relics. If neither potions nor prayers helped, was it that the Lord had some reason to inflict pain on him, or did his prayers go unanswered because his faith was weak?

He dropped to one knee, soiling his dalmatic with dirt and an irremovable grass stain. He dug his fingers into the ground. It was cool and oddly refreshing. *If it weren't for the maggots it might not be so bad to be buried,* he thought. *Much better than lying in a marble sarcophagus in the hard stone vaults of a church. At least I wouldn't be alone here. There are tree roots ... and earthworms. Worms aren't so bad. Actually cute.*

Now one might think that Constantine was entertaining such thoughts out of depression. In a way that was so. The seesaw wars and the seesaw politics between himself and Irene would get anyone down but particularly a Christian trying the impossible. He was trying to love his mother as a good son should and at the same time frustrate her intrigues and rule the empire as God had ordained he do, for the sake not of himself but of the people entrusted to him. Of course, mother felt the same compulsion to rule and she had by far the greater number of adherents to her cause. Marcus Aurelius would have understood the sense of duty that kept Constantine in the game, instead of simply retiring to a life of powerless leisure.

But on another level Constantine was not depressed at all. It may be that he knew he was only dutifully playing out a hand that he could not win. As the poet had written: "It is not possible to fight beyond your strength, even though you strive." There was now, however, one large area of happiness in his life: When the cares of day were put aside, he had Theodote.

There was nothing in this world that Constantine would have wanted more than to finally be free of the cares thrust upon him and his bride; cares that whatever the outcome, he could not simply walk away from and still call himself a man and God's anointed. He lay on the ground listening to the song of insects in the grass and the occasional chirp of one of the Lord's real birds, not the clockwork toys that he had long since tired of. The clouds passed slowly under the mid afternoon sun. One of the guards began to remove his cloak for his emperor to lay upon but Constantine waved him away with a smile and fell asleep.

"Constantine!"

"Hi, girl."

"You're getting too accustomed to my visits."

"To your great ass in that.... What do you call it, a thong?"

"Yes Constantine, a thong; a nice leather thong. These are thongs too." The whip cracked on his thigh, not hard; but now Constantine knew he wasn't dreaming.

"You knew I wasn't a dream. You hoped I wasn't." The valkyrie was smiling her broad smile which had nothing threatening, demonic or cruel in it despite the smack she had just delivered.

"I'm married to someone I love now. You should go away."

"I'm just a dream."

"No you're not." Constantine was gazing at his fantasy with a look of bemusement. Beth was attractive as anything Constantine had ever seen. ... *Saint Christina help me.*

Constantine had to ask. He had to be sure. "Are you a devil?"

"No, and you know it."

"Then what are you? You can't be an angel in that outfit."

"Yes I could be. But I'm not. I am going to tell you a bit about myself. You will not believe me, I fear, but you must act as though you do. This is very important: I won't be born for another twelve hundred years." Beth was no longer smiling; her face was serious, worried. She let the whip drop to her feet. "Just a stage prop to get your attention."

"It did. No, that is wrong. You did."

"Thank you. Was it the thong, then?"

"No. It was you."

At that moment Beth could have reached out and hugged Constantine for those twelve hundred years, but she knew that moment must wait. She looked at him.

"Now stop, or I won't play the bimbo for you. Would you like the whip today?" She picked it up again while affecting a charmingly mean face without a hint of true meanness behind it.

"No, but I got one for Theo to play with. Seriously Beth, the patriarch thinks you are a demon."

"He cannot understand. Just remember in the morning the things I show you now ... And be serious." The whip was gone and Beth held a map in her hand. "I found this map in a book. It is not like any you've seen before. See, it not only shows the roads in Bulgar country and the places along them, but rivers and mountains, the passes and the fords. You will not recall the map itself but you will remember these things when you need to. The theologians would say I'm a guardian angel for showing it to you, but I'll prove I'm not." Beth bent and wiggled her behind. They laughed. "One other thing, Your Serenity, listen to Bertmund. I don't know why."

Constantine looked at the paper and understood though he had never seen anything like it before; only elaborate sketches which simply marked a few towns and features along a single road and indicated nothing of the larger area through which it passed. The junctions of roads and rivers were shown on Beth's map, of course, but also mountain passes, villages and towns; even some contour lines, and geographical features which were not on the main Roman road itself. In his dream Constantine was certain that the strange map from the future would remain forever in his mind. It did not, nor in a few hours would he remember even having dreamed the dream that was not a dream.

"Beth! There is Theo ..."

"I know." For just a moment Beth seemed a little sad. "She will be the joy of your days."

"But ..."

"The Bulgars, Your Serenity."

With the next dawn Constantine joined his troops. Yesterday's dream of Beth was nothing but the remnants of a very pleasant memory which he shook off with the light. Of the map he remembered nothing at all.

Services were held before dawn in the Great Cathedral. Afterwards, as he rode through the crowds that lined his path to the triple walls he thought of how beautiful the earth can seem when death may be near. *"In saffron-colored mantle from the tides of oceans rose the morning to gods and men."* Outside the city defenses he blessed the city and prayed the prayer of victory with his men. John Pikridios had given him another Homeric quote with which to address his troops:

> "Oh friends, be men and let your hearts be strong,
> And let no warrior in the heat of fight
> Do what may bring him shame in others' eyes;
> For more of those who shrink from shame are safe
> Than fall in battle, while with those who flee
> Is neither glory nor reprieve from death."

Only the emperor could see a figure flitting in and out between some cumulus clouds above the marching army, or hear a far away voice singing: "Ho-jo - to - ho!" For just a moment Constantine imagined that the figure swept very close through the sky above him and that the sun reflected off a gilded and bulbous breastplate almost blinding him. He had prayed that Saints Sergius and Bacchus would fight along with his men but certainly this was not one of the military saints. The valkyrie drew a cape across her glinting bosom and when her mount reared in the sky above him Constantine saw or imagined that her legs were bare under the shortest of leather skirts, reinforced with iron plates. Beneath it the straps of a leather panty showed. She was not wearing her usual high heels. Instead her legs were encased in short boots and bound with bands that crossed and recrossed from her pretty feet to the straps of her panty.

"Ho-jo - to - ho! How Say you, Your Serenity? Do you like my battle-dress?"

Nice, Constantine thought in answer, but said nothing. His head hurt. *"Listen to Bertmund."* What was it Bertmund said? *"Belisarius would remind us that a few cataphracts attacking at a decisive moment are of more worth than thousands trying to engage infantry in the woods. He would not hesitate to use those thousands in other ways than combat."* Constantine himself thought that too many cataphracts encumbered the army. *There are also light cavalry and archers. But to rely on them would displease the cataphracts who think they have a right to own the battlefield. They must not feel slighted.*

The Bulgar khan planned an ambush, planned it well to intercept his enemy two day's march from the Via Egnatia, the great stone road along coastal Thrace. The Romans would have to move inland to reach the Struma where according to the blind Nicephorus, they intended to chastise the barbarians who had broken them there four years before, destroying their army and enslaving its remnants. The khan thought he knew every important detail of the Roman attack; its route through the mountains, the strength of the cataphract troop, Constantine and his officers; their strengths and weaknesses.

The sun was not yet very high when advance units of the Bulgar force reached a pretty meadow wet by a shallow stream. The day was bright and seemed yet brighter here where the forest gave way to open marshland. The warriors expected that in another day they would reach the place of their planned ambush of the Roman force moving up the coast. Had they any cause for concern here, Khardam might have sent a few mounted men to scout a rise just beyond the marsh; but his mind was focused elsewhere. *After we eliminate Constantine's army again, the way will be open through Thrace. We'll scare his mother and her gelding general Stauratius plenty. They'll be more than happy to provide us with everything we'll need to reach the Adriatic. Ah, the nice warm sea. My people will forever praise me. A land of grapes and olives with an easy winter.*

The Romans had endured the chill of the previous night without fires. Breakfast had been cold sausage and cold eggs cooked the day before. There was a little wine but the older cataphracts had kept the younger from drinking to the point that they would not be clearheaded. A pink dawn had spread across the sky and lit the marshy field that stretched along the stream a little below them. They had early formed a ragged battle-line hidden among the cypresses. Now they waited, concerned only that their mounts might give them away with a noisy display or that the sun might find a bit of chain mail beneath their cloaks to glint from. Neither happened. If a Roman horse occasionally whinnied to its neighbor, a pat on the neck silenced the mount and the sound was lost among the noise of several thousand moving Bulgars.

The day would be cool; a good day for hard work if entirely too pretty to be killing and mutilating. Some troopers had images of saints painted on their kite-shaped shields. These they kissed. All crossed themselves, their thoughts a mix of fearful devotion and wary attention to the enemy that straggled in bunches of friends into the field below them. Priests moved silently between the cataphracts offering icons to be kissed, prayers for their safety, a few words of faith for the younger men, and absolution. Now Roman battle standards took the morning breeze and their icons were raised before them. A line of dismounted archers, who had been resting on the hill's reverse slope, formed up behind the cavalry.

When the Bulgar men were well away from the tree-line which still hid their families and animals, Constantine, who had been standing beside one of the cypresses, mounted his war-horse and trotted to the line of lancers. He took the banner bearing Christ's Labarum from a standard bearer and rode along the line. He had no brave words of Homer now nor would his soldiers want to hear a speech. He did not even signal the trumpeters but made a hand-signal to the officer commanding the archers.

The air was filled with heavy-headed arrows. After three salvos of agony and death fell on the confused enemy below him, Constantine did give an order to his trumpeters. Before the war trumpets had sounded three notes, many hundred - but not several thousand - cataphracts were forming up in front of the tree-line. Within a minute they were proceeding at a quick walk toward the marsh, being sure to maintain a proper line. The trumpets sounded again and the cataphracts urged their armored mounts to a trot. A third trumpet blast when within a hundred yards of the enemy brought the horses to a gallop and lances to the ready. Now they were so close that they could see the last volley of arrows falling like a summer hail storm before them in the sun.

It was not a pitched battle of thousands but it was a humiliation for Khardam. It was a slaughter but not the slaughter Khan Khardam had planned. His own foot soldiers lay where Roman arrows felled them *en mass*. Roman lances had dispatched hundreds more and Roman spathions several times as many; for Constantine had led an advanced guard into the mountains two days before Khardam.

After much death and many failed attempts to rally his warriors, Khardam and most of his supporting cavalry managed to disengage from their own foot soldiers and escape. Soon the Bulgar infantry followed him into the forest as best they could. A few days later the large and heavy Roman main force finally joined up with their emperor, bringing with them the fire-weapon and the baggage. An attack on Struma had never been intended; nor would the fire-weapon be needed to defend Roman positions against counterattack. Constantine had understood the terrain better than Khardam and had used his light forces effectively without offending the pride of the imperial cataphracts. The Bulgar advance was halted. For seventeen days Constantine's cavalry pursued Khardam with his main army, but the khan would not be brought to combat again. He retreated deep into the forest, then had to face his angry clan leaders. Why was it, they demanded, that he had survived when so many of their kinsmen lay dead? Had he not mocked the Roman emperor for that after the battle near Markella?

Back in the city Stauratius seemed friendly and spoke informally with his emperor in as man-to-man a manner as protocol allowed. The old eunuch now offered advice, rather than discoursing as he had when Constantine had been only a little younger. That might have been because Constantine had proven himself against the khan. It might also have been to promote himself over his rival Aetius in the emperor's mind. In fact it was to put Constantine off his guard.

Despite Constantine's victory, the single-minded monks would not be appeased. To them it was simply Christ's answer to Irene's and their prayers; not the emperor's prowess. A cynic may even wonder if Constantine's divorce and remarriage had truly scandalized them, or did they just want some excuse to depose him. They missed the years of the emperor's minority when Irene had ruled alone? Within weeks of his return there were riots.

"Woe to thee," said Theodote's cousin, quoting Ecclesiastics. "Woe to thee, oh land where thy king is a child." The powerful monk even dared to break communion with his own patriarch over the divorce and remarriage which Tarasios had tacitly allowed. Pleased, Irene began to distance herself from the couple while maintaining the imperial demeanor of a wise ruler.

Though angry with Theodore and the other monks, Constantine tried to mollify them. He even carried to their proper resting place the bones of Saint Euphemia which his iconoclast grandfather had cast into the sea. These had been "miraculously" discovered by the crew of a fishing boat. None the less, Theodote's cousin continued to stand against him, even insulting the emperor in his own palace. Finally Constantine lost patience and began to arrest and exile the monks. But the monks were popular. In Constantinople a huge portion of the population - some estimates say nearly half - spent at least their declining years in monasteries. Their opinion counted.

Within a year Theodote bore a boy child but the babe was born prematurely. In a forlorn attempt to live together in peace Constantine had been relaxing with his mother and many of the court at the hot spring of Prousa. When he heard of the birth he rushed back to the capital. The birth of a grandchild might have drawn another grandmother and father together if only for awhile; instead Irene remained in Prousa with her friends among the strategoi considering how best to remove her son from the throne. His cruelty toward the rebellious cataphracts had been a start. His divorce and remarriage had solidified the opposition. What else might be needed for the crowd to demand that she assert her rule for the sake of the church and the sacred empire?

Constantine's son died before he lived a year. Many blamed that on the boy's parents. It was charged that Constantine had incurred Divine punishment. Although he told himself that his divorce had been best for the empire, he and Theodote worried. Had they just been accommodating themselves? Was it really their desire for each other that had prompted Constantine to believe the charge against Maria? Certainly that was what the monks and populace of Constantinople thought. He and Theodote involved themselves deeper in ceremony to assuage the pain and guilt. Meanwhile, Irene surrounded herself with more stratagoi to whose ambition she was blind, only caring that they be staunch iconodules.

CHAPTER 24

"Basilia, if I may dare say it; but it must be said: The emperor refuses to heed you; and you understand best what is needed."

The empress was listening to one of her generals, a particularly crafty man but an officer of proven ability. He had been one of Stauratius' trusted lieutenants since they had fought against the Sklavians who had ravished Hellas in 782.

"The emperor risks everything by his wars on two fronts. He thinks the Bulgars must be thrown back and a war to wrest all of our lost territories launched against the Saracens. That sounds fine but it is not possible to win."

"We would lose more of our people to Islam?"

"I fear that will be the result, Your Sovereignty."

"But he is the basilios."

"For a time you held that title though you are a woman. It were best for everyone that were the case once again." Those words could cost him his life; but they could also bring promotion and honors.

"Constantine?" Irene asked. The general was deep in treason now. There was nothing more to be lost.

"Let him take holy vows, Empress; or if you will, let him and that girl retire to an estate upon his pledge. I think the emperor has never cared that much to rule. It is a duty he follows and one must respect that. But he could be shown that it is no disgrace that he withdraw and leave affairs in the hands of such capable men as Stauratius and Aetius, and of your holy self, of course. The girl may yet bear him a healthy son to succeed you one day. I believe the patriarch could be persuaded to recognize the marriage and a grandson of yours to carry on the dynasty, so long as Constantine himself not actually rule."

"But would the Asian troops accept that?"

"They would not like it but they have lost faith in him anyway."

Irene dismissed the strategos. He had been forward, true; but not entirely forthright with his empress. But then, Irene was not so simple as to believe he had been. They both knew, though neither would say it, that to convince Constantine to lay down rule in Irene's favor would take more than motherly persuasion.

Possibly that is the way the Lord wishes it. Later that day Irene was on her knees, prostrate in her private chapel.

"Has my son incurred your displeasure, Lord? Do not blame him, please. He is still young and selfish. He does not know that he must think every moment on what is best for the state. I'm sure he and Theodote love each other; they just don't know that it is not important for one who rules. What he must do is trust in me and Stauratius who has never let me down; and in You, of course, who has preserved our city against the enemy. I will go to Studion, Lord, and beg the holy monks to pray for him. He will repent. Then, Lord, will you grant him a healthy son to rule after me?"

It was as though Irene had forgotten her own part. Like Job's friends, she could only believe that her grandchild had died because of sin; yet she would not allow herself to recall that she had encouraged her son's divorce and remarriage. The thing was done. Constantine was unpopular because he had sinned. Her position was stronger now. She could safely fantasize his repentance and an heir, though certainly not his rule.

In April Constantine set out leading a force of twenty thousand against Arab invaders led by Harun al-Rashid himself. There were no heavy cavalry but only more lightly armed horsemen drawn from throughout the empire with which he hoped to entice his enemy to battle. Constantine and his army left the capital without the usual hoopla of church and state. He blessed the city and prayed that Christ would protect it, but there was no grand parade outside the city walls. He left the harbor on a small galley accompanied by his guards and headed directly for the Asian shore. When they landed there was not the usual review of pack animals, archers, cavalry and noble officers of the empire; within hours the army was moving quickly down the coastal road. Even the emperor's baggage was light by Byzantine standards, little more than he would actually need to look presentable: no incense, no hundred dalmatics, no crown for only a helmet would be needed in combat. He carried one very reliable sword and his personal bodyguard a couple of spares. He brought several strong war-horses but not dozens. The only relics he brought were very personal possessions; the only icons were those that would be carried into battle.

Depressed at the loss of her baby, Theodote did not want to remain in the palace surrounded by Irene's rouged and perfumed eunuchs. She accompanied her husband as far as Attaleia where the air was fresh, there to await his return from battle. For long periods she did not ride in her coach. The troops saw their young empress beside their emperor as though ready to do battle herself. That could not be, of course, and the lady did not affect some parody of military dress. That would have been to mock the troops under Constantine's banner. But she did not travel crowned and bejeweled either. She wore baggy trousers after the style of the Arab enemy with only her palla drawn up to cover her face and hair. She sat a horse as well as any of them. Unlike Maria, Theodote was from one of the capital's oldest and most respected families. She had the right to be proud for her family was well-connected both with the aristocracy and the church. The cousin who had turned against her was to win renown as one of the greatest of Orthodox saints. When he was not admonishing the secular authorities about some delinquence of spirituality at court he wrote hymns that are still sung in Orthodox churches. None of that mattered to a hunting cheetah. There was no haughtiness in her. When the chill of evening fell upon their nightly camp she put on a warm black woolen cloak. The soldiers would discuss after what barbarian fashion it might be modeled but none could answer the question. As the army approached enemy-held territory, she was left at a convent to pray with the nuns for her husband's victory.

Stauratius also rode with Constantine. The emperor hoped that if Stauratius alone could not put an end to Arab spoliation of the eastern provinces, possibly they could together. It might be a very great victory. With Constantine's reliance on speedy light cavalry Harun himself might be killed or taken captive. That would increase the emperor's prestige enormously. A victory for Constantine would not help Stauratius or Irene however, so when they approached a village held by the Saracens the logothete of the dromos paid scouts to report that the enemy had departed into their own secure lands.

"How can this be?" Constantine raged, but Stauratius had prepared the lie.

"Harun fears you, Most Sacred Majesty".

"He could easily field twice, three times our forces."

"Weak Saracen archers, Your Sovereignty. He dare not face even our light cavalry in hand-to-hand combat, and so the Arab fades away. There is nothing for it. Their horses are the best in the world while many of ours are of poor stock. They are gone days ago. We can not catch them; nor have you enough men or any artillery to besiege even his frontier fortresses; certainly not anything like we'd need to attack Baghdad itself. We must be patient, Your Sovereignty. There will be other days."

Constantine knew the truth of what his subordinate said. Disappointed, he returned with Theodote to Constantinople. There Stauratius' friends were spreading a rumor to further damage him. They implied that it was the emperor who had refused battle with Harun; that Stauratius' advance had been aborted by Constantine in fear of an Arab ambush. What popularity Constantine might have regained among the populace and the army soon melted away, while Irene continued to discreetly interview those stratagoi who might support a coup. Now it was necessary for Stauratius to act quickly and decisively against his master before the evil intent of these latest lies could become known. In such an event even Irene might not have been unable to save him. Staurarius quietly gathered accomplices with promises of promotion, estates, and honors. He warned the more religious that the emperor might even turn iconoclast to ingratiate himself again with his formerly loyal supporters in the Armeniac theme.

As palace politics gained momentum in Constantinople, in New Jersey, Beth tossed in her bed. She could not sleep. Eventually she gave up trying and lifted her bedside telephone. In a few minutes she had dressed and was enroute to the city.

"What's on your mind, milady?"

Eddy Miller drew up a chair at the *Purring Pussycat* where Beth was already sitting with her face in a mug of straight black coffee.

"I shouldn't have called. It was silly of me to bother you in the middle of the night."

"I'm flattered. Here I'm sitting with the prettiest lady in America and she thinks she's bothering me."

Beth smiled a thin smile, not the broad one she kept for the camera, just one of those smiles that women are expected to have on their faces at all times. Sometimes Beth wished that she were a man so that she could scowl without men thinking it was PMS.

"Do you think a person can love someone she's never met?"

"Yes."

"Really. How?"

"It's easy to love someone you don't have to deal with. It's the people you know who get under your skin."

"It's the guy I dream about ... Trouble is: I don't remember anything much about him in the morning."

"Whoa now! Have you been reading too much lately?"

"No. I shouldn't have called you. It doesn't matter. I know this guy and he knows me ... and we always will. I have to do something for him but I don't know what yet."

"We all love many people in our lives, Beth. We just marry one of them."

Beth reached across the table and took Edward's hand. "But you're real, Eddy; not some dream." Then she laughed. "Hey, I'm supposed to be the fantasy. ...Say, Eddy; can I stay at your place tonight? its a long ride back to Newark."

Weeks passed in Constantinople but on a lovely July day as he

190

returned to the Great Palace after a horse race in the Hippodrome, Constantine was warned that an armed coup to depose him was afoot. His mother had secluded herself in the Eleutherian palace and troops of the Constantinopolitan guard were marching on the Great Palace. Quickly he armed himself and took ship with Theodote to join the few regiments still loyal to him. These were gathering on the Asian shore. These few troops were not to be underestimated for they were at hand while Irene's supporters were afar save for a regiment of guards in the city itself. Furthermore, many of the stratagoi who had pledged loyalty to her were primarily concerned with maintaining their own high positions and would pledge to any passing breeze.

"Soldiers of Rome," their strategos addressed the Asianarmy drawn up within sight of the city with the tutor John Pikridios behind him in a borrowed mail-shirt and with a sword belted to his waist, "that high-handed half-man, Stauratius, has finally done it. As I speak he dares to confront the Elect of God, himself. For too long this city and the empire have been wracked by dispute over some pictures and only our Gracious Sovereign has tried to bring civil peace. Let there be an end to it now. Let us be rid of Stauratius. Let his lady - the Basilios' mother - finally retire from the palace that there may be peace among us. Then as we should, let us follow our Sacred Majesty's battle standard against Christ's true enemies and throw the Saracens back to the sands of Arabia."

It appeared that the coup would fail. At news that her son had escaped the city and was gathering supporters at Chrysopolis across the Bosphorus, Irene was so frightened that she was about to again flee to her son and beg his pardon as she had in 789. However, Stauratius, fearful for his eyes, persuaded her to take heart. Together they frightened those generals who had supported her but now feared Constantine's revenge, warning them that Irene would betray them to her son if they wavered, and that they could not expect clemency from him. The emperor would be resolute as he had been with the Armeniac plotters. For the traitorous generals the coup must go forward or they would face death or mutilation.

They secreted agents among some of Constantine's guards who were leaving the city to join him on the Asiatic side. When they landed there these false friends lied and feigned loyalty. They even swore oaths by the Mother of God. They begged him to return to the palace which they told him would soon be secured by loyal troops. Constantine knew that to be across the Bosphorus was nothing; to hold the city was all important. He believed them. When they returned with him to the emperor's dock in the harbor of Boucoleon they helped their basilios to land with the utmost grace and humility, but inside the Great Palace they laid their hands on the

Anointed of God and ordered him to the porphyry chamber where he had been born twenty-six years before. Constantine succeeded in looking brave before his mother's minions who had come to put out his eyes, even hoping that he would die. For seventeen days the sun was darkened but on the eighteenth his fever broke and the sun shone in the heavens again.

... Theogenius the monk

The weeks following Constantine's blinding were days of terror throughout the city. There was terror and confusion and denial everywhere. The empress, of course, denied any knowledge and assured both clergy and people that the atrocity had been committed against her intent. Of course it had. Who would believe such a horror of any mother much less the pious Irene? Troops and secret police tramped up and down the city, into attics and basements. There were arrests but in the end no one was punished. After all, conventional wisdom - probably emanating from the Great Palace itself - had it that though the blinding of Constantine had been a great sin it had perhaps been best for the body politic. Since no one maimed could rule in Byzantium the good and holy empress would now rule alone. Constantine - fine fellow though he was save for his indiscretions, and certainly brave - was charged with weakness toward the iconoclasts and of fomenting unnecessary confrontation with the barbarian neighbors of the empire. Better to simply contain the Arab threat. Better to pay off the bothersome Bulgars and send them west to trouble that usurper of the imperial dignity, Charles the Frank, who since the previous Christmas had the effrontery to call himself Emperor in the West.

There was rumor that Charles had dared to again raise the possibility of marriage with the empress. That would give the empire back the western provinces and in particular Rome itself, but it would mean a wretched barbarian on the throne of Byzantium. Certainly it were better that he remain in Frankland even with his stolen title. After all, it was just a charade. All agreed that the Bulgars would soon put an end to it.

Constantine, sorely wounded, was taken to the Eleutherian palace, the place of his mother's honorable exile in 791. There he was placed under the care of fine physicians. That could be allowed. After all, he had no direct knowledge of who had ordered his mutilation. He knew no more than anyone else. Now he was without power and near to death. His most trusted supporters had either fled the city or been sent to distant posts and monastic retreats. It was safe to let him live. His mother took solace in that she had been able to preserve his life. She dared not visit him but prayed that the saints would help him and bring him peace. They did.

CHAPTER 25

Theodote held her husband and sank to her knees. "I am smiling," she said softly. He began to braid the hair that fell over her shoulders nearly to her waist. Not only did he feel her and inhale her perfume, he saw her clearly in his mind's eye. She was beautiful.

This is all he'd ever wanted for himself. Some nice sex with someone who really cared about him for himself. He well knew that the days after his blinding had been nearly as hard on Theodote as on him. She'd had to walk the line between antagonizing the empress by outspokenness and being seen as hardhearted. It had not been easy for her, but if she were to keep Constantine alive and give him some kind of peace in acceptance of God's holy will, then she had to act with care. Irene had turned against her too now, just as she had against Maria and her own son. Theodote felt that the only thing which kept the empress from ordering their execution was fear of damnation.

They had retired to a privacy that, as emperor, Constantine had never enjoyed. They were careful not to say anything that might get them killed; not to the servants - no doubt spies of Irene - nor to the few old friends who still dared to visit, bringing with them dainties from their kitchens along with much court gossip. But perhaps it did not matter if these old friends chatted a bit too much. By tradition no one who was mutilated could represent Christ on the throne of Byzantium. It would be useless for Constantine to consider ever regaining it; so Theodote, who until then had not been particularly known for piety, had let it be known that her main concern at this time was prayer that her husband would not die embittered toward his own mother. For herself as a faithful citizen, she would pray for the good of the empire and that Irene would lament her grievous sins and do penance. More than that Irene could not expect and would be suspicious of, less might get them both killed or at least sent to monasteries. That must not happen. Theodote would not be separated from her husband.

When she had done what the church forbade but which everyone did, Theodote and Constantine went to bed. *Do not blame my husband if he cannot control his urges, Lord. We cannot all be monks and saints. I do not believe that sex must be only for bearing children, whatever the monks might say. He has so little else now and, Lord, my husband was not raised to do without. The bishops cast each other into hell just for not agreeing about icons or on the procession of the Holy Persons; but Saint Paul says that none of that is important, only love.* Theodote entwined her legs in Constantine's. She knew that he loved her and that was all that mattered between man and woman and God. Constantine was deep in dreams.

"Not sexy enough, your gracious majesty? This is the sort of thing I like to wear when I'm not with you. Of course it isn't practical for most of the time but I like it. "

Indeed, while not sexy in a conventional manner - not leather or short or revealing - Beth's dress was extremely feminine.

"I told you I'm a nineteen-fifties girl. In the twenties my ma wore much shorter skirts. Hey, maybe someday we'll be able to show our asses in public again … nice tiny skirts and tiny shorts. You'd like that, yes?" Constantine, who his whole life had been surrounded by well-covered women, was nearly overwhelmed by that image and grew stiff again despite himself. "Do you like this though? I'll bet you do. You'll remember I wore it once before when you were only seventeen. We call it a prom dress."

Constantine did indeed remember. Beth's skirt was long and bouncy, a very soft and wide cup that swayed with her movement, stiff but not rigid like imperial vestments for it was made of deep green velvet stiffened by crinolines. The sleeves of the dress were some silk-like material puffed above the elbows, and on her feet were high heels. They were not the high-heeled boots that Beth usually affected, but were instead her high-heeled strappy shoes. Constantine could see that her feet and the calves of her legs were encased in dark nylon hose such as no one else would imagine for centuries.

Beth whirled and when she did her skirt flew high for just a moment, revealing that the tight stockings went all the way past her knees and ended high on her thighs in dark lace bands held by short straps to some kind of belt. Her black panties showed too, and that was more erotic than anything Constantine had ever been able to imagine when he had been able to see - even Beth's thong.

Saint Christina preserve my soul from hell..

Beth curtsied. "You like it, don't you, Your Serenity?" Despite Constantine's fall from power, Beth still used his imperial titles.

"Yes, Christ help me. I do."

"It's mostly velvet. I don't think you've got that here yet. Feel it. Nice, yes?"

The emperor touched the skirt of Beth's dress. It felt as good as a woman.

"A spanking would be nice." Beth lowered her eyes modestly.

"It used to be me who got spanked."

"Not today. An emperor should be spanked from time to time, but I know your mind, Your Serenity. You'd like to spank me in this dress, wouldn't you?

"Yes. But I'll not betray poor Theodote."

"You won't. You won't even want to."

Beth raised the velvet skirt above her stocking tops and lay across the former emperor's lap, her black panties high in the air. Then Constantine awoke to his eternal night. Theodote, beside him in their bed, was rubbing her own young rump.

"I had a dream, my husband. A strange dream. I was wearing the oddest, most beautiful clothing; and you were spanking me." Theodote waited a few moments and then pushed her rump toward her husband for him to touch. "Would you like to do that?"

"Yes."

It might seem weird to suggest that a man who had ruled over much of the western world and reigned over all of it would finally find peace and even happiness, blinded by his own mother and exiled to a minor palace. But he had assiduously studied Marcus Aurelius as a boy and would tell us that what his eyes had seen in twenty six years had been treachery, duplicity, and vain ambition in those who claimed his friendship, even in she who had borne him. Not since he had been old enough to understand danger had he ever gone to sleep feeling completely secure against assassins. In fantasy the emperor had escaped this world and in Theodote he had found what earthly joy he had most wished for. Now he was no longer required to lead the armies of Byzantium and no longer was his daily life circumscribed by rigid ritual. No longer was he lied to. If he could not see the boys who played ball under his window, he could hear their shouts and the laughter of the young girls who watched these young bulls and future husbands prepare by play for manhood. If he no longer participated as the equal of the apostles in hours-long ceremonies in the great cathedral of Hagia Sophia, he could now sit alone in prayerful meditation.

Time passed and Constantine did his best to please his wife. It was a joy to try to please another person; one which had largely been denied him when he had been emperor. They did have a few servants and Theodote quickly learned that her husband hated being fussed over. He'd had more than enough of that in the Great Palace, often by dignitaries with no real liking for him but who could not be dismissed because of their inherited duty and privilege to serve the basilios. Constantine enjoyed playing the Lavouto for Theo, listening together to bawdy stories that no one would have told the elect of God, and occasionally tickling. He would sing to her as blind Homer might have. He dreamed no more of Beth; in Theodote he was content.

Irene triumphed over her son, but her triumph in the political sphere was brief. Within five years of his blinding she was overthrown and exiled to the island of Lesbos where she soon died a bitter, poor, and unpleasant old woman who fed herself by spinning yarn for local shopkeepers. Yet in the way which most mattered to her the empress' ambition was satisfied; for restoring icon worship she is considered a saint in the eastern church.

Time passed. We do not know how many years of peace Constantine shared with Theodote but in God's time he himself lay dying. Unaware of this, his wife was asleep beside him, her hands grasping his arm. Dawn was breaking.

"Come dear."

"I see you, Beth. It's been so long. This truly is not a dream. I can really see. ... Is it time then?"

"Yes. Do you like what you see?" Beth stood bare-breasted looking down at Constantine; bare breasted but with two crystal bells that swung tinkling from her nipples. They took the morning light and broke it into colors which seemed to match the music of the bells. Constantine was glad that he could see again.

"Of course I do. But should I be afraid?"

"You need not be. You once said that with all the glory of being emperor the only thing you really wanted out of life was a little nice sex - which you've had with Theodote - and when you die for Christ to say 'You made it.'"

"You know about that?"

"Yes."

"Beth, you must be an angel."

"No. Something like that to some guys though."

"Yes, I guess angels wouldn't have belled tits."

Beth lifted her whip and put on a mean face. "They're a present for you. I doubt that my fiancée would even like them. She held out a delicate hand on which a small stone sparkled. But you do, don't you? They're just for you, *Your Lusty Majesty*." Beth's face broke out in the familiar grin.

"Is it OK that I like you wearing things like that?" Constantine asked.

"You made it. It's OK."

"But?"

"Would you prefer I didn't?" For just a brief moment Constantine saw, or imagined that he saw, Beth dressed as a proper lady and with her hair put up in a bun.

"No! ....Tell me those lice at the palace won't be coming too."

196

"No. They've got their world, the world of human history; and this is your world now. You will be with God and not know time except as something that has been and can be seen complete now, as one might see a picture. You were in their pitiful world for awhile but God will not allow them in yours - in ours."

"Mother?"

"Does it matter?"

"No. Somehow I don't feel that it does. But shouldn't it matter to me? She's my mother. Tell me that the demons will not get her."

"She bore you but she has always been far from you. There is no reason for guilt."

"But she loves God."

"In her way she reveres some sort of god, I suppose… and she's gotten the satisfaction she sought. Do not feel bad. Because you have loved her and forgiven her sin, she will not be damned; but neither is she blessed. Few are blessed and fewer are damned. Many just cease to be … Jesus said that he'd vomit them out of his mouth. Yet that which is divine - the spark of life even in them - can never die."

"But you, Beth, you were never more than a dream, an imagined thing."

"Would you insult me?" Beth danced to jingle her bells. Her smile was broad, bright as the sun, and happy as a child's. "I am real, just from another time, as you are from another time in my history. I am your dream and you are mine. Hey, we don't have to worry about time - about history now. But if you'd prefer I were from your time you can call me the Rotrud of your fantasy as you did for so long; but not Theodote whom you love. I'm your pinup; I am not your wife.

"Now don't think about those lice, as you call them. We cannot change the hell of time, but we have more, much more."

"I love Theo but Our Lord said that no one will marry or be given in marriage in the life after this life. I don't want to leave her."

"Our Savior was talking property rights, not love, Your Serenity … May I call you Constantine now? There is no time or jealousy or temporal contracts in the Lord."

"Will I see you again?"

"Forever, dearest; and Theodote, and John Pikridios. You'll know Rotrud who is as sweet as you knew she was, if not quite as you liked to imagine her."

"You never called me 'dearest' before."

"Until now it would have been improper. I was just the dream of a frustrated Roman emperor, you thought; and nothing more. But now it shall be different."

Beth stood by the bedside of the emperor of the Romans preparing, as she knew he wished, to carry his spirit to some Valhalla. But this would be better. She slipped off her bells, smiled a warm smile, and became very real to him.

"Into Thy Hands, Oh Lord, I commend his spirit."

Meanwhile in the scriptorium of the convent of Chelles, Rotrud thought of what might have been. She was the daughter of Great Charles and that was enough. Still, she had nearly been empress in the east, able to wield real power like Constantine's mother. No; it was better this way; she would not have herself compared with that woman. Rotrud mused on what might have been, but she was not sad. A presence seemed to always sit beside her on her bench, a cheerful woman that she seemed able to lean on for support when the days wore on and on and the pains and cold of a Frankland winter hung about her malevolently. Taking up her brush and secure in God's will for her and the lover she had never met and never would - or so she thought - she began in the margin of a book of poems to draw little bells that seemed to sway and jingle.

The Isaurian dynasty was ended. The new emperor, Nicephorus I, gave Constantine an imperial funeral.

AFTERWORD

An aged man is but a paltry thing,
A tattered coat upon a stick, unless
Soul clap its hands and sing, and louder sing
For every tatter in its mortal dress.
Nor is there singing school but studying
Monuments of its own magnificence;
And Therefore I have sailed the seas and come
To the holy city of Byzantium.

... William Butler Yeats

In the year 330 of the common era, the Roman emperor Constantine I (the Great) who had legalized the practice of Christianity in the empire, founded a second capital city on the Bosphorus where Europe meets Asia. That city, present day Istanbul, replaced the village of Byzantium. Though Constantine named it Nova Roma (New Rome), it was commonly called Constantinople or simply "the city" in deference to its founder and importance. It would never have been called Byzantium by its inhabitants, nor would they have referred to the Later Roman Empire of the East as Byzantine. These terms are modern usage but they are regularly used by historians and throughout this narrative; though never in dialogue.

Within two hundred years, old Rome itself was in the hands of barbarian invaders and western Europe was politically divided. Yet the empire did not die. The term Roman remained and came to signify both a single Christian unity of all the European and Mediterranean kingdoms vaguely centered politically in Constantinople and spiritually in Rome; and also the Eastern Empire itself: "the Land of the Romans." (The terminology continues today in Romania.) For centuries this empire was the largest and most powerful state west of China. By the time of our story, however, all of North Africa and much of the Middle East had fallen to Moslem Arabs. The Islamic caliphate of the Abbasids held a greater extent of land and equaled Byzantium culturally. Western Europe was culturally far below both.

In the year 800 the Frankish king Charles the Great (Charlemagne) was crowned by the pope "Emperor in the West." This was the beginning of the Holy Roman Empire. Our story is set just before this event which

199

divided the theoretical political unity of the Christian world.

The background is the dispute over icons. Before our story opens three Byzantine emperors had outlawed holy pictures as graven images. Our story makes no mention of Leo III, called the Isaurian, who first banned images, and only tangentially mentions his iconoclast son, Constantine V. His son, Leo IV, also an iconoclast, was our Constantine's father. The monks of Constantinople fiercely opposed iconoclasm. They felt that although the God of the Hebrew Scriptures had forbidden images of God, Jesus was also a man and could be depicted in art. Once that door was opened the depiction of saints and angels followed. When emperor Leo IV died, his widow, Irene, restored icons. This might have been all right. The council restoring icons made it plain that they only represented Christ and the saints and were not in themselves to be venerated. In practice, however, people thought of icons as mystically linked to the persons they represented.

After Irene's rule, icons were again restricted for awhile but not absolutely banned. Effectively Irene and the monks had sounded the death knell for iconoclasm.

At the same time two heresies were rampant. The Monophysites denied the human nature of Christ, for which reason they were iconoclast too. The Paulitians, a Gnostic sect, denied entirely the worth of the material world. To them Christ was only an image, not a man. All material things, and the orthodox church itself, were the work of an antigod. This made them iconoclasts also, though that was the least part of their heresy.

Irene and Leo had a son, Constantine VI. Leo associated the boy with himself as basilios; but Constantine was only ten years old when his father died and Irene became regent for the young emperor. Seven years later when he should have assumed all power, Irene would not surrender it.

The period is sometimes called the Byzantine dark ages. It roughly corresponds with the latter years of the period sometimes still called the dark ages in western Europe. This was the time of the Carolingian Renaissance that is credited with the beginnings of recovery in the west. To call it a dark age in the east is, however, only true by reference to Byzantium's own cultural glory both earlier and later. Byzantine civilization at no time sank to the level of the barbarian West. Still, rather little is known of this time in Byzantium.

Historians have not been kind to Irene's chief advisor, the eunuch Stauratius, for under his ruling hand the empire lost as many battles as it won. Yet these were more skirmishes than critical battles and the imperial borders remained generally intact if fluid. In the absence of greatness he has been charged with being ineffective and irresolute. As a minister he was certainly ambitious and devious and it is hard to see him as ever putting the good of his country before his own good; but possibly, like so many other national leaders, he did not differentiate between them. It seems his strategic vision was shortsighted and directed only at immediate containment of the empire's and Irene's neighbors and sometime-enemies.

And what neighbors! Stauratius administered Irene's empire and fought its battles in the historical shadow of Carolus Magnus - Charlemagne - in the west, and of Harun al-Rashid, of *Arabian Nights* fame, in Baghdad to the East. None of this excuses his devious plots and pettiness. It was Stauratius, fearing the popularity of a now battle-hardened emperor, who would undermine Constantine's last campaign. In doing so he served Irene but betrayed the Anointed of God. It was he and others like him who gave the Byzantines a reputation for double dealing in the west; not to mention a prejudice in western historians against all imperial eunuchs, many of whom served the empire well for over a thousand years.

In the years immediately following our story Stauratius and the other highly placed eunuch, Aetius, continued plotting against each other, hoping to have a relative marry into the imperial family. The aging Irene and the aging eunuchs became increasingly unpleasant, suspicious, and vicious; and none of their plots came to fruition.

Besides the Arab threat and internal feuding over icons, Byzantium in the eighth and ninth centuries faced incursions by Bulgar tribesmen who had already occupied territory north of the Danube. Although their leader, Khan Khardam, failed in his attempts to move further south, within a decade of the deaths of Khardam, Constantine, and Irene, his successor extended Bulgar holdings into Moesia.

Six centuries after our story, Constantinople fell; not to the pagan Bulgars or Moslem Arabs of Constantine's time, but to Moslem Turks. After a history of over eleven hundred years the Byzantine Empire passed into history. In Constantine and Irene's time however, the frontiers just barely held.

Though based upon the chronicle of Theophanes, the story contains important elements of fiction. The fictional characters are noted in the appendix, the most important being Beth, and the Franks Ricolf and Bertmund. All of these are entirely fictional persons, though Beth's persona is loosely based upon the lives of pinup girls in the 1950s, and inspired by Bettie Page. Beth is certainly idealized but one might remember that before the birth control pill there was more inhibition and less intimate sex between unmarried men and women than today; and that religion played a very important part in most people's lives, morals, and fears. Even those who were sexually freer than the erotic but chaste character of Beth usually preferred to pretend otherwise. Bettie Page's smile first attracted this teenage boy's attention decades before her authorized biography *Bettie Page, The Life Of A Pin Up Legend* appeared. Though best remembered today for fetish poses that projected an image of innocent naughtiness, it was that sunshine smile in bikini and lingerie poses that first overwhelmed millions of guys looking at men's magazines in the 1950s. Of course the similarity between Beth and Bettie ends there. Beth was inspired by, but not modeled upon Bettie. That would have been impossible even had the author wished since little is known of Ms. Page's actual thoughts in the '50s. Bettie was Baptist not Catholic, and she is famed for her raven black bangs whereas Beth has blonde hair in braids. The character of Beth is, in fact, a conglomerate of many girls that I knew. I did, however, borrow Bettie's smile. But how to describe that smile? I found the perfect analogy in Townes Van Zandt's lovely *Tecumseh Valley:*

The name she gave was Caroline / daughter of a miner / her ways were free / it seemed to me / that sunshine walked beside her

Charlemagne and Irene did consider marriage for themselves but that was later, after Charles assumed the title of Emperor in the West, whereas in the story it is placed at the beginning of Irene's reign. It is not impossible, however, that they'd also have considered it earlier.

It is reported by Theophanes that Constantine was deeply infatuated with Rotrud whom he never met, but there is no report that he ever received a concussion either as a child or while pursuing Arabs. There was at least one attempt on his life but it too was later and did not resemble the attack described which is provided only to advance the story. Nicephorus did try to take the throne after Constantine's defeat by Khan Khardam, but there is no report that his plot involved the Bulgar enemy. The sexual indiscretions of Irene, Aetius, Stauratius, and Nicephorus are fiction, though in Byzantium as elsewhere, these things might have happened - there is little documentation except for Theophanes' chaste chronicle.

The necessity for sacramental marriage had not been fully enforced in Carolingian Gaul and Rotrud (or Rotrude or Hruodrud, or Erythro in Greek) had a son by one of Charlemagne's courtiers before entering the convent. (Somewhat later than in the story since he was born in the year 800, the same year that the pope crowned Charlemagne as Emperor in the West.) Charlemagne loved his daughters and thought nothing of them having children out of wedlock but would not let them marry. Rotrud's son became an abbot.

I have not set down every known event of Constantine's life, however I have left all the major events. Whether they advance the narrative or not, they certainly complicate it. Historians dispute much of the history of the time: for example, whether it was Irene or Charlemagne who broke the engagement of Constantine and Rotrud; and whether Constantine was a weak or a moderately strong ruler. My own feeling is that he was a personally brave and effective military leader within a framework of the possible. Though details of battles are fictional the results are not. Constantine did make effective use of lighter forces than was usual in Byzantium. He did what was possible; it was impossible to assert himself further.

The major contemporary history is the Chronicle of the monk and historian Theophanes Confessor which has been translated by Cyril Mango and Roger Scott, and more recently by Harry Turtledove (who also authored the alternative history: *Agent of Byzantium* and a fictionalized biography of the Emperor Justinian.) Relatively little has been published in English about Byzantium but for anyone who might wish an overview of the Eastern Empire I recommend Charles Diehl's classic: *Byzantium, Greatness and Decline*. It is a pleasant appreciation and while currently out of print copies are readily available. In the same mode is Tamara Talbot Rice's excellent *Everyday Life in Byzantium*. For a more recent and academic cultural study there is Deno John Geanakoplos' *Byzantium: Church, Society, and Civilization Seen Through Contemporary Eyes*. For a complete history the most recent study is John Julius Norwich's three volume *Byzantium*. All these, however, are general studies and while Byzantine civilization is often viewed as static it lasted over eleven hundred years from the legalization of Christianity in the Roman Empire until within forty years of Columbus sailing to the Americas. There was change. Unfortunately there is sparse information on Byzantium's middle period in which our story is set though Henry Maguire's scholarly *Byzantine Court Culture from 829 to 1204* begins with the period immediately following.

LIST OF CHARACTERS

MAJOR CHARACTERS

Aetius – A eunuch and highly placed advisor and personal favorite of Irene.

Bertmund of Loutern - A younger protégé of Ricolf, six years older than Constantine (fictional).

Beth Pagane - 1950s pinup model (fictional).

Charles, Carolus, Charlemagne, - At this time king of the Franks, later to be crowned by the pope as emperor in the west.

Constantine VI - Son of Byzantine iconoclast emperor Leo V and the Empress Irene.

Irene - Succeeds as iconodule empress regent of 10 year old Constantine on the death of Leo.

John Pikridios - Chief tutor and friend of Constantine.

Khardam - Khan of the Bulgars.

Maria of Amnia - First wife of Constantine.

Nicephorus - Uncle 'foros (with four never seen brothers) - Half brother of Leo IV.

Rotrud - Daughter of Charlemagne. Although only briefly mentioned in our story, Rhotrud bore a son after the breakup with Constantine; ((Charlermagne would not allow his daughters to marry.) Later than in our storuy she did join the convent at Chesses and together with her aunt Gisela appears to have led a pious life.

Ricolf of Bacheim - An advisor and diplomat to Charlemagne (fictional).

Stauratius - Eunuch, First minister, **Logothete of the Dromos**, and general (strategos) of Irene.

Theodote - Handmaiden of Irene and second wife of Constantine.

MINOR CHARACTERS

Alexios Mousoulem - General who at first supports Constantine but then turns against him.

Aaron - Son of the caliph al-Mahdi. Later known as **Harun al-Rashid** (see) which terminology is used in this story even before his ascent to the throne.

Comantes - Client of Nicephorus (fictional).

Cyril - A monk of Studion who has a dream, the only monk of Studion who puts charity before his conception of orthodoxy (fictional).

Elpidios - Byzantine rebel and traitor who flees to the Arabs.

Eunuch (Unnamed) - Appears only once. A Court dignitary who negotiates details of Rotrud's betrothal with Ricolf and Bertmund (fictional).

Eustathius of Dalmatia - Secret police spy (fictional).

Furface – Constantine's cat.

Harun al-Rashid - (Aaron the Just) became Abbasid caliph in 786 succeeding his father, al-Mahdi, and elder brother, al-Hadi.

Lucia - (fictional) The ambitious and depraved slave of Khardam. See also: **Urophagia.**

Miller, Eddy - Photographer and friend of Beth (fictional). It was not too unusual in the '50s when many people were "reserved" out of religious belief, fear of disease, of pregnancy, or scandal to be uncertain about another's sexual orientation. Homosexuality was thought of as far less common than it is today.

Paul - Patriarch to 784 AD.

Platon - A saint and abbot of SaccudionUncle of Theodore of Studion.

Strategos 1 (Unnamed General) - Appears only once suggesting that Constantine be removed just before the final coup (fictional).

Strategos 2 (Unnamed General) - Appears only once to rally troops to support Constantine during the final coup (fictional).

Tarasios - Succeeds Paul as patriarch. Previously he had been a holy layman.

Theodore of Studion - Saint. Succeeded his uncle Platon as abbot of Saccudion near Constantinople. Moved the monks to Studion within the city. Cousin of Theodote.

PEOPLE MENTIONED

Absalom - Old testament son of King David. When entangled by a tree branch, he was killed by his enemies. (Samuel: 2)

Acacius, St. - Patron saint for sufferers from headaches. A perhaps fictional military saint martyred by the Romans who were said to have crowned him with a ring of thorns in imitation of Christ's passion.

Adrian I – Pope, 772 – 795.

Aeneas - Fled burning Troy with his father on his back, went to Italy to what would be Rome, protagonist of the *Aeneid* in Roman literature.

Alcuin of York - English tutor at Charlemagne's court. He was one of the foremost scholars of his day and is regarded as a key figure in the Carolingian cultural revival.

Anna - Wife of Nicephorus (fictional).

Anthemius of Thalles - He and Isidorus Miletis were the architects of Hagia Sophia and were so highly regarded that - unusual for the time - their names have been preserved for posterity.

Antonina - Wife of **Belisarius** (see). Although of doubtful virtue, she bravely accompanied and assisted Belisarius on many of his expeditions.

Aristotle - 4th century BC philosopher. Aristotle's strict methodology is generally regarded as the source of the scientific method. He proved that the earth was round because it formed a curve on the moon during a lunar eclipse. Other proofs were known to the Byzantines, such as a ship's masts appearing on the horizon before the hull.

Attila the Hun - In the fifth century he briefly founded an empire stretching from Germany to the Urals and from the Danube to the Baltic Sea. Famed for their cruelty, the Huns threatened both Rome and Constantinople. Attila was known as the Scourge of God.

Augustine, St. - Fourth century doctor of the church. Primary theologian of the Eastern church.

Bacchus – See **Sergius and Bacchus** and **Sergius and Bacchus, church of.**

Basil, St. - Fourth century monk who laid down the first "rule" of eastern monasticism, so that monks who had previously lived solitary lives could now live together in monasteries.

Belisarius - Sixth century general who reconquered North Africa and Italy for Justinian. Known for his loyalty and sense of honor, he is also credited with being one of the world's ten best generals.

Boudicca - British queen who led a rebellion against Roman rule in the 1st century AD.

Caesar, Julius - General who ended the Roman Republic and wrote his famous commentaries describing his conquest of Gaul. Later caesar became a Roman title, originally for secondary co-rulers but in Byzantine times extended to other members of the imperial family.

Charles Martel (the hammer) - Grandfather of Charlemagne.

Children of Constantine - Two daughters (by Maria) were raised in a convent. One later married an emperor. A son, Leo, (by Theodote) died within a year of his birth. A second son was born to Constantine and Theodote after Constantine's fall but was considered disqualified for imperial rule because the church did not recognize Constantine's second marriage. Even had the church been persuaded to accept that, he would not have been of age to rule before the overthrow of the dynasty.

Christina, St. - Third century martyr, and a very beautiful virgin who was tortured by her pagan father for destroying idols.

Christophorus, Photus, Bardas - Three highly regarded stratagoi who joined Constantine in battle against the Bulgars at Markella. Bardas was killed in this, Constantine's first major battle, together with his iconoclast supporter Michael Lachanodrakon and several other top generals.

Clement I - Pope and saint, patron of boatmen.

Constantine I (The Great) - Fourth century emperor, legalized Christianity and founded Constantinople.

Constantine V – Iconoclastic grandfather of Constantine VI.

Cyril of Jerusalem - Fourth century saint and Doctor of the Church .

David, King – C. 1000 BC. As a youth he slew the Philistine giant Goliath. Later as king he drove the Philistines out of Israel.

Demetrios, St. - Military saint martyred in Thessaloníki during the Roman persecutions.

Diana the Huntress - Pagan Greek deity, patron of the hunt. Although Constantinople was a Christian city from its foundation and the mosaic representation in this story is fictional, it would not have been unusual. Not only was the Great Palace built when the practice of Christianity had just been legalized in the Roman Empire and artistry was still in pagan mode, but classical motifs and references were common throughout the history of Byzantium. Classical learning was far more honored than in the barbarian west, the connection with the ancient world never having been severed.

Drungarios of the watch – A brigade commander and responsible for the security of military camps.

Eisenhower, Dwight - U. S. president 1953 - 1960 during an era of unmatched prosperity in the country following World War II and the Korean conflict. But this was also a period of cold war with the Soviet Union and cultural stagnation and sexual repression at home, enlivened by the beatnik movement in the arts. Almost anything showing a woman with even her navel uncovered was considered marginally pornographic; much more fetish photographs which were never shown publicly.

Elissaeus - Tutor sent by Irene to teach Rotrud Greek.

Euphemia, St. - Female Roman martyr.

Faustina – Wife of the Roman emperor and philosopher **Marcus Aurelius** (see). Just as Antonina was to accompany Belisarius on his military expeditions, Faustina accompanied Aurelius on his.

Flacilla - Nurse of Constantine (fictional).

Flagstad, Kirsten - Famous Wagnerian soprano of the 1930s, '40s, and early 1950s.

Gibbon, Edward - (1737-1794) Author of *The Decline and Fall of The Roman Empire*. Despite his great erudition, Gibbon's regard for the classical world and his anti clericalism caused him to label the medieval paradigm as a "triumph of barbarism and religion." Although today's scholars consider this a shallow attitude it colored the view of the medieval world and especially the Byzantines negatively for two hundred years.

Gobel, George - Popular comedy show host of the 1950s.

Grant, Cary - Movie actor, Romantic leading man.

Hector - Hero of the Trojan war.

Helena, St. - Constantine the Great's mother. She toured the Holy-land returning relics of the Christ to Rome and Constantinople. Some are lost and others were probably frauds. However, the Holy Stairs, still extant in Rome (In a building across from St. John Lateran) were quite likely the actual steps to Pilot's palace and as such the place where Jesus stood during his condemnation.

Hildegarde - Wife of Charlemagne. Charles had four successive wives and at least five concubines. Although he outlawed divorce he still practiced it himself. Europe was still struggling with monogamy for the well bred and celibacy for the clergy. (Celibacy meaning not marrying, not necessarily being chaste.)

Homer - Ancient Greek poet (quoted). Classical learning was far more valued in Byzantium than in the West. The Byzantines never ceased to study and imitate ancient models in literature and history.

Horatius - Saved the Roman republic from reconquest by the Tarquin king by holding a Tiber bridge with only two companions.

Herodotus – Fifth century BC. Called the father of history.

Hospicius of Thier - Hermit from near Nice whose bone is brought from Gaul. He lived in the sixth century CE, kept himself chained, wore a hair shirt, and lived upon herbs, dates, and coarse bread.

Hroudland, Count - Roland, hero of the *Chanson de Roland*, killed in battle at Roncesvalles.

Iosephius, Brother - Scribe (fictional).

James the Greater - Patron saint for sufferers from arthritis and rheumatism.

Job - Biblical figure who, though righteous, was brought to ruin by Satan. His friends insisted that his loss of family, wealth, and health were a punishment for sin though he had committed none.

John Chrysostom - Patriarch and Doctor of the church, a saint very highly regarded in the Orthodox church. Famous for his homilies, John was called chrysostomos meaning the golden mouthed.

John of Damascus - Supporter of icons (quoted).

Joshua - Biblical commander of Israel who brought down the walls of Jericho by Divine intervention.

Justinian - Sixth century emperor whose general, Belisarius, retook Italy and North Africa. In his reign the bubonic plague broke out which for several succeeding centuries wracked Europe. He is well remembered for codifying Roman law and building many beautiful churches including Hagia Sophia, the masterpiece of late Roman / early Byzantine architecture, still extant in Constantinople.

Lachanodrakon - Iconoclast strategos who had persecuted monks and nuns under Leo IV. He however served Irene for a time. A close supporter of Constantine VI he helped him gain power with the support of his Armeniac army. Killed while campaigning with Constantine against the Bulgars.

Laocoon - He and his sons were crushed to death by sea serpents by the will of Apollo (or Athena) for warning the Trojans to destroy the Trojan horse.

Leo, son of Constantine - See **children of Constantine.**

Leo IV (and father Constantine V) – Iconoclast father and grandfather of Constantine VI, Constantine V's father, Leo III, actually began iconoclasm.

Lilith - A demon in the Cabala. Originally an angelic first wife of Adam. Damned by God for refusing to submit to a human, she goes about the world seducing men and devouring children by the thousands. Probably also confounded with other pre-Christian myths.

Lombard Deacon – See Paul, the Lombard deacon.

Machiavelli, Niccolo – Sixteenth century political philosopher. His treatise, *The Prince,* was realistic advice for a ruler instead of the religion-based idealism of medieval works.

(al)-Madi - Abbasid caliph to AD 784.

Marcus Aurelius (quoted) – second century pagan military emperor and noted stoic philosopher. He deeply loved his wife, Faustina (see) though reports of her behavior are mixed. In this they were alike to **Belisarius** (see) and his wife Antonina. Marcus and Faustina were parents of Commodus certainly one of the less worthy Roman emperors. Commodus thought himself a god; killed wounded soldiers for sport; and renamed Rome in his own honor. Marcus Aurelius was mourned and deified when he died; his son was assassinated.

Maurus, St. Patron saint of copper smiths, relics lie at Glanfeuil in Gaul.

Michael, St. - Archangel, patron of many things. Patron of soldiers because he defeated Satan in battle.

Mohammed – The prophet of Islam was originally seen as a Christian heretic. By this time it should have been clear that his was a new religion but one that distorted the Christian scriptures. It would have been natural to believe that he had been misled by diabolical forces. Certainly the armies of Islam had robbed Christianity of its most sacred sites.

Monk (unnamed) - Tried to assassinate Constantine (fictional). Several other unnamed monks are in the narrative, usually for having visions that please Irene. These others are in agreement with the sources.

Moses – Since Gnosticism identifies the god of the Hebrew scriptures as being the Demiurge, the revelation to Moses is rejected as misleading man into identifying with God's earthly rather than his spiritual being.

Nero and Caligula - Roman emperors: Nero murdered his mother and disemboweled his pregnant wife; Caligula slit open his pregnant wife and fondled his great-great grandmother on her deathbed.

Odysseus - Greek hero of the Trojan war who spent ten years adventuring before he was able to return home, noted for his craftiness.

Pamphilus - Bulgar spy and conduit between Khardam and Nicephorus (fictional).

Paul, St. - Credited as the founder of Christianity, apostle to the gentiles.

Paul the Lombard deacon - Agent sent by Irene to Charles' court to educate Rotrud.

Paul of Samosota - Heretic, founder of the **Paulician** heresy (see).

Paul the Silentiary - Sixth century scholar at Justinian's court. (quoted).

Pepin - Father of Charlemagne.

Peron, Eva – Wife of Argentine dictator Juan Peron. She was extraordinarily popular with the poorest citizens who perceived her as their champion because of her public charity and support of labor and women's rights in the late 1940s and early 50s. The Broadway musical Evita uses the affectionate diminutive of Eva as its title.

Phidias and Praxitiles - Ancient Greek sculptors. (See note under **Arts**.)

Philip and Alexander of Macedon - Alexander the Great and father.

Phillipus and Meletius - Childhood friends of Constantine (fictional).

Photographers, unnamed - Besides the photographer Eddy Miller, two others are mentioned only once each (fictional).

Plato - Fourth century BC philosopher. More mystic than Aristotle, some of his theory is reflected and distorted in Gnosticism and neoplatonism.

Platters, The - Extremely popular Doo-Wop songsters of the 1950s. (*The Great Pretender, Only You,* et c.)

Procopius - Historian of Justinian and Belisarius (quoted).

Romulus - With his twin Remus, the mythical founders of the city of Rome.

Sergius and Bacchus - Military saints martyred during the Roman persecutions for whom a church (Now the mosque kucuk Ayasofya) is named in Constantinople.

Simon Magus - A Gnostic magician said to have joined the church to learn Christian magic.

Socrates - Ancient Greek philosopher (quoted). See note under **Homer**.

Tatzantes - Early in Irene's reign he defected to the Arabs out of hatred for Stauratius.

Theodosa - Female saint, murdered for protecting an important icon of Christ in Constantinople during the iconoclastic period.

Theodosius II– Emperor responsible for construction of the triple walls of Constantinople. The forum of Theodosius, however, commemorates Theodosius I (The Great).

Theogenius the monk - Chronicler (Fictional). An actual contemporary history of this period is *The Chronicle of Theophanes Confessor.*

Theophanes – Not in the story itself, but mentioned in the afterword. See **Theogenius** above.

Theophilos - General sent against the rebel Elpidios in Sicily.

Wagner, Richard – German composer of operas including Tristan *und Isolde* (quoted), an operatic version of the well known medieval love triangle, and of *Die Walkure,* a restructuring of ancient legends of the Germanic gods.

PLACES, TERMS, ET C.

Aachen (Aix la Chapelle) - The city, cathedral, and palace where Charles usually held court, although he regularly visited other places. Although Charlemagne's Aachen structure is now included in a larger church which includes Gothic elements, the heart of the church is in the more colorful domed tradition of late Roman and Byzantine models. The author expects that craftsmen from Constantinople would have decorated the church but much of the material came from Rome and Ravenna.

Abbasid caliphate - Ruled North Africa and the Near East. Its capital was Baghdad.

Abrams - Still a publisher of art books.

Acacius, Church of – see name entry: **Acacius, St.**.

Adrianople - City west of Constantinople, site of the first Roman loss to barbarian invaders, some four hundred years previous to our story.

Ahriman – In Persian dualism, the principle of evil.

Amnia - A minor town on the south coast of the Black Sea. The birthplace of Maria, Constantine's first wife.

Anadendradion – A palace garden.

Anatolia - A theme (military district) in southwestern Asia Minor but the term is often used for the whole of Asia Minor.

Aquaducts – A section of one of Constantinople's aquaducts remains in the city's center; as do a number of cisterns, including a so-called Underground Palace near Hagia Sophia.

Arab – The term is used interchangeably with Saracen.

Armeniacs - Troops of the Armenian theme.

Armenian theme - Located in eastern Asia Minor and extending from the Black Sea to the center of the peninsula.

Artillery - By which is meant ballistae and other ancient torsion weapons. Gunpowder was not introduced until the fifteenth century. Also see: **Fire weapon.**

Arts, ancient and Byzantine - Mosaic is the quintessential Byzantine art form. However fresco painting was as highly developed, following the same forms as mosaic. Figures were deliberately stylized and sculpture in the round practically disappeared except in excellent ivory work. This was so that icons would not be beautiful idols but only representative of the person portrayed with stylized characteristics to indicate unreproducible virtue and holiness. (However, ancient sculptures were displayed and highly regarded.)

As you judge, so shall you be judged. As you are kind, so shall kindness be shown to you. - Do not condemn, and you will not be condemned. Forgive, and you will be forgiven; Give and it will be given to you. A good measure, pressed down, shaken together, running over, will be put into your lap; for the measure you give will be the measure you get back. (Luke 6:37)

Atroa – A plain, probably near Prousa in Asia Minor.

Attaleia – A major city on the southern coast of the Anatolean penninsula.

Attic Greek – The language of ancient Athens. Generally the literary language of Greece imitated by learned Byzantines.

Augusta - Wife or widow of the basilios, not necessarily a basilia.

Augustaeum - The forecourt and first hall of the palace precinct. This square dated to the time of Constantine the Great.

Autocrator - Military title of the emperor, equivalent to the Roman Imperator. Generally replaced by the more inclusive title Basilios.

Augustus - The original title of the Roman Emperor, replaced in Byzantium with the more inclusive Greek title of **basilios**. When **Constantine I (The Great)** divided the empire administratively between Rome and Constantinople. There were to be two senior augusti and two junior caesars who were to succeed the augustus on his death. The arrangement was not very successful and in time the term augustus was replaced by basilios in common usage. **Caesar** (see) became primarily an inherited position of honor and little actual power, much as did that of **senator.**

Ax-men - The Byzantines regularly employed foreign mercenaries as guards. These ax-men are fictional but presumed predecessors of the Viking Varangian guards who are first identified in the tenth century.

Bacheim - Present day Bochum in North Germany.

Baghdad – Baghdad. Located on the Tigris River and only about thirty miles from the Euphrates River was essentially a new city, having been made the capital of the Abbasid Caliphate only a few years before the ascent of Harun al-Rashid to the throne. He is responsible for its splendor, immortalized in the *Arabian Nights* stories.

Ballista - A Roman artillery piece resembling a huge crossbow used to fire darts and stones.

Basilia - Empress by virtue of being raised to the throne by the basilios. As with Theodote this was generally done before their marriage. Constantine's first wife. Maria of Amnia, was augusta but was never raised to the status of basilia.

Basilios - Emperor, King of Kings, God's Anointed. The Eastern Empire is often termed Greek. A more accurate identification would be Hellenistic for it was composed as much of oriental as Greek traditions ... and, of course, of Roman elements. It was in the east that Roman emperors were first deified, and though that did not fit in a Christian state, the emperor as the Anointed of God and Equal of the Apostles was the next best thing. The emperors ruled with a mandate from heaven, for which reason an unsuccessful revolt was sacrilege as much as treason, while a successful one meant that the mandate had passed to a new ruler.

214

Be it done unto me according to thy word. - Luke (1:38) The Virgin Mary's response to an angel announcing to her that she was to be the mother of Jesus.

Beards – Beards were common among Byzantine aristocrats, and obligatory for the clergy since Jesus was bearded. Thus to say as the Master of Horse does to Aetius: "you have no beard" indicates a eunuch.

Beatniks - Originally disenchanted veterans of World War II, somewhat analogous to the "Lost Generation" of WW I. By the mid nineteen fifties members of the "Beat Generation" can be considered an art-literary-philosophical movement. Beatniks were preoccupied with the philosophy of Jean Paul Sartre, the poetry of Lawrence Ferlinghetti and Allen Ginsberg, the novels of Jack Kerouac, and the nonrepresentational art of such painters as Jackson Pollock and Willem de Kooning. In music they favored "Modern Jazz." The term "Beatnik" may originate from the "beat" of the music or from a remark by Jack Kerouac who when asked how he felt after the world war is said to have replied "beat." Nik was a suffix sometimes added to words in the wake of the Soviet sputnik launch, just as 'orama was added to words following the appearance of Cinerama, a motion picture screen with a 146 degree arc that filled the viewers' field of vision. Bettie Page appeared in the sexploitation film *Striporama*. In New York City, Greenwich Village was a popular residential area for beatniks and would-be beatniks.

Belgae, Aquitani, and Celts – As every schoolboy once knew these were the tribes which inhabited the three parts of Gaul in the time of Julius Caesar, before the Gothic and Frankish invasions. That was ancient history even to Constantine.

Belladonna - Nightshade. Used in the middle ages to dilate the eyes and make them more attractive. Overuse or ingestion can, however, cause blindness and death.

Bithynia - Area of north west Asia Minor. The military theme (province) there.

Blachernae District - In later times A palace was constructed here near the northern part of the land walls. At this time, however, it would have been relatively rural but containing the church the Panagia, a title of the Virgin Mary.

Bohemia - Part of modern Czechoslovakia.

Bosphorus - The narrow stretch of water connecting the Black Sea to the Sea of Marmara, with Constantinople on the European side and the much less important Chrysopolis on the Asian side. (I might remind the reader that distances which seem small to us were substantial to the ancients, particularly when going by sea against the wind)   .

Boucoleon - Imperial harbor and district where the Great Palace was located.

Boyars - Bulgar noblemen.

Bulgars - A group of Asiatic tribes that fought the Byzantines from at least the sixth century.

Bulwark of Islam – Not a title, but a nickname the author has invented and put into Harun Al Rashid'd imagination.

By your sweat you shall earn your bread – (*Genesis*). God to Adam when Adam was ejected from Eden.

Byzantine, Byzantium – Constantinople was founded on the site of the ancient Greek city of Byzantium, but that is the only connection with that word. The Byzantines never called themselves Byzantine, or their city Byzantium. This is a more modern term coined by historians (see Roman.)

Byzantine Art and Archeology - O. M. Dalton. Oxford University Press, 1911. Reprinted by Dover 1961. Currently on-line by Google.

Caesar - The highest rank next to the throne itself, often but not necessarily inherited. Originally a rank of importance second only to the Augustus himself, by the eighth century the titleholder had no real power but still had great prestige. (see also: **Augustus.**)

Camera clubs - In the 1950s amateur photographers would sometimes band together to hire a model for the day. Some were inhibited young men who allegedly didn't even have film in their cameras.

Campus Martius – The annual gathering of the chief lords of the Franks; not to be confused with the Roman training ground and later site of many public buildings.

Cappadocia - a rugged desert area of Asia Minor where monks often lived because of its hardship.

Cataphracts, cataphracti - Heavy cavalry - the usual troops of the empire. Infantry and archers usually only supported these.

Celibacy – see: **Holy Orders**.

Chalcedon - Modern Kadikoy, Located on the Sea of Marmara near Constantinople on the Asiatic shore of the Bosphorus. Chalcedon was the site of the Fourth Ecumenical Council in 451 CE.

Chalke gate - The entrance to the Great Palace where a portrait of Christ hung until removed at the beginning of the Iconoclastic period. The holy Theodosa and other women were beaten or martyred defending the portrait against troops sent to remove it.

Chelles – An abbey near Paris famous for the work of its female scribes. An abbess was Charlemagne's sister Gisela but she may not yet have held that office at the time of our story..

Chi-Rho – Christ's monogram in Greek. First used by the emperor Constantine the Great on his banner at the battle of the Milvian bridge to encourage the many Christians among his soldiers. This banner, or labarum, continued in use by his successors.

Christ Pantocrator - Christ, The Ruler Of All; the central figure in the dome of Orthodox churches.

Chrysopolis - City opposite Constantinople on the Asian side of the Bosphorus.

Chrysotriklinos Palace - A part of the Great Palace where foreign dignitaries were received. It was especially furnished to impress barbarians with great artistry and with clockwork bird and animal figures. A few years after this story the imperial thrones were even engineered to rise into the air.

Cilicia, Cilician Gates - Cilicia is on the far North East coast of the Mediterranean Sea. The Cilician Gates form the main passage through the Taurus Mountains. Their southern opening is north of Taurus. This pass links the Mediterranean coast and the low plains of Cilicia with the central Anatolian plateau.

Claudia Augusta Pass - Modern Brenner Pass.

Commander of the Faithful – A title of the Caliph   .

Comes – Count. At this time a high military title both among the Franks and the Byzantines.

Consistoria - A meeting room.

Constantinople – (See: **New Rome.**) The population of the city at one time reached over one million persons. However at the time of our story it is considerably less. Parts within the **Walls of Theodosius** (see) had reverted to farmland.

Convent - a convent for women can also be termed a monastery in Eastern Christendom.

Council – In our context the term refers to an ecumenical or general council that determines matters of Church governance and discipline and is considered infallible in matters of faith or morals (see also: **Synod**.)

Count – Comes.

Count no man happy until he is dead - According to **Herodotus**, Solon the Athenian lawgiver gave this advice to the Lydian king Croesus, who later lost his kingdom and was executed by the Persians. In this story the phrase takes on a rather different meaning,.

Croats - A Slavic people who seem to have begun trickling into Dalmatia about the seventh century CE.

Cubicularia - a lady in waiting.

Curiosi and agentes in rebus - Secret services of the Byzantines.

Dacia - North of Moesia.

Dalmatic - Outerwear worn both by men and women of rank over the tunic, often ornamented. Although properly the term is for a male garment, by the time of our story there is so little difference between the dalmatic of men and the **stola** of women that the term is sometimes applied uni-sexually.

Dalmatia - Roman province on the Adriatic.

Danube frontier - The Roman emperor Octavius Augustus set the rivers Rhine and Danube as a defensible frontier for the empire beyond which it should not expand.

Darenos - Site of an early defeat of Arabs by Lachanodrakon.

Demiurge – In Platonic and neoplatonic philosophy the Demiurge is the fashioner of the material world but not evil. In Gnostic dualism he takes on some resemblence to the Persian Ahriman, an evil power.

Doctors and Fathers of the Church – In general, the early theologians who hammered out the content of orthodox Christianity.

Doux - Duke, a high military rank.

Dromon - A Byzantine war galley, normally with two banks of oars, a fighting platform for archers, and sometimes equipment for throwing Greek fire (see: **Fire weapon.**)

Drungarius of the Watch - A military official in Constantinople.

Druzhina - One of the peoples making up the Bulgar host.

Dualism – Various theological forms having in common the belief that there are two great beings: one the father of all that is spiritual, the other the creator of material things. Commonly there is a plethora of lesser divinities. The Paulician and Gnostic heresies were dualist.

Duke - see **Doux**.

Dyrrachium - City on the Via Egnasia in modern Albania.

Ektachrome and plates - 35 mm color photography first became popular in the 1950s because of its quality and convenience, generally replacing the previously popular 116 - 120 films. By this time studio cameras were still in use but they used cut film rather than glass plates.

Eleutherian palace - Built by Irene in the Eleutherian district on the southern (Marmara) coast of Constantinople. She lived there during her brief exile and Constantine retired there after being dethroned.

Empress-regent - Irene's husband, Leo IV, had never raised her to the dignity of Basilia but at the death of Leo she retained the rank of augusta and ruled for her son during his minority. She could do this since Constantine, had been raised to the position of emperor (basilios) by Leo.

Envy is the ulcer of the mind – The sayings of Socrates (c. 469 – 399 BC) are known only through the writing of his pupil Plato.

Eucharist - Properly the term refers to the Real Presence of Christ under the appearance of bread and wine in the Divine Liturgy, usually known in the west as the Mass (from the closing Latin words: ete missa est.) The term is often used to designate the entire liturgical service and I follow this usage in the story. The Eucharist itself is also known as Holy Communion to emphasize the social aspect of the service.

Eunuchs - In accordance with its Oriental character, eunuchs were much more common in Byzantium than in the West. Many were from the middle classes but some were aristocrats. Since they could never hold the position of emperor and had no children to advance, they were considered relatively safe to appoint to high positions. They often held important administrative and even military rank, and very many served the empire loyally and well. Others, like Aetius and Stauratius however, were constantly conniving to advance other members of their families. Eunuchs did not necessarily appear more effeminate than others at court as it was normal even for manly and courageous military emperors to wear cosmetics and perfume. There is some question too whether all eunuchs were entirely devoid of sexual desire. Supposedly those castrated after puberty could achieve an erection and enjoy coitus, but not ejaculate. There is also the possibility that men who were homosexual from an early age were lumped together with the castrated; the theory being that these were natural or holy eunuchs.

Euxine (Euxinus) Sea - The Black Sea.

Evil eye – The Byzantines were quite superstituous. Besides holy images, they would employ amulets, and gemstones on their clothing believed to protect against evil spirits and the evil eye.

Exarchate of Ravenna - A long-time center of power for Byzantium in Italy, still noted for its mosaics. On the Adriatic coast, it controlled some but not all of Byzantium's holdings in Italy until 727 when it was taken by the Lombards. After being held briefly by Saracens it fell to the Franks in the reign of Charlemagne's father Pepin. Pepin donated it to the papacy and the donation was supposedly confirmed by Charlemagne. This formed the beginning of the Papal states and the temporal power of future popes in Europe.

Fire-weapon - Known in the West as Greek fire, it was the most effective weapon before gun powder and often saved Byzantine forces. It was used on land but was especially effective in sea battles where it would be spewed from "siphons" and could not be extinguished with water.

Forum of Bovis - Named for the sculpture of an ox, it was one of several forums on the Mese, the main thoroughfare of Constantinople

Frankland - Gaul. The Franks superseded Gothic rule. Their kings ruled the Franks as king, but in theory ruled the land and ancient inhabitants as representative of the empire.

Franks - A Germanic tribe originally living along the Rhine river who in the fifth century moved into Roman Gaul. Their king ruled his people as king but in theory ruled the conquered people there as the representative of the Roman Empire.

Gallia est omnis divisa in partes tres. (The whole of Gaul is divided into three parts.) - With these words Julius Caesar begins his commentaries on the conquest of Gaul. Ever since Caesar penned this line his dispatches to the Roman senate and people have been the bane of students of Latin. Yet it is the clear and forthright style of a soldier which impressed the citizenry then, and makes the commentaries an excellent first Latin text now.

Garment District - An area of light industry in New York City extending roughly from 34th to 44th streets and from Fifth Ave. to the Hudson River

Gaul - The Roman emperor Augustus had set the Rhine and Danube rivers as the frontier of the Empire in Gaul, though Bavaria too was part of the Frankish state that now effectively ruled in its place. Charlemagne set to conquering the wild and heavily forested Saxon, Bohemian, and Moravian lands to the north and east.

Gnostics - A duelist heresy with mystical neoplatonic interpretation of Holy Scripture.

Golden Gate - The gate at the southernmost end of the triple walls of Constantinople, reserved for use by imperial processions only.

Golden Horn - An inlet from the Bosphorus forming the northern boundary of Constantinople.

Gothic - A derogatory term from the Renaissance applied to art and architecture from the 12th century onward in western Europe. The defining feature is the Gothic arch. See **Aachen**.

Goths - German tribe who ended the Roman Empire in the west and ruled Italy until the coming of the Longobards

Great (Sacred) Palace - The palace complex overlooking the Bosphorus and adjacent to Hagia Sophia cathedral and the hippodrome, a race track for chariot races but also used for many other events.

Grecia, Italia, Roma – Greece, Italy, Rome. No attempt is made to be consistent in using obvious Latin and English place names. The author has used what seemed best in the context.

Greek fire - see **Fire-weapon**.

Greenwich Village - Bleeker Street - A residential and tourist area in lower Manhattan with a certain old world look; favored by artists, intellectuals, and beatniks.

Hagia Sophia, Great Church - The cathedral church of Constantinople. Built in the late Roman style of architecture, the emperor Justinian certainly intended that it be an impressive imperial structure. Later churches more truly reflect the Byzantine attitude toward worship. While northern Europe was creating Gothic cathedrals that reached toward the heavens but were fairly monochromatic inside, the Byzantines and Italians preferred less ostentatious exteriors, employing colorful decoration for the worshiper to contemplate inside.

Hay and Horses - Horse manure had therapeutic qualities in the Middle Ages, but not lately.

Heiaha! Der freude, et c. Quote from R. Wagner's *Tristan und Isolde*.

Hellas - Basically, the part of Greece that was ancient Greece.

Heriban - A Frankish militia inherited by Charlemagne to which every able-bodied man could be summoned.

Hellespont - Ancient name of the Dardanelles separating Asia and Europe at Gallipoli south of the Sea of Marmara.

Hippodrome - The race track but also used for many other events and gatherings.

Ho-jo-to-ho! - Battle cry of the Valkyries in Richard Wagner's *Die Walkure.*

Holy - Often attached to the names of saintly persons, alive or dead, or of objects dedicated to religion (holy icons, holy church). It has a slightly broader sense than the English "saint" which is reserved for deceased persons of undoubted holiness. In the Roman church being declared a saint (canonization) has for many centuries only followed after a strict investigation.

Holy Orders - The priesthood. While monks were celibate, eastern rite priests were not usually so. Priests who were also monks were, of course, celibate. Even in the West where the church was trying to enforce celibacy, priests were often married in Charles' time. It might be noted that to take a vow of celibacy means to forgo the comforts and distractions of married life. Chastity is required of all Christians, but violations, while sinful, were considered to be normal and natural. Moreover in the Carolingian Middle Ages there were few opportunities for excess progeny. To avoid excessive division of inherited land many sons would become clergymen, but not necessarily priests. This did not have much to do with spirituality. Celibacy did become important for the western church so that priests and, bishops particularly, could not pass on their wealth and power to heirs, or develop into a priestly caste.

Hudson Tubes - The old name for the PATH system of trains running under the Hudson River. These connect New York City with parts of New Jersey on the opposite shore.

I see my love leaping upon the mountains et c. - *The Song of Solomon.*

Icon - A holy picture usually painted on wood and often covered in silver and decorated with pearls and gem stones. That icons not become objects of worship in themselves, they are always stylized representations. For the same reason, sculpture in the round is also frowned upon in the eastern tradition. That pictures and statues are merely artistic representations is also emphasized in the West. Religious representation is very natural but kept more distant from the devotee. For this reason Pope Adrian may not have grasped the magnitude of excessive veneration of icons in the Eastern Empire.

Iconoclasts - Those who thought icons idolatrous. Traditional Islam also prohibits representation of the human or divine form.

Iconodules - Those who venerated icons.

Illustrious, Illustrati - A high rank of late Roman aristocracy, held by Belisarius.

Imperator - Emperor. Originally a Roman military title, rarely used officially at this date.

In saffron-colored mantle, et c. - Homer: *The Iliad.*

In the beginning God created the Heavens and the earth – (Genesis 1:1) The opening words of the bible. The meaning is clear and advanced for its day. There is but one Power and He is a supreme intelligence that is responsible for all that is "seen and unseen" in the later words of the Nicene Creed. Common cosmology had more often posited a primeval blob which unexplainedly split into sky and earth, the male and female principles; not unlike the Big Bang theory of creation. Persian dualism held that the material world was the work of generations of spirits; and Roman astromysticism that there were many spheres between the fire that is God and the mud that is earth. Roman paganism considered Jupiter to be the king of the gods but the primal force was Deus Aeterna (Eternal Time).

In the morning when thou art sluggish at rousing, et c. - Marcus Aurelius Meditations V 1.

Into Thy hands, et c. - A variant of Psalm 31:5. Into your hands I commit my spirit, O Lord, the God of truth.

Isapostle - Literally Equal of the Apostles, a title of the emperor.

Isaurian dynasty - Founded by Leo III, Constantine VI's great grandfather. Ended with the deposition of Irene.

It is not possible to fight beyond your strength et c. - Homer: The Iliad.

Joyosa - Charlemagne's favorite sword, arguably still extant and used at the coronation of Napoleon.

Justinian plague - Bubonic plague. The first known pandemic, it struck Europe in 541 and returned with each generation until about 750. The initial outbreak may have killed one quarter of the population in the eastern Mediterranean. Later outbreaks were less severe but still very serious.

Karaman – The modern town near the Waterless Towers (the exact location of which is not known.) The Waterless Towers guarded the silk road through Asia Minor.

Khan – A common Asian title with varying importance depending on the time and place. In the context of this story, the khan is the military leader of a tribe or group of tribes. In such a context it was not necessarily hereditary nor held in settled times. It was seen as important, however, to have a autocratic ruler during periods of war and migration.

Khazars - Turkik mercenaries of Byzantium.

Knight, Sir, Seigneur - In the time of Charlemagne, a class of mounted noble warriors, with their status based on land holdings, began to develop among the Franks separate from mere cavalry.

Knotted silk cord - Titillating rumors of far eastern erotic practices could have made their way to the West via the silk road.

Koine - The vulgar derivative of Attic Greek, the *lingua Franca* of the Hellenistic world. The term is used here to mean common Greek, the ancestor of the modern language, as opposed to Attic Greek which continued to be the language of literature where medieval authors tried to imitate the language and style of the ancients. Technically, however, modern linguists differentiate between the koine of the Hellenistic world and the medieval street Greek of Constantine's time.

Kontakion - A hymn. In this case one written for the dedication of Hagia Sophia.

Kotrag - A minor Asian tribe conquered by and incorporated into the Bulgars.

Kowtow – A Chinese act of deep respect shown by kneeling and bowing so low as to have one's head touching the ground.

Kyrie elision - Literally, "Lord be with us"; frequently repeated in Orthodox chant.

Labarum - The two letters Chi-Rho comprising Christ's monogram originally formed as the standard for Constantine I's army when he recognized Christianity. This standard continued to be carried in successive centuries.

Lamellar armor – Made from hundreds of metal plates and sometimes worn over chainmail, it produced a deflective surface for blades to skim over, rather than strike and pierce.

Lavouto - A lute.

Lector – Properly a lector is a cleric in minor orders who reads scripture at the Eucharistic service. The word is used here in a slightly more general sense.

Lesbos – The island to which Irene was exiled was not some isolated rock but a large sunny and verdant island in the far eastern Mediterranean just off the coast of Asia Minor.

Logothete of the dromos - The first Minister in Byzantium. Since all power resided in the Anointed of God, there is no position quite equivalent to Prime Minister.

Longobards, Lombards - A German tribe which settled in North Italy and superseded the Goths.

Macedonia - The area west of Thrace.

Magistros - A title of honor for a few very high dignitaries of the empire.

Markella - An important Byzantine fortress built by Constantine to control the Struma valley.

Marmara, Sea of - The southern boundary of the Constantinoplian peninsula. The ancient Propontis, though for clarity the modern name is used here.

Master of horse - Military official in charge of cavalry.

Merovingian - The original royal line of the Franks in Gaul, deposed by Charles' father Pepin.

Mese - The main boulevard in Constantinople. Long, wide, and straight, it ran from the Forum of Constantine (the Great) just outside the Great Palace to the Golden Gate in the triple walls. It was the usual processional path of the Basilios when he left the city for war or other purposes, except when he left by sea.

Military Saints - Saints Sergius and Bacchus were prominent soldier-saints of the early Church, having been martyred during the persecution of Christians by the Roman emperor Galerius. So too had been Saint Demetrios and perhaps St. Acacius. The church recognizes only a few others.

Moesia - North of Thrace.

Monks - While lone holy men were very respected in Byzantium, by the time of our story most monks lived a communal life in monasteries. Eastern monks were often very political, undisciplined, and riotous; and only nominally submissive to their bishops. In our story, the monk Theodore breaks communion with the Patriarch Tarasios, though both were in their way very holy men.. This is reported by the real-life chronicler Theophanes, Confessor.

Monasteries - see **Monks**.

Monophysites - Believed that Christ was of one Divine nature only, not man. As such they shared an abhorrence of images with the Jews and Moslems.

Nestorianism - Taught that there were two separate persons in Christ, Divine and human.

Newark - A major New Jersey city only a few miles from the Hudson River, across from New York.

New Rome - The official name of Constantinople given to the city by Constantine the Great when he created the city as a second capital for the Roman Empire. The term was usually used only in official documents which would state: "Nova Roma (New Rome) which is Constantinople."

Nicea - City in Asia Minor where the seventh ecumenical council reconvened after being interrupted in Constantinople by riotous troops. The seventh council should not be confused with the fourth century First Council of Nicea which generally defined orthodox doctrine and which promulgated the Nicean Creed, still recited in most Christian services.

Nobilissimus - A high ranking advisor to the emperor, generally restricted to the imperial family.

Now deep in ocean sank the lamp of light and drew behind the cloudy veil of night. The conquering Trojans mourn his beams decay'd; the Greeks rejoicing bless the friendly shade – Homer, *The Iliad*

Oh friends, be men and let your hearts be strong, et c. - Homer: *The Iliad.*

One Fold and one Shepard – Other sheep I have that are not of this fold: them also I must bring. And they shall hear my voice: and there shall be one fold and one shepherd" (John: 16)

Orthodox - Since these events transpired before the schism between the

Eastern and Western Churches, the term refers to anyone not a heretic. The "Orthodox Churches" of today do not yet exist. Still, the gap between Constantinople and the pope was opening despite efforts to prevent it. That the Patriarch of Constantinople insisted on placing the legates of the pope in first place at the council to restore icons was a recognition of the pope's status, even while his actual authority in the East was diminishing.

Palanquin - A covered litter carried on poles by four bearers.

Palla, Pallium - A Roman cloak-like overgarment for both men and women which could extend to the hem of the dalmatic but was often draped over the arm. It could be used to cover the head. In time it became an imperial garment and is now an ecclesiastical garment derived from that usage.

Panagia, Church of the – Located in the Blachernae district of Constantinople near the great walls. There were kept relics of the Virgin Mary brought from Jerusalem and greatly revered, as were all relics in Constantinople. In fact there were so many relics – real and fraudulent – that Constantinople might be called a city of relics. Many were to be brought to western Europe by knights of the fourth (robber) crusade which in 1204 AD was to deviate from its mission of conquest of the holy land to seize Constantinople and hold the city for fifty seven years. They stripped the city of most of its spiritual and material wealth. (See also note under **Relics**.)

Pantocrator, Christ - Christ, the Ruler Of All; the central figure in the dome of Eastern churches.

Patriarch - Originally there were three patriarchates in Christendom: those of Rome, Antioch, and Alexandria. Constantinople was added when the city was founded as a **"New Rome"** (see). These patriarchs oversaw other bishoprics. The patriarchates of Antioch and Alexandria, ceased to exist when these cities were conquered by the Arabs, leaving only Rome and Constantinople. At the time of Constantine VI, the Patriarch of Constantinople still (sometimes reluctantly) deferred to the primacy of Rome. As the political head of the church, the basilios called and presided over councils since the office of emperor had long since ceased to exist in Rome.

Patricius - Charles' title as Roman governor of the non-Frank population of Gaul.

Patrician - An aristocrat. This ancient Latin title originated in Rome during the republic.

Paulitians - A dualist heresy which denied the human nature of Christ. For these extremists even the elimination of images was not enough. Paul of Samosota had taught that not only icons but even the cross must be rejected; that only an image of Jesus had died on the cross for he had not been a man at all but of one Divine nature only; that the bulk of the Christian and all the Hebrew scriptures were the false revelations of the devil or the

Demiurge. Both Constantine and Irene would oppose such heresy not merely with persuasion but with all the military might of the empire since the Paulitians threatened the very authority of the government.

Peloponnese - West and south Hellas. Classical Greece.

Pentecost - Feast commemorating the descent of the Holy Spirit upon the apostles and others after which they went forth fearlessly preaching the Gospel, healing, and speaking in tongues. It is celebrated seven weeks after Easter.

Pharos Chapel - An important chapel within the Great Palace which held many alleged relics of Christ including the crown of thorns and nails from the crucifixion.

Philistines - Biblical enemy of Israel who, possessing iron weapons, were able to intermittently control southern Israel until defeated by King David.

Philosophy - The schools of pagan philosophy were closed in the sixth century but many intellectuals, including Church leaders, were well versed in philosophy. However the orthodoxy of those who tried to reconcile Christianity with philosophy was always suspect.

PMS – Premenstrual syndrome.

Praetorium - A barracks for the Praetorian guards in the imperial palace complex.

Prayers for Victory and on leaving the city - These historically accurate prayers demonstrate that the empire in a sense was the city of Constantinople with much of the rest of the empire serving it. They also indicate that usurpers were at least as much a threat to the dynasty as foreign armies.

Probaton - A minor Macedonian fortress.

Propontis - The Sea of Marmara.

Prostration - In the ritual of the Orthodox Church, at Divine Services most of the time is spent standing; only the enfeebled sit. There is little kneeling as in the west but there is prostration. This is akin to the Moslem ritual. The worshiper kneels on the floor with his hands before him and touches his head to the floor. It is unlike prostration at the ordination of priests in the Western Church who lie entirely flat.

Protospatharius - A very high dignitary and advisor to the throne. Both Aetius and John Pikridios were thus dignified.

Prousa - Modern Bursa in Asia Minor, about sixty miles from Constantinople.

Purring Pussycat - A fictional Greenwich Village (NY) coffee shop.

Quaestorium - A military section of the Great Palace.

Ravenna - the Exarchate of Ravenna containing the city of Ravenna on the Adriatic sea. (see **Exarchate of Ravenna**.)

Red footwear - Could be worn only by the basilios and basilia.

Relics - Bones of saints, a nail from the "True Cross" of Christ, and other relics were greatly revered throughout the medieval world. Though certainly regarded as being what was claimed, surely most from biblical times had to have been faked. Yet two reservations may be made: First that medieval people had no critical grasp of history or sense of time, and secondly that it might not have mattered to them. Even today, most of us will be respectful in a place of worship even of a religion that we may despise. We feel the place is sanctified by the holiness of those who have expressed their own spirituality there. (See also note under **Panagia, Church of the**.) A reliquary is a container for the relics, often made of silver or gold and formed in the shape of the limb contained.

Rhineland - Charlemagne established his capital at Aachen near the Rhine probably to be better placed to conduct his Saxon war in North Germany; but possibly also because of the thermal baths there. He did suffer from joint pain.

Roman - Byzantine, Hellenistic, Christian. The term Roman was the Byzantine's term for themselves. It came to signify a Christian unity centered politically in Constantinople; and also the Eastern Empire itself: "the Land of the Romans." They never called themselves Byzantine and were offended when called Greek. This is not unreasonable since the empire extended over non Greek territory in Asia and, at times, in Sicily, North Africa, and parts of Italy; all of which were Christian.

Rosary Beads - Commonly used by Roman Catholics to keep track of prayers said – Basically one *Our Father* and ten *Hail Mary's* for each of five "decades". Each decade recalls an event in the life of Jesus as seen through his mother's eyes.

Saccudion- A very politically important monastery on the Asian shore of the Bosphorus.

Sacred - Often used as an adjective for imperial properties (Sacred Palace, et c.) since the emperor was considered Christ's deputy on earth and the political head of the church and the Christian people.

Saint Gregory's salt - Presumably named for Saint Gregory the Great who suffered from Gout. Known in the Greek Church as Gregory the Dialogist.

Saint Patrick's Cathedral - The neo-gothic cathedral church of the Catholic Archdiocese of New York, located on Fifth Ave. at 50th street. That a woman cover her head in a Catholic church was *de rigueur* at that time.

Saint Stephen's church - Beth's Catholic church in Newark (fictional). Also an actual church within the Great Palace complex used for important state functions. Constantine wed Theodote there.

San Apollinare, San Vitale – Two of the beautiful churches still surviving in Ravenna, Italy. Their extensive mosaic decoration give a good idea of what the churches of Constantinople must have looked like before being stripped of representational art in accordance with Islamic law when that city fell to the Turks.

Saracens - Arabs.

Saxon war - It took Charlemagne thirty years to pacify Saxony.

Scythaean - An ancient people east of Asia Minor sometimes employed as guards in the Byzantine empire. The term is often used generically for west Asiatic tribal groups.

Seigneur- Title for a Western knight or lord. (See knight.)

Senate, Senator - By this time the Roman Senate was powerless, however being a senator still carried prestige.

Sergius and Bacchus, Church of - Still in use as the mosque Kucuk Ayasofya.

She walks in beauty, like the night / Of cloudless climes and starry skies / And all that's best of dark and bright / Meet in her aspect and her eyes … The smiles that win, the tints that glow / But tell of days in goodness spent, / A mind at peace with all below, / A heart whose love is eloquent. … Lord Byron.

Sicily - Still held by Byzantium at this time along with parts of south Italy.

Silifke - A coastal city in Cilicia where a Byzantine fortress guarded the approach to the Cilician Gates.

Sinope - Port on the Black sea.

Sklavian - Slavic marauders. The Peloponnese was so frequently invaded by Slavs during the Middle Ages that some scholars think the present population is of mainly Slavic descent.

Slavic - Various Slavic mercenaries were employed in Byzantium. Many Slavs were being enslaved in the West at about this same time; so much so that the term *Slav* became *slave* superseding the Roman *servus*.

Solidus - The standard gold coin of Byzantium accepted at face value throughout the Western world because it was not devalued for eight hundred years.

Solomon song – Properly known as the Song of Solomon or Song of Songs. Although usually interpreted as an allegory of God's love for his church, it is also an erotic celebration of human sexuality and love; as though the Lord was correcting an omission in Genesis where people are merely required to "increase and multiply."

Spathion - A Byzantine cavalry sword.

Stola – A women's upper garment that in early Byzantium fell to the waist. In later centuries it became longer and is effectively indistinguishable from the men's **dalmatic** (see). There is little evidence of how far this transition had proceeded at the time of our story and I use the terms a bit loosely.

Strategos (stratagoi) - General(s).

Stratigicon and Tactica - Byzantine books of strategy and tactics.

Struma valley - In modern northern Bulgaria, the site of Constantine's defeat near the fortress of Markella.

Studion - A very politically important monastery in Constantinople. The

228

ruins are still partially extant.

Synod – An ecclesiastical gathering of church officials. In our context it refers to an ecumenical council of all the bishops of the Church who are able to attend. (See: **Council**.)

Tang Dynasty - Ruled China (Cathay) from 618 to 907 AD.

Tarsus - City in Asia minor, birthplace of Paul the apostle.

Teuton tongue - **Teutonic,** old German from which modern German, English, and the Scandinavian languages evolved.

Theme, Greek: Thema, (Plural: Themata) - Military districts and provinces. As with the Thracian (Thrakesion) theme, the name could be from where the original troops or general commanding came from. It is not necessarily the same geographical location. (Thrace is in Europe, the Thracian theme in Asia.)

There shall be one fold et c. - Sheep I have, which are not of this fold: them also I must bring, and they shall hear my voice; and there shall be one fold, and one shepherd. (John 10: 16)

Therma - Public bath.

Thessaloníki – Still the most important city in Macedonia.

Thrace, Thracia - The area west of Constantinople.

Thracian (Thrakesion) theme - A theme in Asia minor originally defended by troops from Thrace but now by Asiatic troops.

Thracian Long Wall - Forty miles west of Constantinople, the Long Wall. supported by forts and towers, extended across the Thracian Peninsula from the Black Sea to the Sea of Marmara

Thrakesion (Thracian) theme - The Thracian theme is in Asia Minor. It is not to be confused with Thrace in Europe. (See **Theme**.)

Titter, Wow, Rogue, Wink - Rather mild "girlie" magazines of the 1950s.

To the steeds of Pharaoh's chariots, et c. - *The Song of Solomon* (1: 9 - 11)

Tonsure - head shaven when taking vows as a monk.

Torture and atrocities - Some of the atrocities attributed to the Bulgars are based on stories of other invaders from the East, others are entirely fiction. All could have happened and likely did. It was a rough age. The same can be said of Byzantine punishment, particularly their inclination to blind wrongdoers. In their defense it can be said that before the modern age long term incarceration was unusual. The usual punishments were death, exile (including internal exile in monasteries), and mutilation. Having one's hands removed does discourage theft and having one's tongue removed does restrict slander and the spread of seditious plots. None of this was new. Cruel punishments were inherited from the Romans and from the customs of Rome's conquered Eastern provinces. The Byzantines did not create cruelty; they simply did not eliminate it. Little by little, however, Christian charity did demand better treatment. It would be wrong to view these punishments only as cruelty. If there was little long-term incarceration in prisons (which might have been a blessing), wrongdoers might be sent to monasteries. At times, prostitutes were offered or sent to group homes which can be viewed as prisons or as rehabilitation centers depending on one's point of view. The blinding of a traitor rather than his execution left him alive to repent his sacrilege against the elect of God so that he might avoid eternal damnation at the judgment.

Trebizond - Important city on the Black (Euxine) Sea. Located near the (fictional) estate of Nicephorus and near the monastery from which a (fictional) monk who attempted to assassinate Constantine came.

Triclinium - A formal dining room. In the Great Palace, guests (males only) would dine in the Roman manner on seventeen couches presided over by the basilios in a mix of sacred and profane traditions.

Tunica, Tunic - The undergarment of the upper classes and the only garment of the lower. Men's tunics came to the knee, women's to the ankle.

Urophagia, Urine – usually limited to fetishism in the west, Urophagia is sometimes practiced in India, China, parts of Russia, and other Asiatic countries where drinking urine - but usually one's own - is thought to have medicinal qualities - the Mahatma Gandhi practiced it. Urine is nearly sterile and in the middle ages was used to cleanse wounds. Lucia's perverted attempts to please may not be far fetched in a Kotrag.

Valhalla - A glorious hall where Germanic heroes who die in battle fight by day and feast by night.

Valkyrie - Handmaidens of the Norse god Odin who carry heroes who die in battle to Valhalla.

Venetia - Venice.

Vespers - Sunset, the eighth canonical hour. The prayers ordained for that time.

Via Egnasia - Main Roman road through Moesia and Thrace to Constantinople.

Vigla - Slavic mercenaries employed as imperial guards.

Walls of Theodosius - Built in the fifth century after the city of Constantine the Great had expanded to a population of perhaps as many as one million, the triple land walls - still extant today - were a marvel of medieval defense. They withstood numerous attacks until 1453 AD when the Turks after a prolonged siege finally breached them with artillery. The story makes mention of a fort where the land and sea walls meet near the Sea of Marmara. These original towers were supplemented by the Turks but resemble some other Byzantine forts such as the tower still extant in Thessaloniki.

Waterless Towers - An unknown site on the trade route across Asia Minor, likely in Cappadocia.

Waterloo, Battle of - The remark attributed to Wellington implies that the duke and his subordinates both shared a common background and understanding gained in school, and would have known what to expect of each other.

Weeping may endure et c. - His anger is but for a moment. His favor is for a lifetime. Weeping may endure for a night, but joy cometh in the morning. (Ps 30:5)

What God has joined together et c. - Matt 19:6

Who is this arising like the dawn, et c. - The *Song of Solomon* (6: 10)

Willow bark - Willow bark contains salicylic acid, the operative chemical in aspirin.

Woe to thee, oh land where thy king is a child - Ecclesiastes (10:16).

Your Father knoweth that you have need of these things et c. - Matt (6:32-34) This quote is from the 1750 AD revised Douay-Rheims translation of the Bible used by Catholics after the counter reformation until new authorized versions appeared in the 1960s following the Vatican II council. Sometimes, however, I take the liberty of using other translations - though Beth probably wouldn't have unless the quote was in popular use outside purely religious service. Quite frankly, the Douay-Rheims version did not have the poetic quality of the Protestant King James translation.

Your Sovereignty, Your Serenity, Your Clemency, Elect of God, Anointed of Christ - Many actual imperial titles have an odd sound in translation, so I have limited usage to these together with an occasional western form (Highness, Majesty, Gracious Sovereign) or the expression Ruler Of The World which I invented because it seems in keeping with Byzantine political theory.

Zeuxippos, Baths of - Famous for their statuary, the largest baths in Constantinople though probably losing popularity at this time. Following the Roman tradition, Constantinople had numerous public baths as well as some indoor plumbing.

www.ingramcontent.com/pod-product-compliance
Lightning Source LLC
LaVergne TN
LVHW011346080426
835511LV00005B/156